MW00860605

# THE SUSTAINABILITY MYTH

# The Sustainability Myth

*Environmental Gentrification and
the Politics of Justice*

Melissa Checker

NEW YORK UNIVERSITY PRESS
New York

NEW YORK UNIVERSITY PRESS
New York
www.nyupress.org

References to Internet websites (URLs) were accurate at the time of writing. Neither the author nor New York University Press is responsible for URLs that may have expired or changed since the manuscript was prepared.

Library of Congress Cataloging-in-Publication Data
Names: Checker, Melissa, author.
Title: The sustainability myth : environmental gentrification and the politics of justice / Melissa Checker.
Description: New York : New York University Press, [2020] | Includes bibliographical references and index.
Identifiers: LCCN 2020016803 (print) | LCCN 2020016804 (ebook) |
ISBN 9781479835089 (hardback) | ISBN 9781479855278 (paperback) |
ISBN 9781479840069 (ebook) | ISBN 9781479859245 (ebook)
Subjects: LCSH: Sustainable urban development. | Urban ecology (Sociology) |
Environmental justice. | Gentrification. | City planning—Environmental aspects.
Classification: LCC HT241 .C434 2020 (print) | LCC HT241 (ebook) | DDC 307.1/416—dc23
LC record available at https://lccn.loc.gov/2020016803

LC ebook record available at https://lccn.loc.gov/2020016804New York University Press books are printed on acid-free paper, and their binding materials are chosen for strength and durability. We strive to use environmentally responsible suppliers and materials to the greatest extent possible in publishing our books.

Manufactured in the United States of America

10 9 8 7 6 5 4 3 2 1

Also available as an ebook

*Frontispiece:* The five boroughs of New York City. Credit: Vector Images

*In memory of my parents, Armand Mendel and Ruthie Jane*

# CONTENTS

# LIST OF ABBREVIATIONS

ADM     Archer Daniels Midland
AFSZ    Asthma-Free School Zones
BIB     Build it Back
BOA     Brownfield Opportunity Area
BPC     Battery Park City
CB1     Staten Island's Community Board 1
CPC     Central Park Conservancy
D-LMA   Downtown-Lower Manhattan Association
DCP     (NYC) Department of City Planning
DEC     New York State Department of Environmental Conservation
DOE     Department of Energy
DOT     Department of Transportation
EJ      environmental justice
EJO     Office of Environmental Justice
FEMA    Federal Emergency Management Agency
FIRE    finance, insurance, and real estate
FOIA    Freedom of Information Act
HCDC    Harlem Community Development Corporation
IAP     Industrial Action Plan
IBZ     Industrial Business Zone
IOC     International Olympic Committee
LEED    leadership in energy and environmental design
MLM     multilevel marketing
MTA     Metropolitan Transportation Authority

MTS   Marine Transfer Station

NCLDC   Northfield Local Community Development Corporation

NEJAC   National Environmental Justice Advisory Council

NFIP   National Flood Insurance Program

NPIC   nonprofit industrial complex

NRSTP   North River Sewage Treatment Plant

NSCCEJ   North Shore Community Coalition for Environmental Justice

NSWC   North Shore Waterfront Conservancy

NYCEDC   NYC Economic Development Corporation

NYCT   New York Community Trust

NYLPI   New York Lawyers for the Public Interest

OER   Office of Environmental Remediation

OSLRP   Office of Sustainability and Long-Range Planning

PANYNJ   Port Authority of New York and New Jersey

PCE   perchloroethylene

SAB   Sustainability Advisory Board

SBA   Small Business Administration

SFN   Stop FEMA Now

SIE   Staten Island Expressway

SITA   Staten Island Taxpayers' Association

SNAP   safe for nature, animals and the planet

TCE   trichloroethylene

UPROSE   United Puerto Rico Organization of Sunset Park

WEACT   West Harlem Environmental Action

WPA   Works Progress Administration

# Introduction

## *The Big Green Apple*

In late 2012, exactly two weeks after Hurricane Sandy pummeled the Atlantic seaboard, some 150 weary and shaken Staten Island residents shuffled into the Music Hall at the Snug Harbor Cultural Center. Many had only just regained electricity. A mid-November draft chilled the auditorium. With its faded red velvet seats and chipped paint, the 120-year-old theater itself seemed to embody a "down, but not out" mood. With so many people attending in the aftermath of a crisis, the meeting might have been about flood protection or emergency management procedures. But that was not the case. Instead, it offered residents a chance to comment on a plan to build the world's largest Ferris wheel high atop Staten Island's northern shoreline. "The New York Wheel" was the brainchild of Mayor Michael Bloomberg, who claimed that it would be "an attraction unlike any other in New York City—even unlike any other on the planet."[1] The Wheel was set to rise eighty-four feet higher than the Singapore Flyer (currently the title-holder for the world's largest Ferris wheel), and would beckon riders twenty-four hours a day. Next to it, a 340,000-square-foot designer retail outlet complex and a 130,000-square-foot hotel would summon shoppers and tourists alike.

I arrived at the Wheel meeting just as it started and scanned the audience for Beryl Thurman, who was saving me a seat. Catching my eye, Thurman's face lit up with one of her warm, contagious smiles and she beckoned me over. In her mid-fifties, she had smooth, caramel-colored skin and big, brown eyes. Her short, natural hair was threaded with the occasional silver strand. She dressed casually but precisely, in sharply pressed, solid neutrals accented with a colorful scarf or a piece of jewelry. Since 2005, Thurman had presided over the North Shore Waterfront Conservancy (NSWC), a local environmental justice organization. She was known for peppering her frank comments with witticisms.

I first met Thurman on a fateful morning in mid-March in 2009 when she pulled her grey Mercury Sable into the pick-up lane at the St. George ferry terminal on Staten Island. I had contacted Thurman a few weeks earlier for an interview, and she had offered to take me on a "toxic tour" of her neighborhood instead. As I settled into the passenger seat, she looked over and greeted me slyly. "Welcome to the North Shore. I like to call this place an industrial *Girls Gone Wild.*"

For over three hours, Thurman drove me along a five-mile stretch of the Kill Van Kull, a narrow tributary that divided the North Shore from Bayonne, New Jersey. Along the shoreline, she pointed to a dizzying array of industrial properties—twenty-one in all. These included a sanitation garage, an electric power plant, a waste transfer station, a sewer treatment plant, an industrial salt manufacturer, a salvage yard, several former factories and ship-repair yards, and the site of an old warehouse that contained levels of uranium nearly ten times higher than the acceptable limit. All of these sites sat within seventy feet of dense and diverse residential neighborhoods, and most were within flood zones. I had seen plenty of examples of environmental injustice across the United States, but never had I witnessed the volume, density, and proximity of toxic sites and residential neighborhoods that I saw that day. Long before Hurricane Sandy slammed into New York, Thurman had warned federal, state, and local officials that climate change presented a triple whammy for Staten Island. First, flooding was a continual and worsening problem, to the point that residents had to rearrange their basements annually, moving valuables to higher and higher shelves. Second, those floods constituted a toxic soup made from the heavily contaminated Kill Van Kull, street runoff, sewer overflows, and, potentially, pollutants from the soil surrounding nearby toxic sites.

Third, locals did not necessarily have the resources to get out of harm's way. Approximately 17 percent of residents on the North Shore (officially known as Staten Island Community District 1) had incomes below the federal poverty line (as compared to 13.6 percent in New York City). The North Shore also housed Staten Island's most racially and ethnically diverse populations—approximately 51 percent identified as Black or Latinx and 37 percent identified as White (and non-Hispanic).[2] Such demographics, combined with the North Shore's high number of toxic sites, led the EPA to designate the area as one of its ten "environmental

Map of polluted sites on the North Shore of Staten Island, 2018. Created by Ruchika Lodha.

justice showcase" communities in 2010.[3] The EPA designation would have little traction, however, when it came to convincing local and state officials to clean up the district. "If Staten Island is the 'forgotten borough,'" Thurman would say, "then we are way down on the food chain."

This was not my first toxic tour. For nearly two decades, I had studied environmental racism, the ways in which people of color experience environmental hazards and pollution at higher rates than white individuals.[4] (Low-income African Americans, for example, are three times more likely to die from exposure to air pollutants than their white counterparts.[5]) As an anthropologist, I was interested in learning what environmental racism meant to the people who confronted it in the course of their daily lives. My initial research focused on a low-income, African American neighborhood in Augusta, Georgia. Surrounded by seven polluting facilities, residents referred to their neighborhood as "the hole in a toxic donut." After discovering unusually high levels of PCBs, arsenic, lead, and other heavy metals in their soil and groundwater, these community members launched a multi-decade fight for environmental justice.[6] I found that residents' experiences of race and class shaped their definitions of and struggles for environmental resources. For them, environmental justice was an extension of the same civil rights battles they had been fighting for decades.

My research in Augusta led me to visit numerous communities across the US, where I saw a strikingly similar pattern of environmental disparities. My own New York City neighborhood of Harlem, a global center of black culture, housed five out of Manhattan's seven bus depots, two waste treatment plants, and scores of former factory sites (known as "brownfields") that contained toxic chemicals. But nothing prepared me for the density of toxic sites with proximity to low-income communities of color that I saw on Staten Island's North Shore.

Even more startling was that just across the New York harbor, Manhattan sparkled like an emerald city. State-of-the-art, energy-efficient buildings pierced the sky, and the city was scattered with new parks, bicycle lanes, farmer's markets and hybrid taxi cabs. Waterfronts in Manhattan, Brooklyn, and western Queens, previously strewn with abandoned rail yards, factories, and warehouses, were now lined with glassy high-rises and lofts boasting LEED (leadership in energy and environmental design) certifications, photovoltaic paneling, and filtered air, and offering rooftop gardens, bocce courts, canoe launches, and individual composting units. Boutiques, restaurants, cafes, and food stores beckoned upwardly mobile professionals and members of the "creative class" with organic wares and promises of "greener" lifestyles. This book investigates the contrast between the dense cluster of industrial sites lining the North Shore and the high-end luxury developments and greenspace amenities that constitute the sustainable city.

In creating a tourist attraction, a profit-generating gem on the polluted and imperiled North Shore, Bloomberg's Wheel epitomized the paradoxes of urban sustainability. Even the timing of the meeting was paradoxical. Amid warnings from climate experts to limit further coastal development, the Wheel site was located on a floodplain. In the neighborhoods surrounding it, scores of North Shore businesses were still digging out from Sandy's massive floods. This contradiction outraged most of the meeting-goers. One by one, residents took to the mic to voice their misgivings.

Nearly everyone worried about increased traffic on Bay Street and Richmond Terrace, the only two streets that could carry cars to the Wheel. Congestion was already heavy along these routes. "They're just two small roads, with lights every four streets," said Lawrence Cohen, of New Brighton. "[The traffic] will all bottleneck into these two roads."[7] The CEO of New York Wheel LLC, Rich Marin, a local resident and former Bear Stearns banker, assured meeting-goers that he expected 90 percent of visitors to take either ferries or water taxis to the site. In addition, he pledged that the entire project would be lit with LED lightbulbs and powered with wind, solar, and water-based energy. The outlet mall would feature almost five acres of green roof. Altogether, developers expected a Platinum LEED certification, the highest standard for sustainable construction.

But meeting-goers were not reassured. "Will those LED lights shine on us all night?" demanded Bernice, who lived about half a mile away in St. George. "Part of our island was just devastated in the floodplains. And this is actually going to be built in the floodplain," said local resident Stephanie Woodard, shaking her head in disbelief.

"The Wheel will actually act as a buffer," Marin explained. The structure itself, he claimed, would boost storm protections by blocking storm surges and cutting high winds. Moreover, its architects were designing it to withstand the three-hundred-mile-per-hour winds and surges from storms as super-sized as those created by Sandy. But North Shore residents were not mollified, knowing all too well that hard buffers redistribute, rather than absorb, flood waters. "Won't this displace flood waters onto the properties around it?" Bill, another St. George resident, wanted to know.[8]

Even if the Wheel was as green as promised, its environmental costs were considerable. In addition to the natural resources required to construct it, the Wheel's waterfront location would disturb the Harbor's

Architect's rendering of the New York Wheel. Credit: S9 Architecture /
Perkins Eastman

flora and fauna, and the construction period would generate dust and
debris for several years. Moreover, the project would be built from pre-
fabricated parts manufactured around the world that would arrive at
the harbor via oil-spewing supertankers. Finally, the city required that
developers create hundreds of new parking spaces to accommodate visitors to the Wheel.

In the end, those parking spaces and the outlet mall were all that came
of the New York Wheel. Cost overruns, complicated legal battles, and
the physical challenges of erecting such an enormous structure proved
to be insurmountable. By 2018, project costs had ballooned to $1 billion,
four times the initial estimate. At that point, the project's last remaining investors pulled out and developers pronounced its demise. North
Shore residents were left with a 325,000-square-foot garage that blocked
their view of the Harbor, an outlet mall, and the Wheel's concrete base.[9]
The saga of the New York Wheel serves as a dramatic example of short-
sighted and ill-conceived urban development. No part of the project,
including its development and construction phase, was sustainable. For
the purposes of this book, the New York Wheel offers an excellent vantage point for examining the ruptured logics of pairing sustainability
with urban redevelopment. I argue that these logics, based on win-win
scenarios in which sustainability advances private economic interests,

created a pernicious double bind that had significant consequences for both urban residents and the climate.

The idea of the "double bind" was first proffered in the mid-1950s by the anthropologist Gregory Bateson, who used it to describe conflicting systems wherein resolving the conflict only creates another contradiction. Bateson and his colleagues originally applied double-bind theory to child psychology, explaining how children raised on multiple, contradictory logics develop a range of psychological dysfunctions, including schizophrenia.[10] Later on, Bateson applied double bind theory to environmental problems. For example, in evolutionary history, human organisms adapted internally to survive environmental changes, whereas contemporary humans survive changing environmental conditions (land loss, droughts, deforestation) by adapting their external environments to the change. As Bateson noted, however, these external alterations typically generate further environmental changes, which then require more external adaptation—and so the cycle continues.[11] More to the point, urban and economic growth depend on the exploitation and eventual depletion of natural resources, which then precipitates an ecological crisis. Resolving that crisis with the same kind of growth only exacerbates it. More simply, no matter how green it is purported to be, constructing an enormous tourist attraction (or a residential or commercial development) on a floodplain is not the way to protect a coastline, or to mitigate the causes and effects of climate change. My research shows that the more these solutions stimulated economic growth, the more they extended environmental problems and sacrificed the health, safety, and livelihoods of communities of color and people living in low-income neighborhoods.

The term "sustainaphrenia" describes the inherently contradictory promise of urban sustainability: that we can stimulate economic growth while mitigating the effects of climate change, without any sacrifice. Importantly, sustainaphrenia spills over into politics at the grassroots level. It includes the paradoxes facing environmental justice activists who fight for healthier neighborhoods that are also affordable. It also includes forms of civic engagement that invite public participation only to ignore it. In the early twenty-first century, New York City became a nexus for sustainaphrenia's double binds.

\* \* \* \*

In 1994, I moved to New York City to enter New York University's PhD program in cultural anthropology. In September 2001 I had returned from my fieldwork in Augusta and was midway through writing my dissertation when two hijacked planes hit the twin towers of the World Trade Center—and everything changed. For the next three months, my neighborhood in lower Manhattan stank of burned plastic. South of 14th Street, any view of the horizon included a gray plume of smoke snaking toward the sky, a wraith of the fallen towers. Outside of firehouses, and in the walkways of public parks and plazas, flickering candles encircled strewn flowers and framed photos of the dead. "Missing" flyers and photos taped to chain-link fences weathered rain, wind, and sun. Like the smoke that shrouded lower Manhattan, a collective hush muted the city's usual hustle and bustle. In grim slow motion, New Yorkers held doors, offered seats, looked one another in the eye, and whispered "thanks."

I moved away to take my first academic position but returned to New York on New Year's Day in 2007. By that time, the city bore almost no traces of 9/11. Its population had swelled to an all-time high of 8.2 million, and the local economy had come booming back. Everywhere, glassy new condominiums reflected the sky, and more were going up all the time. Waterfronts along Brooklyn, Queens, and Manhattan, once dotted with the remnants of their industrial pasts, now sparkled with lush landscaping, benches, and playgrounds. Old manufacturing buildings were now outfitted with one-, two-, and three-bedroom apartments offering gyms, green roofs, and organic supermarkets designed to shelter the hipster elite and keep them healthy. The city was blossoming, and its new color was a vibrant green.

Former Mayor Bloomberg was riding the crest of this "green wave." On taking office in 2002, he vowed to bring New York out of the post-9/11 recession by rebranding it as a "luxury city." When some New Yorkers pushed back against the luxury concept (was there room in it for the city's low-income communities?), Bloomberg took a different tack. In 2007, he merged growing concerns about climate change with his redevelopment agenda. That same year, he launched PlaNYC 2030, a sweeping program for achieving a robust urban economy while cleaning up environmental pollution and reducing greenhouse gas emissions.

Bloomberg's zeal for such "win-win" scenarios attracted worldwide attention and accolades, and his name became almost synonymous with urban sustainability.

Between 2007 and 2010, however, the city's bright, green tide took a turn. Mortgage lending companies began filing for bankruptcy, one after another. Eventually, US housing markets froze, creating a giant fiscal iceberg whose chill reverberated throughout the global economy.[12] The recession hit New York City especially hard, thanks to the demise of major companies like Bear Stearns, AIG, Lehman Brothers, Merrill Lynch, Wachovia, and Washington Mutual. The city's private sector lost approximately 100,000 jobs in twelve months, and construction work on many of those new condos came to an abrupt halt. For the first time in years, average city rents decreased.[13] A green city did not come cheap. Would diminished tax revenues put the kibosh on Bloomberg's shiny new sustainability initiatives?

Two years later, such questions already seemed obsolete. In some ways, New York City rebounded from the recession with a vengeance.[14] Construction dinned even louder as tourists thronged to the city's iconic spaces, and rents and home values floated back into the stratosphere. For working-class, middle- and low-income New Yorkers, however, the recession's effects would last far longer. In 2012, the top 10 percent of Manhattan's earners made eighty times more than the bottom 10 percent, and nearly half of all New Yorkers lived at or near the poverty line, while the incomes of the city's wealthiest residents topped $20 million.[15] As the gap between rich and poor widened to a chasm, a new protest movement gathered steam. In September 2011, a group of self-described anarchists took over Zuccotti Park, a small, rectangular patch of sidewalk and evenly spaced trees near Wall Street. For nearly two months, these "occupiers" drew worldwide attention to the gaping inequalities endemic to neoliberal policies and economics. Bloomberg made no attempt to hide his disdain for the protestors. Early one morning in mid-November, he sent the NYPD to evict them while barring press from the area. After the eviction, Occupy Wall Street protestors decamped and many went on to work on neighborhood-based problems, helping to form anti-eviction and grassroots movements.[16]

About a year after the Occupy eviction, the city faced another kind of crisis. Hurricane Sandy submerged parts of Manhattan's Lower

East Side, southern Brooklyn, and eastern Queens. The storm killed forty-four New Yorkers and destroyed thousands of homes as well as an estimated 250,000 vehicles. In the days following Sandy, leading climate scientists warned that if development continued to encroach on natural flood barriers and sea levels rose, the city could be set for further destruction. But Bloomberg remained defiantly pro-development. "Let me be clear," he stated shortly after the storm, "We are not going to abandon the waterfront."[17] Bloomberg's zeal for economic growth would shape the city for years to come. In particular, by the time he left office, Bloomberg had rezoned one-third of the city. Most of those rezonings lifted height and use restrictions in low-income neighborhoods, paving the way for new residential and commercial developments.

Like urban development plans in other major cities around the world, Bloomberg's embraced a win-win scenario that promised economic growth and also promoted environmental sustainability. Accordingly, redevelopment plans featured green spaces and waterfront parks; cleaner manufacturing businesses and the remediation and repurposing of contaminated properties. I use the term "environmental gentrification" to describe the use of such sustainable initiatives to serve high-end, luxury commercial and residential development.

Michael Bloomberg did not invent environmental gentrification. It is a global phenomenon that has been well documented by researchers in cities around the world.[18] It is also not limited to fiscally conservative mayoralties like Michael Bloomberg's. In fact, as I demonstrate in this book, sustainability especially appeals to progressively minded urbanites and is a particular darling of liberal political administrations. Bloomberg's successor, Bill de Blasio, for example, rode into office on a tide of dissatisfaction with income polarization and economic inequality. Far to Bloomberg's left, de Blasio's campaign was centered on social justice and featured photos of his mixed-race family marching together in protests against police violence. During his first year in office, de Blasio issued "Housing New York," a ten-year plan for creating and preserving affordable housing. The plan emphasized building heights and density and also called for mandatory inclusionary zoning, which required private developers to create or fund a certain number of affordable residential units as part of any new market-rate residential building. Local housing advocates agreed that de Blasio's housing record constituted a clear improvement over his predecessor's.

Even so, redevelopment continued more or less unfettered. A 2017 report found that 85 percent of the residents living in areas rezoned under de Blasio were predominantly black or Latinx, and over 50 percent of their households earned less than $35,000 annually.[19] Rezonings allowed for higher density—and higher priced—residential development. New mandates for preserving affordable housing mitigated only a portion of the displacement generated by rising property values. In January 2019, the Coalition for the Homeless reported that the city's homeless population had reached an all-time high of nearly 64,000 men, women, and children sleeping in shelters each night. In no uncertain terms, the report blamed gentrification for this increase.[20]

Similarly, de Blasio's answer to PlaNYC 2030, known as OneNYC, extended many of the former's ambiguous and often contradictory measures. In his second term, de Blasio successfully recycled some of Bloomberg's failed ideas, such as a version of Bloomberg's congestion pricing initiative to charge vehicles for entering central Manhattan, which passed the Democrat-dominated state legislature in the spring of 2019. De Blasio also reconstituted Bloomberg's proposal to extend the southern tip of Manhattan hundreds of feet into the East River. Using landfill, the plan would fortify the Wall Street area and protect it from sea-level rise and flooding. Days before declaring his candidacy for US president in 2019, the mayor announced the Climate Mobilization Act (or New York City's own Green New Deal). The Act was meant, in part, to keep the city in line with emissions reduction targets set by the Paris Climate Agreement and the city's pledge to achieve a 40-percent reduction in carbon pollution by 2030 and an 80-percent reduction by 2050. Most of these reductions would come from new building codes mandating that owners cut their carbon emissions within ten years or face fines.[21] As a concession to outraged building owners, the bill left open the possibility of a cap-and-trade system whereby they could offset their use of fossil fuels by purchasing renewable energy credits.

While the mayor received national praise among progressives for these policies, local environmentalists complained that he overpromised and under-delivered.[22] A plan to protect the Lower East Side of Manhattan from flooding met with great controversy. The plan involved building flood gates in the East River and reinforcing the shoreline by refurbishing a waterfront park. After many years of input from community members, including tenants' councils from nearby public housing developments, the city abruptly changed its design for the park. The new plan, which passed the City Council in November 2019, removed almost 1,000 trees, and added eight feet of landfill, much of which would cover existing park amenities. Construction required shuttering sections of the park over several years with no interim measures in place to protect residents from floods that might occur during that period.[23] More generally, environmental justice activists criticized the mayor for not paying enough attention to protecting low-income communities from flooding and coastal erosion.[24]

Indeed, answers to OneNYC's call to address both environmental justice and environmental gentrification remained faint. Two pieces of legislation acknowledged the existence of environmental disparities— the first established an Interagency Working Group on the issue, and the second required a city-wide survey to identify potential environmental justice areas—but they provided no means of establishing or enforcing environmental equity. Only the third and fourth bills had teeth—both regulated the commercial waste industry in ways that would protect the health and safety of workers and communities where waste transfer stations are clustered. Both of these bills also grew out of years-long efforts by labor, environmental, and social justice coalitions.[25]

While individual leaders influenced and shaped the city in sometimes significant ways, urban policies always operated in conversation with global financial systems, political interests, and social discourses, as well as local constituencies. This book takes a close look at how this conversation played out over time, in the everyday lives of low-income communities of color.

* * * *

In my own Central Harlem neighborhood, I watched environmental gentrification unfold in real time. Like most residents, I enjoyed many of its benefits: restored and renovated parks, new street trees, farmer's markets, and bike-sharing stations. A Whole Foods opened on the corner of Malcolm X Boulevard and 125th Street in 2017. But these changes did not come in a vacuum, nor were they neutral. Between 2000 and 2015, the share of white residents in Central Harlem increased by 846 percent while the black population decreased by 17 percent.[26] These demographic shifts accompanied economic ones—the average price for a multifamily dwelling more than doubled between 2012 and 2018.[27] As a white, middle-class woman, I played my own role in these changes, and the tensions they bred. To address some of these tensions on an interpersonal level, I had frank conversations with my neighbors, both old-timers and newcomers, as well as local business owners, and by engaging in small, neighborly acts. I also participated in the efforts of local environmental justice activists.

In some ways, the greening and whitening of Harlem boosted the efforts of its environmental justice organizations. In 2007, for instance, after a multiyear process, West Harlem Piers Park opened on the site of a large parking lot adjacent to a former waste transfer station. The project was both spearheaded and led by West Harlem Environmental Action (WEACT), a grassroots environmental justice organization. Seven years later, another WEACT initiative came to fruition when the Metropolitan Transportation Authority (MTA) finished rebuilding and retrofitting the Mother Clara Hale Bus Depot,[28] which featured a green roof, rainwater collection, and a LEED certification. Both projects were at least a decade in the making. Over in East Harlem, a 2017 rezoning plan included a seven-acre greenway along the East River and the lifting of height and density restrictions along four of the area's major thoroughfares. I saw similar patterns in other waterfront neighborhoods. In Williamsburg and Sunset Park, for instance, activists finally won hard-fought battles for green space and other environmental improvements, only to find that those initiatives led to new development that threatened to price them out of their own neighborhoods. Without diminishing the hard work and commitment of grassroots environmental justice activists, I wondered whether their successes were being co-opted. Had their activism unintentionally caused environmental gentrification?

My experiences on the North Shore begged even more questions about the relationship between sustainable development and environmental justice. While the EPA completed three Superfund cleanups in the early 2000s, nearly two dozen additional polluted sites, including the radioactive site, had yet to be remediated. During this time, the city opened world-renowned parks on Manhattan's west side and in central and northern Brooklyn. But on the North Shore, soil in Veteran's Park contained unsafe levels of arsenic and lead covered only by thin layers of burlap and gravel. Moreover, funds had yet to be allocated for the re-building of Staten Island's largest recreation center, which collapsed into the New York Bay in 2010.[29]

During the course of my fieldwork, public agencies issued permits for a new cement plant, a facility to treat remediated materials dredged from local bodies of water (including, for instance, the Gowanus Canal Superfund site), the expansion of the container port, and a natural gas pipeline. In addition, construction began on a multiyear project to raise the Bayonne Bridge to allow super-sized container ships to pass below. Not only would the construction be a long-term nightmare for nearby residents, but larger ships would increase local air pollution exponen-tially. Finally, in 2013, the NYC Economic Development Corporation designated an Industrial Business Zone (IBZ) along several miles of shoreline, offering attractive tax incentives to bring industrial businesses to the area.

Perhaps the North Shore had not been forgotten after all. Perhaps the luxurious green city had needed a place to house its heavy industries and municipal waste facilities. This proposition was not lost on Staten Island's environmental justice activists. As Victoria Gillen, a longtime North Shore activist told me,

> Creating all the wonderful new playgrounds and high-value waterfront residential areas pushes *heavy* industrial use into parts of Queens and Staten Island . . . while our taxes support these changes, we do not share in the benefits, and find ourselves, here on Staten Island, once again a dumping ground for the City's unwanted garbage.

Gillen's statement about the dynamic relationship between gentrification and environmental degradation captures one of the essential questions driving my research and this book: how did the greening of some parts of the city also lead to the browning of other parts?

At the same time, the story of brown and green also played out within the boundaries of the North Shore. As permits for new industrial sites mounted, city planners and developers were eyeing certain North Shore neighborhoods for commercial potential. Between 2005 and 2015, the city planning department issued half a dozen studies reimagining certain North Shore neighborhoods using the "industrial chic" aesthetic that had made Brooklyn one of the country's hottest real estate markets. Planners' pastel renderings featured peaceful pedestrians strolling along shoreline paths that had been greened by bike lanes, farmer's markets, and grassy, open spaces, while industrial cranes and containers rose from the water to create a picturesque backdrop. In 2017, "Urby Staten Island" opened in Stapleton, a neighborhood just east of the ferry terminal. Built to resemble a former factory, Urby featured a five thousand square-foot farm complete with an on-site commercial vegetable stand and a farmer who doubled as a chef—for an extra fee, the farmer would transform the vegetables into a take-out meal. Between the IBZ and such hip new developments, city planners and developers seemed to be hedging their bets on which economic engine would prevail.

* * * *

To understand how sustainability and real estate development have affected the everyday lives of grassroots environmental justice activists and those living in their communities, I used an ethnographic method. I spent extended periods of time spent observing and participating in the activities of a particular group, or groups, of people. Because I also wanted to explore the dynamic relationships that sustainaphrenia—the contradictory politics of sustainability—creates both within and between urban neighborhoods, my ethnography moved across several locations.

I spent most of my time on Staten Island's North Shore, where the sheer volume and density of toxic sites provided an ideal setting for exploring uneven development and environmental injustice, both past and present. As one of the last, active industrial waterfronts left in New York City, the North Shore also provided a unique window into the underside of sustainable initiatives and their unseen effects on non-gentrifying neighborhoods. In contrast, Harlem offered me an opportunity to study the historic relationship between rising property values and green space. To identify larger, citywide patterns of redevelopment and sustainable initiatives, I have fleshed out my ethnographic cases with examples from other New York City neighborhoods, especially in Brooklyn and the Lower East Side of Manhattan. Finally, the urgent and dire situation facing survivors of Hurricane Sandy impelled me to explore the plight of homeowners on Staten Island's southern and eastern shorelines, as well. Both before and after Sandy, these homeowners joined activists from the North Shore and elsewhere to lobby public officials for better environmental protections. Such partnerships crossed sometimes vast political, racial, ethnic, and class lines, defying prevailing logics about the political divisions splitting the country apart.

A great deal of my research involved traipsing after activists as they raced around from public hearings to workshops, from charrettes and information sessions to any number of meetings. Indeed, the sustainable city offered endless opportunities for public participation. Yet for all the steering committees and advisory boards on which activists were asked to sit, testimonies they gave, and comments they contributed to public projects, their input seemed to have little effect. Plans, permits, and projects moved forward regardless of local concerns about their impacts on environmental or climate justice. I began to see civic engagement as another symptom of sustainaphrenia. Rather than fostering democratic action, participatory politics re-channeled, and drained, activists' time and energy, siphoning it away from their long-term goals. Ultimately, this process undermined local activism and democracy itself.

* * * *

In January 2017, I attended a meeting of the New York State Department of Environmental Conservation, along with representatives from each of the city's environmental justice organizations. The Department of Environmental Conservation was revamping its environmental justice guidelines and they wanted input from experts. I sat between Beryl Thurman of Staten Island's NSWC and staff from El Puente, the venerable environmental justice organization started by the late Luis Garden Acosta, a former member of the Young Lords. Nearly twenty years before, I had conducted research with El Puente, when Williamsburg was still predominantly Latinx, although rapidly filling with twenty-something hipsters. Within the next decade, Williamsburg transformed from gritty, to grungy, to an icon of gentrification. With some of the city's most exclusive restaurants, boutiques and apartment buildings, it was hard to imagine that El Puente was still there. "Wow," I said to the El Puente staffers. "Great to see you guys here. And kind of surprising."

One of the women replied, "Yeah, I know. Everyone thinks we don't exist anymore, but there are still low-income, Latinx families in South Williamsburg, and we still have environmental problems."

Her words reminded me that gentrification, even the hyper-gentrification like Williamsburg has experienced, is rarely a uniform process—and rarely does it displace every low-income family in a neighborhood. Back in 2009, Garden Acosta and I were talking about disparities between the beautifully restored Williamsburg waterfront and the highly polluted waters of the river it fronted. Radiac, a nuclear waste transfer facility, was still operational near the waterfront, and many toxic sites, leftover from Williamsburg's industrial past, had been turned into the neighborhood's new multimillion dollar apartment complex. "Babies!" Garden Acosta had exclaimed at the time, "the gentrifiers are having babies!" His concern was not just for El Puente's remaining constituents, but for the neighborhood's newcomers. Garden Acosta worried that the neighborhood's splendid waterfront, eco-friendly condos, and organic restaurants and stores lulled these new residents into thinking that its environmental problems had been rectified.

The environmental justice activists in this book refuse the lull of sustainability's false promises. Their struggles to call out the contradictions of environmental gentrification and the fallacies of participatory politics lie at the heart of this book. Perhaps these struggles also lie at the heart of our collective future. Short-sighted and profit-driven sustainable policies and practices undermine the very goals of sustainability itself. As Beryl Thurman wrote in a furious email to her elected officials,

> [We] plod along as if we have all the time in the world for these problems to be resolved and come to a reasonable conclusion. And to be honest we don't have a lot of time, we are on the same clock as the developers, businesses and mother nature, it's whoever gets here first.

The sustainaphrenic city is built upon its own undoing.

# PART I

## Environmental Gentrification

1

# Sustainability and the City

On a late August evening in 2009, I stepped into the parlor of the Indigo Arms in Central Harlem. A mansion-turned-guest house that dated back to the Harlem Renaissance, the Indigo Arms had just undergone an "eco-friendly" renovation. In addition to featuring sustainable flooring and energy efficient fixtures, the ground floor of the guest house could now be rented for yoga classes, parties, and other events. That night, UrbanGoGreen, a local organization devoted to championing "eco-preneurship" in Harlem and elsewhere, had rented the space for a networking event. Around the room, about fifteen vendors had set up tables showcasing products and services from organic skin care to nutritional consulting, to homemade vitamins, to green construction materials. As I roamed from table to table, I stopped to talk with a vendor named Carol.[1] Unlike the other mostly African American vendors who wore the same casual attire as those of us milling around, Carol was dressed in a dark purple business suit and black pumps. Her table displayed just two different cleaning products, each in a plain white plastic container. Pasted onto the front, a small label decorated with yellow daisies and bright, green lettering read, "SNAP."

"It stands for "safe for nature, animals and the planet," Carol explained, "because it's made of all-natural ingredients, so it won't pollute the water supply." As she spoke, I picked up one of the containers and turned it over in my hand until I found an ingredient list pasted to the bottom of the container. In very small typeface it read: "cleaning agents, no phosphates, biodegradable." Wondering how that label passed regulatory muster, I asked Carol for the name of the product manufacturer. "Market International," she said, handing me a card.

Market International's parent company, Amway, was one of the world's largest "multilevel marketing" (MLM) companies. Based on a "pyramid" model, these companies derive revenue from non-salaried salespeople who typically buy the products outright and then earn back commissions by selling them and recruiting other salespeople. According to the Federal Trade Commission, many MLMs skirt the edge of legality,[2] and offer products that are overpriced, make false claims and/or are unsafe.[3] Sure enough, the Environmental Working Group gave Amway's green cleaning products its lowest ratings for environmental safety. Still, Amway was technically within its legal rights to label SNAP products as "green," because no federal standards existed for determining what constituted a green, or eco-friendly, product. Any manufacturer, in other words, could slap a green label onto a product and call it sustainable. No wonder Amway saw an opportunity and seized it.

In their haste to create recycling and toxic waste disposal programs, legislators have also left open opportunities for exploitation. In 2018, California authorities broke up a recycling fraud ring that was collecting used beverage containers in other states and driving them back to California to claim that state's higher bottle return.[4] A 2017 investigation by the state of New Jersey found that loopholes in recycling laws made it possible for mob-connected haulers to collect toxic construction debris and dump it into erosion control projects or resell it as mulch.[5] Outside the United States, organized criminals have taken advantage of similarly vague policies and programs geared toward sustainability. Canadian officials found that crime organizations were collecting e-waste and reselling it to developing countries.[6] In 2013, Europol (the European Union's law enforcement agency) found that mafia affiliates had received European Union subsidies for solar panels and wind farms across southern Italy. Instead of reinvesting proceeds from energy sales in jobs and/or agricultural businesses as promised, these organizations pocketed the money.[7] How did sustainable policies and practices become so profitable that organized crime syndicates could not refuse them?

This chapter explores how "sustainability" became capitalism's darling in the early twenty-first century. I begin with a quick overview of how economic and ecological crises are built into the very fabric of capitalist economies. New York City's history as a rapacious economic center exemplifies the ways, before, during and after the industrial era, economic and environmental crises became opportunities for capitalist expansion. By the latter half of the twentieth century, these cycles of crisis and expansion had increasingly serious—and global—ramifications. Recognizing the need to rethink their imperatives for unbridled economic growth, multinational organizations and leaders adopted the concept of sustainable development, which continued to prioritize economic growth, but with an eye toward mitigating resource depletion, as well as social and political inequities. Sustainability thus rose to prominence on a neoliberal tailwind—and, in practice, became another mechanism enabling economic expansion to re-inscribe environmental, economic and political inequities.

## The Sorcerer

In *The Communist Manifesto*, Karl Marx likens capitalism to "the sorcerer who is no longer able to control the powers of the nether world whom he has called up by his spells." To reproduce itself successfully, Marx argues, capitalism must continually generate profit and growth. Available capital and natural resources stimulate production; commerce stimulates profit and builds forward momentum. But the system is flawed. Eventually, it leads to a surplus of production, which lowers prices and diminishes profits. To resolve this issue, a portion of surplus profit must be directed toward expanding existing markets and creating new ones. If markets become saturated and cannot absorb surplus profit, the flow of capital is interrupted and the economy as a whole slows down—or halts. Marx explains that in order to overcome such crises of overaccumulation, capitalism remakes itself in two ways: "on the one hand, by enforced destruction of a mass of productive forces; on the other, by the conquest of new markets, and by the more thorough exploitation of the old ones."[8] This is capitalism's central contradiction— its triumph also brings forth crisis, creating an ongoing cycle of creation and destruction.

In the twentieth century, new technologies in transportation and engineering enabled a massive expansion of buildings and suburbs both within and outside of urban centers. Real estate became an increasingly common solution to crises of overaccumulation. Geographer David Harvey refers to this as the "spatial fix":

The built environment that constitutes a vast field of collective means of production and consumption absorbs huge amounts of capital in both its construction and its maintenance . . . Capitalism finds a "spatial fix" for its periodic crises of overaccumulation through investment in fixed assets of infrastructure, buildings, etc. . . . [9]

Real estate expansion thus served as an ideal solution to capitalist crises—it soaked up investment and prevented surplus capital from flooding the market. In addition, real estate investment supported a myriad of subindustries, such as construction, sales, advertising, and so on.

But the spatial fix only exacerbated Marx's second concern about the expansion of capital—that it required the depletion and degradation of natural resources. In the mid-1800s (as Marx was formulating his ideas about capitalism), advances in organic chemistry, especially in understanding the composition of soil nutrients and their metabolic relationship to human consumption and waste, alerted scientists to an impending crisis. As the industrial revolution expanded, more and more people were moving to cities. Whereas rural populations consumed what they farmed and then returned their waste to the soil to replenish it, city inhabitants only imported agricultural products. Over time, this one-way relationship was leaching the soil of its nutrients.[10] In *Capital*, Marx describes this crisis as a "metabolic rift." He explains that capitalist production "disturbs the metabolic interaction between man and the earth, i.e., it prevents the return to the soil of its constituent elements consumed by man in the form of food and clothing."[11] Yet, the crisis of the metabolic rift also created an opportunity. In the mid-1800s, the market for natural fertilizers exploded, catalyzing a global rush on guano. Capitalists staked out mines in faraway places and hired Chinese, Polynesian, and Easter Island laborers to work for nearly slave wages and under grueling conditions.[12] Marx was deeply concerned about the exploitation of these workers and about the environmental impacts of soil depletion. "All progress in increasing the fertility of the soil for a given time," he warned, "is progress toward ruining the more long-lasting sources of that fertility."[13]

Bateson's double-bind theory echoes Marx's prescient warning. That is, technology appears to offer win-win solutions to environmental crises, or solutions that do not involve compromising convenience, consumption, or capital growth. However, these solutions rely on the same kinds of natural resource exploitation that generate crisis in the first place. Solar and wind energy systems, for instance, take up enormous amounts of land. In addition, solar panels are frequently manufactured in China using toxic materials, while onshore wind farms can harm bats and birds, which can have reverberations up and down the food chain. Offshore wind farms similarly disrupt aquatic systems, and so on. "Green" consumption convinces consumers that they can purchase their way to environmental safety and out of climate crisis.[14] Yet green labeling is nebulous at best. Moreover, green consumables are caught up in the same cycles of production, transportation and waste generation that have harmed the environment in the first place.

Even so, the market for sustainable products continues to grow by leaps and bounds. In the US alone, profits from such products reached $128.5 billion in 2018 and were expected to rise to $150 billion by 2021.[15] Why does the promise of green products and lifestyles resonate so powerfully with environmentally concerned consumers? Part of the answer can be explained through a Freudo-Marxist perspective, that is, the dynamics between psychological drives and market capitalism. Briefly, psychoanalyst Jacques Lacan theorized that at around six to eighteen months (the "mirror" stage), a child begins to understand that there is a split between its internal drives and impulses and an outer self that is part of the social world. The child also recognizes that the fulfilment of its needs and desires depends on another person, usually its mother. These interrelated realizations create a sense of alienation and anxiety that Lacan refers to as *lack*. As individuals mature, they retain a sense of lack and are therefore driven—and constituted by—a relentless quest for reintegration, wholeness and unadulterated joy, which Lacan calls *jouissance*. The anxious pursuit of *jouissance*, however, is inherently contradictory and futile, because we can never actually reintegrate and return to our pre-mirror stage. Nonetheless, we persist in our pursuit, projecting images of expected *jouissance* onto various others, people, objects and experiences.[16]

Lacan believed that the pursuit of *jouissance* is part of the human condition and that people will seek it through whatever channels are available to them. Capitalism, Lacan proposed, is an especially well-suited channel. The capitalist imperative to find new avenues for profit syncs up perfectly with individual drives to find ways of salving anxieties and lack. The result is an ever-unfolding array of new products, experiences, and services that promise self-actualization, joy and contentment. In other words, as political philosophers, Gilles Deleuze and Felix Guattari argue, capitalism abstracts, fragments, and rechannels our desires into consumption. Over time, consumers become overwhelmed by choices and distractions, which ultimately reinforce the very neuroses we are trying to resolve. This contradiction, in turn, produces a distorted reality, which Deleuze and Guattari refer to as a kind of schizophrenia.[17] Importantly, in their formulation, schizophrenia is primarily a social condition that is brought about by the ways contemporary capitalism interacts with individual psyches. Their intention (and mine) is not to diminish the seriousness of the psychological illness known as schizophrenia in which individuals become detached from reality, but to use that illness as a metaphor for a more general state of fragmentation and abstracted reality produced by capitalism.

*Sustainaphrenia* builds on this metaphor to describe how public concerns and anxieties about climate change are abstracted and reconfigured into consumer-oriented behaviors, technologies, and policies that do not actually address the root of the problem. As Marx found with the metabolic rift, capitalistic quick fixes for environmental crises only lead to more extensive and more destructive crises that generate new opportunities for quick fixes, and on and on. Over time, capitalism's cycles of crisis and resolution speed up and the "sorcerer" becomes more entrenched and powerful.[18] Eventually, capitalism comes to exist perpetually "on the edge of chaos."[19] This book delves into the heart of that chaos, investigating how the capital-driven solutions to both economic and climate crisis came together in the late twentieth and early twenty-first century.

## Empire State of Mind

From the time Dutch colonists forced the Lenape peoples off of their land, New Yorkers refused to see natural borders as a limit to growth. As historian Ted Steinberg explains, when European settlers arrived in the early seventeenth century, founding New Netherland, the area was brimming with rich salt marshes that supported a vast ecosystem. As the British colonies expanded over the next century, economic competition drove New Yorkers to extend the very land underneath their feet into those waterways. Residents habitually deposited their garbage and other waste products just off land's edge, into the shallow waters of the Hudson and East Rivers, or the New York Bay. It soon became clear that they could pile more dirt on top of mounting waste piles and transform them into actual land. In the mid-1700s, city leaders responded to an increasing demand for more commercial space by allowing private owners to purchase these underwater lots and turn them into commercial spaces.[20] By 1900, Manhattan's original footprint had expanded by almost one thousand feet on each side, narrowing the East and Hudson Rivers, as well as New York Bay.[21] As Steinberg writes, "nearly three Manhattan Island's worth of open water was filled, and an area of tidal marsh and underwater land in the Hudson estuary amounting to almost half the size of the five boroughs was lost to urban development."[22] Such manipulations to the land were key to expanding the city's capacity as a trade center, which in turn attracted droves of laborers, merchants, and others. Soon, the city was bursting with labor power, capital, and other goods. To sustain this level of growth, city leaders had to access more and more land and natural resources, extending the city even further into local waterways.

The fervor for expansion decimated a robust oyster industry and wreaked havoc on the city's underwater ecology in general. This, in turn, destroyed the city's supply of clean water. Waterborne diseases were multiplying, as was fire damage. Moreover, without a supply of fresh water, local industries could not survive, let alone grow. Plenty of fresh water was available north of the city, however. After several years of deliberation and opposition from residents of Westchester County, the state of New York permitted the city to construct an aqueduct, which opened in 1842.[23] An elaborate system of pipes diverted water from the Croton River and fed it into New York City, allowing the city to grow unimpeded. The aqueduct, however, did no favors for the city's waterways. Unfettered economic growth meant that unlimited amounts of human and industrial waste were put directly into New York's harbor and rivers. By this time, the industrial era had arrived in full force. The city's human population boomed, and steamships filled its waterways, importing raw materials and exporting finished goods.

City leaders now confronted another spatial crisis. The robust economy needed more room to grow, but further expansion into the city's already narrowed rivers was out of the question. Thanks to advances in engineering, New York expanded upward, its buildings climbing toward the sky. Not only did skyscrapers resolve a crisis of space, they also resolved an oncoming crisis of accumulation. Real estate became a flourishing industry unto itself, creating a mechanism for reinvesting surplus capital while also generating new sources of revenue and employment. In urban centers like New York City, the spatial fix continually bumps up against the limits of physical space. Continued expansion thus requires an ongoing process of creative destruction, of remaking the old (or the less-old) into the new.[24]

This process had enormous environmental impacts. Not only did it require vast amounts of raw materials, it also involved paving over more and more surface area, including small rivulets and waterways that ran throughout the city. During heavy rains, there was nothing to absorb stormwater, so it combined with overflows from the city's sewers and drained into the rivers, further destroying marine life. Water also collected underground until it rose into the streets, causing the street corner floods and potholes that continue to plague today's New Yorkers. In addition, sky-piercing buildings trapped heat, creating an "urban heat island" effect, which would eventually raise the city's overall temperature.

In the 1930s, the accumulation and concentration of wealth generated by the industrial era ran headlong into the Great Depression. This time, it took federal New Deal programs and nearly a decade to bring the city out of crisis. In particular, the Works Progress Administration (WPA) funded public works and infrastructure programs, such as the La Guardia airport, the Lincoln Tunnel, as well as hospitals, public parks, and pools. However, New Deal programs did not benefit all New Yorkers equally. African Americans were banned from over twenty-four of the city's trade unions, and African Americans, Puerto Ricans, and other immigrants were frequently denied WPA jobs.[25] The situation improved somewhat during World War II, as New York City served as the main point of military embarkation and hosted a number of wartime industries, including media outlets.[26]

After World War II, the federal government continued to play a substantive role in economic development. The Federal Highways Act, the Federal Housing Authority, and the GI Bill sponsored the expansion of the suburbs and made it possible for white families to buy homes, build

equity, and achieve higher education. Certain ethnic communities—
Jews, Italians, Irish, Polish—especially benefitted from such programs
and were able to establish solid footing in American's middle classes.
However, once again, black and brown-skinned Americans were excluded from federal benefits, missing the opportunity to accumulate
wealth to pass down to future generations.[27] In the next chapter, I discuss the effects of suburban expansion on people of color and on New
York City in general. For now, it is important to note that the post-World
War II cycle of accumulation eventually found its crisis in the 1970s.

Throughout the 1960s, new technologies in shipping, refrigeration,
and logistics made it easier for companies to globalize and expand (or
move) their operations overseas.[28] New York City's politicians and corporate leaders foresaw the bleak future of US manufacturing and began
discouraging industrial development in favor of real estate investment.
They campaigned to bring corporate headquarters to downtown Manhattan, and to expand the finance, insurance, real estate, and media sectors. But tax revenues had yet to catch up with this transition. In fact,
the city's coffers were suffering mightily from deindustrialization and
white flight to the suburbs. New York City began to rely more and more
on state and federal aid to finance its ample social welfare programs. By
1969, nearly 47 percent of the city's revenues were coming from external public funding.[29] Municipal bonds, issued by the country's largest
banks, also supplied a sizeable chunk of the city's revenues. As the city's
debt increased, the banks raised their interest rates.

In the early 1970s, export competition from Western Europe and
Japan, increased industrialization in the global south diminished rates
of production in New York City and across the US. Then, the 1973 oil
embargo spiked fuel prices, which slowed production even more, driving the city further into financial crisis. In 1974, the banks recalled about
40 percent of New York's municipal bond debt.[30] City leaders initially
appealed to New York Governor Hugh Carey, who agreed to advance
funds to the city provided that the city turn over its financial management to the state.

It was around this time that the ideas of economist Friedrich Hayek
began to enjoy a renaissance. Hayek had argued in the 1930s that a
free market required that the state play an active role in supporting
business growth.[31] Hayek's philosophy, which became known as neo-

liberalism, held that free market capitalism was not just an economic approach, it was an all-encompassing way of looking at, and being, in the world. Through this lens, humans and businesses both follow natural logics based on competition, supply and demand, and self-interest. Regulations—whether environmental, labor, or corporate—were unnecessary and only interfered with this natural order. In fact, it was in the state's best interest to roll back regulations and create an architecture that allowed businesses to flourish so they could act as good citizens, reinvesting in public education and other programs that fuel labor and consumer markets. Neoliberal logics held, moreover, that markets will always try to broaden their consumer base and exercise race, gender, and ethnic neutrality. Hierarchies exist, of course, but they are based on an individuals' ability to compete, not on their ascribed social status. After the upheavals of the 1960s and in the throes of the 1970s recession, Hayek's ideas garnered a new fanbase among up-and-coming conservative politicians such as Margaret Thatcher and Ronald Reagan, as well as business leaders. In 1972, a group of the country's most powerful CEOs formed a lobbying group, known as the Business Roundtable, with the explicit aim of influencing public policy to minimize government interference in business affairs.

Back in New York, Governor Carey appointed a similar entity, the Financial Control Board (FCB, to oversee New York City's finances. Modeled after the Business Roundtable, the FCB was comprised of high-ranking corporate leaders, including some of the same bankers who had raised interest rates and then recalled the city's loans. But whereas the Roundtable was established to lobby for a pro-business agenda, the FCB had direct power to implement that agenda. Immediately, the FCB implemented austerity measures such as a public worker wage freeze, a subway fare hike, the closing of several public hospitals, and massive reductions in public services—including ending free tuition at the City University of New York. Even so, within a few months, the city was once again on the verge of bankruptcy. This time, its leaders appealed to the federal government for assistance. While Congressional representatives were sympathetic to the gravity of the situation (if the city defaulted on its loans, the ripple effect on banks as well as bondholders would be enormous). President Gerald Ford, however, vowed to veto[32] any bailout that came before him, forcing the FCB to implement even tougher austerity measures.[33]

One example was the austerity policy termed *planned shrinkage*, which New York's housing commissioner Roger Starr proposed in 1976. To conserve public expenditures, this policy directed city services to central business districts and white middle and upper-middle-class enclaves and away from communities of color.[34] Fire protection, trash collection, and schools were all reduced in poor neighborhoods such as Harlem, the South Bronx, and Bedford Stuyvesant. By the mid-1970s, the Bronx reportedly had 120,000 fires per year—an average of thirty fires every two hours. Forty percent of the housing in the area was destroyed.[35] These conditions, along with increased racial unrest due to desegregation, drove even larger numbers of white families from the city—during the 1970s, New York City lost more than eight hundred thousand people.[36]

The fiscal crisis of the 1970s ushered in a new era for New York City and for the nation as a whole by empowering a group of corporate elites to serve a quasi-political role. Under the rubric of austerity, this group operationalized the idea that private investment was the only vehicle that could drive the city. New policies privatized public services and generally made the city more hospitable to business. At the same time, they blamed the fiscal crisis on profligate municipal spending, especially on salaries and benefits for city workers and on entitlement programs for low-income residents. Such narratives would prop up neoliberal configurations of power for decades to come.

## The Spatial Fix(es) Are In

In 1964, British sociologist Ruth Glass coined the term "gentrification" to encapsulate one form of the spatial fix. Glass used the term to describe how real estate investment in working-class neighborhoods in central London was transforming them into enclaves for affluent young professionals:

> One by one, many of the working-class quarters of London have been invaded by the middle classes—upper and lower. Shabby, modest mews and cottages—two rooms up and two down—have been taken over, when their leases have expired, and have become elegant, expensive residences. Larger Victorian houses, downgraded in an earlier or recent periods—

which were used as lodging houses or were otherwise in multiple occupation—have been upgraded once again . . . The current social status and value of such dwellings are frequently in inverse relation to their size, and in any case enormously inflated by comparison with previous levels in their neighborhoods. Once this process of "gentrification" starts in a district, it goes on rapidly until all or most of the original working-class occupiers are displaced, and the whole social character of the district is changed.[37]

Gentrification was an ideal vehicle for the spatial fix in urban centers because it established new housing markets within the confines of existing space. In addition, land speculation both stored and created excess capital.

In his 1978 inaugural speech, New York City Mayor Ed Koch announced his intention to promote gentrification and rescue neighborhoods previously targeted by planned shrinkage and other austerity measures. Koch came through on his promise, launching a multibillion-dollar housing program that funded affordable housing (especially for middle-class residents) in some of the city's most neglected neighborhoods. More controversially, he offered tax abatements to private developers, who took advantage of bottomed-out land values in areas targeted for redevelopment.[38] These tax abatements helped to widen what geographer Neil Smith refers to as the "rent gap," or the difference between "the actual capitalized ground rent (land price) of a plot of land given its present use, and the potential ground rent that might be gleaned under a 'higher and better' use."[39] The wider the rent gap, the more investment capital pours into an area. Eventually, that area becomes saturated, and investors move their capital to another part of the city where the gap is growing. As Smith writes, "Capital jumps from one place to another, then back again, both creating and destroying its own opportunities for development."[40]

Post-crisis policies also helped to consolidate and centralize the finance, insurance, and real estate (FIRE) sectors. This brought new populations of affluent white-collar professionals into the city during work hours—but city leaders also wanted them to stay for dinner, drinks, and dancing. Even more, they wanted these people to move in. The crisis-ridden 1970s had turned New York's tagline into "the most dangerous city in the world." To attract white collar workers—and tourists—the city would need a new brand. In 1978, the state's Department of Commerce launched the "I Love NY" campaign. Within a few years, the campaign successfully shifted New York's image from a place of danger to the place to be, a center for culture, night life, fashion, and sophisticated culinary expertise.[41]

The I Love NY campaign, and New York's post-fiscal crisis agenda more generally, represented a sea change in urban planning and policies. While municipalities never shied away from business growth and development, prior to the 1970s, urban policy was primarily concerned with infrastructure planning and the provision of housing, health and education, as well as services not provided by the market.[42] After the 1970s, many services were either cut or privatized, making municipalities into purchasers of services rather than providers of them. In addition, a significant retraction in federal funding meant that the aggressive and entrepreneurial pursuit of investment and capital became central to the mission of urban governments. The importance of real estate development to this mission cannot be overestimated—not only did it provide a spatial fix for excess capital, it also created new places to live, work and play, all of which generated more capital. Branding and marketing played an essential role in this process, especially as intercity competition grew increasingly fierce. The next two sections explain how sustainability came to be part of this fray.

## A Brief History of Sustainability

The end of World War II ushered in a new era of globalism, especially when it came to economics. Many of the world's nations entered into multilateral trade agreements, treaties and organizations designed to rebuild the economies of war-devastated nations. New international aid programs were also established, promoting the idea that "first world" countries had a responsibility to rescue "third world" countries from poverty and repressive governments. This new economic world order significantly benefitted the US and later Europe and Japan, as well. Stabilizing export trade markets ensured profits for companies in the global north. International aid provided a rationale and mechanism for outsourcing manufacturing operations to resource-rich, developing nations while accessing their raw materials and cheap labor. Often, developing countries became ensnared in complex webs of debt and dependence.[43] For example, programs designed to support agriculture introduced pesticides, monocropping, and technologically advanced equipment, all of which had to be purchased or rented from companies in the global north.[44] When revolutions and political unrest in Africa and Central America threatened to disrupt these relationships in the 1960s, nations in the global north stepped up their funding for international aid programs in the hope that reducing poverty would mean fewer revolutions.

But as the next two decades wore on, the failure of these programs to eradicate poverty and the environmental degradation they triggered became inescapable.[45] In 1983, the UN Secretary General convened a commission to set an agenda for better development practices that prioritized social, economic, and environmental goals over such devastating growth. In 1987, the commission published "Our Common Future," also known as the Brundtland Report (named for the former Prime Minister of Norway, Gro Harlem Brundtland, the commission's convener), stating:

> A world in which poverty and inequity are endemic will always be prone to ecological and other crises. Sustainable development meets the needs of the present without compromising the ability of future generations to meet their own needs.[46]

The Brundtland Report's call for ecologically and socially conscious growth appealed to free-market capitalists.[47] For instance, water distribution in developing countries was subject to tribalism, political rivalries and inefficiencies. Sustainability principles boosted the efforts of development agencies that were trying to solve this problem by privatizing water systems. Private companies, the thinking went, could manage such services in efficient and neutral ways.

The authors of the Brundtland Report were also influenced by the principles of ecological modernization, a set of ideas put forward in the early 1980s by a group of German scholars. Briefly, these scholars argued that the productive and more efficient use of natural resources also led to future growth. Developing tools for those productive uses required research and development, production, and distribution—all processes that helped stimulate the economy.[48] Sustainable development was thus closely linked to technology and capitalism from the beginning. The faster these technologies came online, the better. As geographer Erik Swyngedouw explains, white papers circulating among policy makers and development officials shared "the basic vision that techno-natural and socio-metabolic interventions are urgently needed if we wish to secure the survival of the planet and much of what it contains."[49] A language of crisis implied that it was imperative to turn to the private sector to develop these technologies quickly and without getting bogged down by red tape and bureaucracy.

The Brundtland Report instigated a series of global discussions. Some of the most influential of those took place during the 1992 United Nations Conference on Environment and Development in Rio de Janeiro (known as the "Earth Summit"). There, participants adopted Agenda 21, an action plan for carrying out the sustainable development ideals of combatting poverty and pollution and conserving natural resources.[50] The agreement was nonbinding, and essentially offered a prescription for how local and national governments could achieve sustainability. One hundred and seventy-eight countries, including the United States, signed on in support of the agreement, and the United Nations, the World Bank, and other international organizations began using it as a guideline for international development programs.

Multinational discussions and agreements on sustainability effectively repackaged neoliberal development agendas and staked out new territory for the expansion of capital. By stressing the need to address deforestation, monocropping, and other kinds of ecological devastation in developing countries, they reinvigorated the very international development apparatus that had created that devastation in the first place. The urgency of climate change justified quick fixes and vague regulations which in turn led to environmental opportunism. By emphasizing ecological modernization and privatization, these agreements established new markets for products and services. Finally, a commodified, consumer-oriented approach to sustainability resonated with neoliberal ideologies about individual choice and responsibility.

My point here is not to diminish the empirical facts and realities of climate crisis. Rather, my aim is to illustrate how, and with what effect, neoliberal capitalism has dominated solutions to climate change from the global to the local to the individual. For instance, in 2006, Al Gore's award-winning documentary, *An Inconvenient Truth*, riveted and alarmed viewers with clear facts about climate change. The film became one of the most watched documentaries in the world and helped Gore win a Nobel Peace Prize. While Gore calls for the "political will" to develop alternative energy sources and new technologies that will decarbonize the atmosphere, the film's conclusion centers on personal responsibility:

> Each one of us is a cause of global warming, but each one of us can make choices to change that with the things we buy, the electricity we use, the cars we drive; we can make choices to bring our individual carbon emissions to zero. The solutions are in our hands, we just have to have the determination to make it happen.[51]

The film amplified an already loud message that buying green products was both a political and a moral issue, well worth the higher cost of green products.

Paradoxically, studies on the impact of green consumerism raise questions about its efficacy. A recent study of German consumers, for instance, found that "individuals with high pro-environmental self-identity intend to behave in an ecologically responsible way, but they typically emphasize actions that have relatively small ecological benefits."[52] These results are striking considering that Germany has an extensive and regularized system for green labelling, especially in comparison with the US. The study also points out that consumers themselves tend to offset even the small benefits of eco-consumerism through other kinds of consumption like frequent air travel, owning large homes, and buying a lot of products, often imported. In fact, the main predictor of an individual's carbon footprint is not the kind of cleaning solution they purchase or the car they drive, but their wealth. A 2015 study by Oxfam found that over half of the world's carbon emissions could be attributed to the wealthiest 10 percent of the world's population.[53]

Sustainability thus came to represent far more than the development goals set out by the Brundtland report. It came to embody a host of morally coded but vaguely defined technologies, services, and consumer markets.[54] And, it came to represent a pro-environmental identity that appealed to the progressively minded, affluent professionals Mayor Bloomberg hoped to bring to his luxury city in the early 2000s.

## "The Green Emperor Is Butt Naked"

Environmentally Friendly, LEED Certified, GREEN, Ultra Luxury Townhouse
You don't have to pretend to be environmentally friendly anymore; with ownership of this trophy landmark you are entitled. You can now live in decadence and snub your nose to all when you purchase this GREEN Masterpiece.
—Real estate listing for a renovated 1910 Harlem townhouse, 2008[55]

Shortly after taking office in 2002, Mayor Michael Bloomberg and his Deputy Mayor of Economic Development, Dan Doctoroff (an investment banker-turned-civil servant) submitted a bid to the International Olympic Committee (IOC) to hold the 2012 Olympics in New York City. Like all IOC bids, the submission included a comprehensive plan for creating the spatial arrangements necessary to accommodate the Olympics. Such bids provide city leaders with an opportunity to push forward a redevelopment agenda and to market their city globally as well as nationally. However, the IOC rejected New York City's proposal because it did not comply with the organization's standards for sustainability.[56] The rejection put Bloomberg and Doctoroff on alert. Rival cities—London, Paris, Stockholm, and Munich—had already begun implementing Agenda 21, which sought to make sustainability central to urban planning. If New York was going to compete with these cities, it would have to follow suit. A few years later, Bloomberg and Doctoroff reapplied. To repackage the plan, they hired TwoTwelve, a public information design firm specializing in sustainability.[57] Although New York's bid now incorporated more sustainability goals and measures, the IOC rejected it a second time.

Again, the bid had as much to do with implementing Bloomberg's vision for redevelopment as it did with hosting the Olympics. Accordingly, the mayor reconfigured it and released it to the public as the "Five Borough Redevelopment Plan," which proposed rezoning dozens of low-income, waterfront neighborhoods to create high-end residential and commercial space. Community groups voiced strong opposition, citing concerns about its harmful impacts on low-income residents, neighborhood character, and historic buildings. After months of negative press suffocated the plan, the administration backed off and regrouped.

Bloomberg and Doctoroff turned to McKinsey and Co., a management consulting conglomerate that specializes in international development and public sector projects.[58] They also hired former City Planning Commissioner Alex Garvin to conduct a study of the city's long-term growth potential. Garvin reported that New York's population would add a million new people by the year 2030, and that the city's industrial waterfronts and rail yards could be developed to house them.[59] Building on the data in the Garvin report, McKinsey and Co. recombined the redevelopment goals from the Five Borough Plan with a long list of energy-efficiency and greening initiatives. They then joined forces with TwoTwelve to repackage the whole agenda as "PlaNYC 2030."[60] On Earth Day, 2007, Bloomberg launched *PlaNYC: A Greener, Greater New York,* declaring that it would "prepare the city for one million more residents, strengthen the economy, combat climate change, and enhance the quality of life for all New Yorkers."[61] Specifically, the plan set a goal for reducing citywide carbon emissions by 30 percent below 2005 levels and laid out 127 measurable objectives and milestones for building market rate and affordable housing, and for fostering economic and sustainable development.[62] Sustainable initiatives included instituting greater efficiencies in managing storm water overflows and energy use, as well as reducing air pollution and creating new waterfront parks, green spaces, bike lanes, farmer's markets, and other environmentally minded amenities.

Bloomberg's timing could not have been better. 2007 was the same year that *An Inconvenient Truth* won the Academy Award, and the popularity of green branding was reaching new heights. Framing his redevelopment strategies as part of a larger vision for sustainability resolved Bloomberg's previous problems with pushback. Sociologist Miriam Greenberg argues that PlaNYC was essentially a public relations effort to rebrand New York: "Greening, with its connotations of quality of life, transparency, innovation, and resilience, was the ideal antidote to image crises."[63] Old-school New York liberals feared that "the luxury city" was a regressive attempt to expunge the city's low-income populations. "The sustainable city," however, was aimed directly at liberals' concerns for the environment and climate change, and it resonated with their pro-environmental identities. Greenberg quotes a high-level marketing official from the NYC Economic Development Corporation, who clarifies the advantages of the sustainability brand:

> If you think of a city as being sustainable and green, you think of it as cleaner, safer, friendlier—it does a lot to undermine negative perceptions of the city . . . If you are going to be moving big businesses with all of their upper-level employees, you have to show them that their kids will be provided for, that they're going to be able to breath clean air, ride their bikes somewhere . . . [Sustainability] works really well for us, in everything we do, to have this kind of reputation.[64]

Sustainability thus became shorthand for developing the kind of city that "upper-level employees" desired—one that provided health, recreation, and well-being. In this vision, just being a New Yorker would mean participating in a healthier, greener lifestyle.

PlaNYC 2030 was a game changer. Two Twelve's branding and marketing expertise ensured that the Plan's reputation extended well beyond New York City. Within a few years, Bloomberg was hailed as a global leader in the fight against climate change, and New York City appeared regularly on various lists of the "world's most sustainable cities." Notably, Greenberg finds that such lists are often created by either trade organizations or consulting firms, which then partner with public relations firms to publicize the awards. Competition to appear on these lists then feeds more business to both industries. In sum, PlaNYC and other sustainability agendas both feed and are fed by an incestuous network of trade organizations, consulting and marketing firms, economic development agencies, and real estate professionals.[65]

This is not to reduce PlaNYC to a mere marketing ploy. Its Cool Roofs program re-covered over ten million square feet of city roofs with reflective paint, which cooled inside temperatures and reduced the need for air conditioners. New requirements forced building owners to make energy-efficient upgrades, to phase out highly polluting heating oil blends, and to switch to natural gas. Buses, taxis, garbage trucks, police cars, and other city-owned vehicles were changed to hybrid or natural gas vehicles. In addition to lowering air pollution and asthma rates, these measures lowered the city's carbon emissions. Between 2005 and 2015, greenhouse gas emissions decreased in New York City by approximately 14.8 percent.[66]

At the same time, researchers have questioned the source of those reductions. For instance, carbon emissions in the US fell by 11 percent between 2007 and 2013; experts attribute about 75 percent of this decline to decreases in production and consumption caused by the 2008 recession.[67] As the recession has abated, emissions have crept up again. In 2018, carbon dioxide emissions rose by 3.4 percent in the US,[68] and by 2.7 percent on a global level, the largest increase in seven years.[69]

Bloomberg's "win-win" strategy for climate-friendly redevelopment was similarly questionable. By the time the mayor left office in 2016, his administration had rezoned over one-third of the city, lifting height and use restrictions to make way for a massive number of high-rise and high-density residential and commercial buildings.[70] Despite energy efficiencies imposed during Bloomberg's administrations, buildings accounted for approximately 67 percent of New York City's carbon emissions in 2017.[71] In particular, the glass-covered buildings that became ubiquitous during the Bloomberg era did a poor job of insulating energy.[72] Even sustainable building materials (Italian marble, bamboo flooring, solar panels) had to be imported from faraway places, and construction, of course, required the use of fossil fuels.[73] The city's swelling population also taxed its already inefficient sewer and storm water drainage systems, while new waterfront properties encroached on natural flood protections. But these points often got lost in the din of positive press the Bloomberg administration received for adding a million street trees to the city's sidewalks, carving 250 miles of new bike lanes into the urban landscape, and adding scores of new parks, plazas, and greenways.

A year prior to the release of PlaNYC, Bloomberg and Doctoroff created an Office of Sustainability and Long-Range Planning (OSLRP), charging it with developing and implementing PlaNYC. They hired an ex-McKinsey executive to direct the organization. Almost immediately, the new director convened a Sustainability Advisory Board (SAB) comprised of seventeen business and community leaders.[74] WEACT's Executive Director, Peggy Shepard, was one of those invited to sit on the SAB. She recalled:

It soon became clear that the long-term vision for the plan would focus narrowly on infrastructure needs and metrics that would enable the city to effectively track and evaluate its progress. PlaNYC was never envisioned as a broad-based planning process that engaged area residents.[75]

As Shepard notes, PlaNYC skirted the detailed public approval process prescribed in the New York City Charter.[76] Rather, between January and March of 2007, OSLRP organized focus groups with selected nonprofits. They also held eleven town hall meetings in which they presented a slideshow that included background data on the challenges facing the city and highlighted ten main sustainability goals.[77] OSLRP also then solicited public comments.

Considering that OSLRP held these public meetings right up until the month before the plan was finalized, there was a preset limit to how many, and to what extent, public input would be integrated into the final version. This kind of highly controlled public engagement is known as "participation by consultation," according to James Pretty, a biologist who has published widely on his work in sustainable development and civic engagement. Pretty defines participation by consultation as "people participating by being consulted or by answering questions. External agents define problems and information gathering processes, and so control analysis." However, Pretty continues, this process "does not concede any share in decision making, and professionals are under no obligation to take on board the people's view."[78] In terms of assessment, PlaNYC similarly offered a transparent and publicly accessible system. But assessment procedures relied exclusively on metrics, milestones, and quarterly targets.[79] The public could review this quantitative data online, but there were no metrics or opportunities to evaluate PlaNYC's social justice implications or its qualitative effects on everyday lives.

In this way, PlaNYC 2030 synced perfectly with neoliberalism's technocratic approaches to both sustainability and governance. Just as neoliberal ideals valorize the neutral logics of a self-regulating, market-based economy, technocratic models endorse procedures of governance that rely primarily on highly specialized expertise, technical knowledge, and quantifiable data.[80] In addition, these models of governance uphold politically liberal values such as transparency, consensus, and civic participation.[81] However, as many critics caution, in practice, these values never come to fruition. Rather, technocratic models mute or marginalize dissention, inequality, and cultural distinctions.[82] Ultimately, a language of participation, transparency, and engagement becomes a veneer that masks the consolidation of power, wealth and privilege among a small number of elites.[83] As Beryl Thurman once said, "the green emperor is butt naked."

## Environmental Justice and the Politics of Co-option

Consolidating power and privilege is one thing—sustaining it is another. In liberal democratic political systems, one mechanism for maintaining power is through the appropriation of political opposition. Critical environmental scholars argue that green consumption does just that. In his book *Shopping our Way to Safety*, sociologist Andrew Szasz finds, "Consumers believe [green] products will protect them, which creates a kind of political 'anesthesia' that severely reduces their willingness to participate in collective political action to generate real change."[84] Because much of the discourse around climate change emphasizes individual consumer choices, environmentally concerned people believe that their purchases constitute political acts.[85] Philosopher Slavoj Zizek elaborates on this insight:

> The point is that, by buying [organic apples], we do not just consume a product—we simultaneously do something meaningful, show our caring selves and our global awareness and participate in a large collective project.[86]

According to Zizek, by paying slightly more to buy fair-trade coffee, consumers take a stance "against the ruthless capitalist exploitation of natural resources." However, in so doing, the consumer "is already caught in the commodification of experiences."[87] Green consumption thus provides a way to both express and displace anxieties about climate change. In that sense, it co-opts consumers' good intentions, using them to prop up capitalism and maintain the status quo.

Sustainability has also co-opted the language and, in some cases, the efforts of environmental justice activists. Indeed, environmental justice activists officially made sustainability one of their primary organizing principles in 1992, at the Earth Summit in Rio de Janeiro. This conference drew grassroots environmental justice activists from around the world to discuss and disseminate "The Seventeen Principles of Environmental Justice." Among other things, the Principles urged mainstream environmental groups to embrace a social-justice-oriented concept of sustainability.[88] WEACT staff members described how grassroots environmental justice activists influenced the spread of sustainability discourse in a 2008 article for *Reimagine Magazine*:

> Sustainable development is often presented as a traditional environmental issue, but the forces that led to its emergence are not the traditional "greens." Any credible analysis of sustainable development will reveal that it was social justice movements that propelled the "greens" into thinking in terms of equity and justice for present and future generations.[89]

On the face it, the popularity of sustainability seemed like a significant "win" for the environmental justice movement. Yet, approximately thirty years into the movement and after the Rio Summit, people of color around the globe continue to face greater environmental risks than their white counterparts.

In the United States alone, ample studies document that race continues to be the main predictor of the clustering of hazardous waste sites.[90] A 2019 study by the National Academy of Sciences found that blacks and Hispanics respectively experience 56 percent and 63 percent more pollution than their consumption generates. Whites, however, experience 17 percent less pollution than their consumption generates.[91] The EPA itself released a study in 2018 which found that black Americans are exposed to about 1.5 times more particulate matter than whites, and that Hispanics had about 1.2 times the exposure of non-Hispanic whites.[92]

Year after year, and decade after decade, the statistics rarely vary. Racial disparities are as deeply ingrained in the landscapes of cities, suburbs, and rural areas across the United States as capitalism is ingrained in the US political economy. American Studies professor Julie Sze writes that "environmental violence is built into the history of the United States. It is not an aberration, but part and parcel of a political economic system based on racialized extraction of land and labor, including from Indigenous peoples."[93] In other words, capitalism relies on the exploitation of land and natural resources, *and* the simultaneous exploitation of people of color, whether by dispossessing their land, exploiting their labor, or organizing the landscape so that these communities take the brunt of environmental hits generated by overproduction and overdevelopment.[94] However well-intentioned the sustainability era seems, after more than a decade, little has been done to advance the cause of environmental justice.

What sustainability *has* done, this book shows, is to rearrange uneven geographies of race, space, and waste. As early as 2006, environmental justice activists expressed concern about the "unintended impacts" of brownfield and Superfund cleanups. That year, the National Environmental Justice Advisory Council (NEJAC) published a study outlining five case studies in which cleanup efforts paved the way for gentrification and displacement. (Two subsequent studies found correlations between the location of publicly funded brownfield or Superfund cleanups and a rise in proximal property values[95]). The NEJAC report offered six recommendations for avoiding the unintended consequences of cleanup programs. Three of them centered on the need to improve public opportunities "for *meaningful* involvement in redevelopment and revitalization projects."[96] However, as sustainability became a ubiquitous part of urban planning over the next few years, the unintended consequences of environmental improvements intensified and participatory opportunities seemed to grow more superficial.

Taking notice of these trends, urban and environmental justice scholars began exploring the process known as environmental gentrification: the ways sustainability initiatives serve high-end redevelopment, and threaten to displace low-income communities of color.[97] Such studies examine what Gould and Lewis call "the green growth machine," a cadre of elite real estate developers and governmental officials whose aim is to "harness environmental concerns to generate publicly funded environmental amenities and restoration" for the purpose of raising property values. Not only do higher property values return greater tax revenues, they also increase the financial gains of investors.[98] Some of these studies focus on the ways that new parks or other green spaces have accompanied rising property values and demographic shifts.[99] Others investigate how environmental restorations, or "ecological gentrification" have displaced homeless people[100] or low-income communities.[101] Transportation improvements, including the transformation of old, elevated rail lines or problematic intersections into parks,[102] or the installation of bike lanes[103] and/or transit-oriented developments[104] also provide environmental amenities that serve gentrification. Similarly, research on "food gentrification" finds associations between redevelopment and healthy food establishments, like Whole Foods[105] or farmer's markets.[106] The cleanup and repurposing of former industrial sites offers another kind of opportunity to gentrify urban neighborhoods.[107] Some scholars also proffer solutions for less co-optive and more equitable revitalization. Curran and Hamilton offer a "Just Green Enough" strategy,[108] and Zavetovski and Ageyman suggest the idea of "Complete Streets" as a way to think more holistically about the effects of environmental improvements.[109]

Building on these and other studies of environmental gentrification, this book takes a deeper dive into the consequences it holds for environmental justice activism.[110] Putting environmental justice activists at the front and center of my narrative enables me to understand the dialectics of the co-option and contestation in which they engage. In addition, by locating my research primarily on Staten Island's North Shore, a *non*-gentrifying neighborhood, and comparing it to other neighborhoods around the city, I explore both the drivers and the consequences of environmental gentrification. In this way, I make a case for viewing the city as an interdependent system in which change in one area triggers change in others. Finally, I pay careful attention to the discursive power of sustainability and the ways it seeks to neutralize narratives about environmental racism. Altogether, I demonstrate that the contradictory dynamics of urban sustainability are designed not just to create profit opportunities for developers, but also to disable grassroots activism.

Importantly, I do not wish to represent this research as "traditional ethnography." Due to professional and personal constraints, I neither lived nor worked on Staten Island, and there were long periods when I was unable to travel there. Instead, I supplemented my field data with data from local media sources, blogs, Facebook groups, online comments, discussion forums, email blasts, and the websites of various city agencies. I also conducted extensive historical research using various books, articles, and public records, and analyzed them through the same ethnographic and political economic lens that I applied to all of my data. That is, I looked across my sources for patterns, contradictions, and discrepancies in the ways people discussed and represented issues of urban sustainability, environmental justice, economic development, zoning, and resilience, as well as how those issues played out in daily life. I compared the ways public agency websites described Brownfield initiatives, how agency representatives presented them at public meetings, how local activists reacted, and how the outcomes of those meetings were then reintegrated into agency websites. In the case of Brownfields, I was further able to track the first few years of the program's implementation, citywide. This last effort led me to a quantitative project, conducted with colleagues and students at the Queens College Department of Urban Studies, Office of Community Studies in the summer of 2015. This project sought to document environmental gentrification by mapping a decade's worth of rezonings, park development, and city-funded brownfield projects, and then connecting them to demographic changes in census tracts across the five boroughs. In the end, I consider my research to be less of an ethnography of a particular place or group as it is an ethnographic approach to a particular trend and moment in time.

I have divided the book into two parts. The first part identifies three distinct subcategories of environmental gentrification. Each chapter takes a historic view, probing the ways discourses of progress, revitalization, redevelopment, or sustainability veiled the accumulation of privilege for some, and environmental injustice for others. Chapter 2, set primarily in Harlem, examines "green gentrification" and tells a much longer story about green space and its relationship to property values, race and privilege. Chapter 3 develops my definition of "industrial gentrification" as an economic development strategy that replaces traditional, "heavy" industrial facilities with small-scale manufacturers.[111] Here, I use examples from the North Shore and across New York City to track the history of industrial versus residential zoning. This chapter also introduces my arguments about the consequences of environmental gentrification for non-gentrifying neighborhoods. Chapter 4 focuses on "brown gentrification," where private developers use public incentives to clean up and repurpose brownfield sites. Concentrating on the North Shore, I show how activists have challenged environmental gentrification and the selective ways that sustainability was put into practice. In

Part II, I stay on Staten Island in order to take a close look at grassroots activism in an era of sustainaphrenia. Chapter 5 analyzes the paradoxes of participatory politics. Tracking the ways neoliberal agendas appropriated civil rights discourses about civic engagement, I show how a growing emphasis on participation has co-opted and disabled grassroots activism. In chapter 6, I examine how climate instability fostered unlikely partnerships and coalitions that crossed multiple boundaries of geography, class, race and political affiliations. It is my hope that these partnerships speak for themselves in offering a way forward.

## Conclusion: The State of Sustainaphrenia

In *Democracy, Inc.*, political philosopher Sheldon Wolin offers an apocalyptic vision of politics under advanced capitalism. Using the term "inverted totalitarianism," Wolin describes how market-based economics have finally overtaken politics, commodifying both natural resources and living beings. For Wolin, inverted totalitarianism turns on the management of the populace. Debate, disagreement, and dissent are eschewed as unseemly and unproductive.[112] Instead, public participation is channeled into carefully managed opportunities for expression. Once everyone has had their say, consensus is assumed. As a managed democracy, Wolin argues, the public is shepherded, not sovereign.[113] Beryl Thurman has similarly referred to public meetings as "PR opportunities to make the government look like it's doing its job." I likewise argue that carefully orchestrated participatory opportunities reconfigured citizenship as consumerism. This left little room for conflict, dissent, or negotiation—the messy stuff of actual politics.

Participating in this façade has extracted a heavy cost—it has sucked up activists' time and energy and diverted them from their original goals for environmental justice even as it co-opted some of those goals to serve environmental gentrification. But refusing to "take a seat at the table" means being ostracized and characterized as being uncooperative or self-serving. This has left activists in an untenable position. Either they agree to "participate in their own repression" or they stand totally outside of the system.[114] As Thurman once told me, "You find out that the system that you think works one way actually works in a way that is not for you. And you're out there by yourself."

For Deleuze and Guattari, this dilemma is a product of late-stage capitalism and one of the hallmarks of schizophrenia. At the same time, however, ostracization also represents an opportunity for emancipation.

> Schizophrenia is the exterior limit of capitalism itself or the conclusion of its deepest tendency, but that capitalism only functions on condition that it inhibit this tendency, or that it push back or displace this limit. . . . Hence schizophrenia is not the identity of capitalism, but on the contrary its difference, its divergence, and its death.[115]

If Marx likened capitalism to a sorcerer whose spells will eventually run amuck, then schizophrenia marks that loss of control. In other words, it represents the point at which the sorcerer—capitalism—has produced the source of its own demise.

Sustainaphrenia tells the story of how sustainability got tangled up in these spells, driving the very crisis it was supposed to mitigate. The environmental activists who animate these pages refused to be lulled into that future; they called out the fallacies of sustainable development, the realities of environmental gentrification, and the false promises of participatory politics. This book details the very real stakes of their struggles.

2

# Wiped Out by the Green Wave

*Green Gentrification and the Value of Urban Nature*

In a 2016 editorial for the *New York Times*, historian Michael Henry Adams remembers joining a picket line, several years earlier, to protest the rezoning of 125th Street, Harlem's main commercial thoroughfare. Also known as Martin Luther King, Jr. Boulevard, 125th ran due west from the East River to Morningside Avenue, then in a northeast diagonal until it reached the Hudson River. At the time Adams's editorial was published, 125th Street still housed a few historic sites like the Studio Museum and the Apollo Theater, as well as the Adam Clayton Powell, Jr. state office building. But mostly it offered Harlem residents places to shop and eat. In addition to assorted fast food restaurants, "big box" stores, such as Staples, Old Navy, H&M, and a Gap Outlet, stood alongside city-based chain stores like V.I.M., which sold sneakers, hoodies, and other casual wear. In between, small storefronts testified to Harlem's role in the African diaspora. Here one could buy West African teas, Jamaican soaps and lotions, African American soaps and lotions, wigs, vegan Caribbean food, traditional soul food, pawned jewelry, and so on. On the sidewalks outside these stores, vendors—mostly from West Africa—sold t-shirts, socks, incense, handbags, jewelry, and other everyday items. Towards the eastern end of the street, a Metro North train station took commuters to Westchester and the Hudson Valley, and a variety of homeless shelters, food banks, methadone clinics, and rehab facilities served some of the city's lowest-income populations.

Adams and his fellow protestors feared that rezoning jeopardized this eclecticism. By lifting height and density restrictions, it would allow the construction of high-rise—and high-priced—hotels and condominiums. Adams recalls,

Even then, a few boys passing by on their bikes understood what was at stake. As we chanted, "Save Harlem now!" one of them inquired, "Why are y'all yelling that?" We explained that housing's good, in theory, but because the median income in Harlem is less than $37,000 a year, many of these new apartments would be too expensive for those of us who already live here. Hearing this, making a quick calculation, one boy in glasses shot back at his companions, "You see, I told you they didn't plant those trees for us."[1]

"Those trees" were courtesy of PlaNYC 2030's popular One Million Trees campaign, which planted new street trees on nearly every Harlem block.

The boy in Adams's narrative was indeed on to something. Along with street trees, city leaders were planting the seeds of change in Harlem. Already, the proportion of whites living in Central Harlem had more than doubled, and more dramatic changes were on the way. In 2015, the median household income in Central Harlem hovered around $38,621, reflecting its high number of public and subsidized housing units, while the median home resale price was $565,690, up 11.9 percent from the year before.[2] Three years later, northeast Harlem made it to number five on a national list of gentrifying zip codes (based on increases in home values, median income, and population of college-educated residents).[3] As Harlem whitened, it also greened. New parks lined both the Hudson and East Rivers, while Mt. Morris, Morningside, Jackie Robinson and St. Nicholas parks received upgrades. In 2017, a Whole Foods opened on the corner of 125th Street and Malcolm X Boulevard.

In some ways, none of this is news. Green spaces, including parks, squares, greenways, riverfronts, gardens, street trees and median plantings, have helped spike property values for centuries. And yet, the relationship between greening and real estate values intensified in the sustainaphrenic era. Using Harlem as my primary example, this chapter shows how struggles over green spaces mirrored larger political and economic shifts as well as the very localized concerns of nearby residents. At the same time, one of the main aims of this book is to show how green space investment (and dis-investment) in certain neighborhoods was intimately linked to investment in other neighborhoods. To elucidate these interdependent relationships, and to tell a more complete story

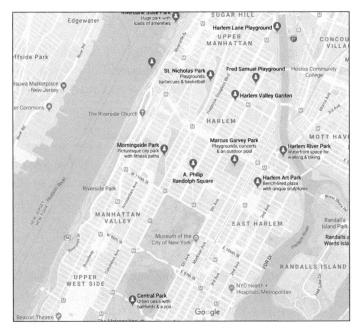

Map of Harlem parks. Credit: Map Data © 2019 Google

about green gentrification, I complement my Harlem case study with examples from other neighborhoods. Threaded through the spaces and time periods covered in this chapter are powerful ideologies about the symbolic and public value of urban nature and green space. The chapter tells the story of how these ideologies both fed and were in tension with the market value of urban land.

## Parks, Populism, and Property Values: Industrialism and its Discontents in the 1800s

As cities densified during the industrial era, their inhabitants struggled to adapt to new conditions of overcrowding, pollution, and noise. Romantic poets and artists in Europe responded to industrialism by praising nature's majesty and ability to inspire spirituality and sublime experiences. US artists followed suit, exalting nature as an antidote to the crowded, dirty conditions of urban life. Transcendentalists like Henry David Thoreau and Ralph Waldo Emerson pursued nature outside of cities, especially as advances in transportation during the Industrial Era made travel to remote places accessible to those who could afford it. Others focused on urban nature, still upholding the repose and uplift that it offered. In an editorial for the *Brooklyn Daily Eagle*, poet Walt Whitman mused on the power of the Fort Greene park to quiet all who came into contact with it:

> In cities, what a tumultuous thing is a mob! How coarse and clattering! So were not the thousands last night on Fort Greene. Quieted, refined by the poetic repose of Nature, they "behaved" after a method that would not have been unseemly in the parlors of nobles.[4]

For Whitman, the beauty of Fort Greene could bestow even the rowdiest mobs with the kind of refinement that nobles possessed.

For urban reformers like Whitman, nature did not just civilize the masses, it also imbued them with a certain morality, which then led to good health. A passage written by Dr. John H. Rauch, who helped pioneer the field of public health, illustrates how discourses about social refinement and moral uplift became indistinguishable in the mid-1800s.

> The moral influence of parks is decided. Man is brought in contact with nature, is taken away from the artificial conditions in which he lives in cities; and such associations exercise a vast influence for good.[5]

These writings motivated New York City elites to convene a Central Park Commission and charge it with creating the country's first landscaped public park.

But the conveners of the Central Park Commission also had a subtler, economic mission, one inspired by recent developments in industrial England. For nearly a century, London's poshest neighborhoods featured small parks or plazas, surrounded by elite residences. Those who owned these residences also held keys to the square. As the industrial era expanded, so did the number of wealthy families ready to purchase expensive homes. Accordingly, London's leaders decided to scale up the private square model and converted a large expanse of agricultural land into a high-end housing development that surrounded a large park, known as Regent's Park. Initially meant to be private, London's booming population eventually impelled its leaders to open Regent's to the public. Even so, the park continued to drive up the value of surrounding properties.[6]

With the English model in in mind, New York City's Central Park Commission held a design competition for Central Park. Unsurprisingly, they chose the designs of social reformer Frederick Law Olmsted and his mentor, Calvert Vaux. Olmsted was American but Vaux was British born, and their initial designs were modeled after English gardens. To that end, Olmstead designed most of the Park around wide paths that cut through lush, landscaped gardens. To complement these, he also designed the more rugged "ramble," a series of narrow, winding trails that travel over rocky, un-landscaped terrain. Olmstead believed that visiting the park would cure all New Yorkers of the symptoms of city life, which included "nervous tension, over-anxiety, hasteful disposition, impatience, [and] irritability."[7]

Despite the widespread appeal of this rhetoric, some New Yorkers were skeptical of the park's true purpose. A letter to the editor of the *New York Tribune* questions the motives of park developers:

> Will anyone pretend the Park is not a scheme to enhance the value of uptown land and create a splendid center for fashionable life, high rents, etc. Without regard to, and even in dereliction of, the happiness of the multitude upon whose hearts and hands all the expenses will fall?[8]

As this letter writer implies, park creators' disregard for "the multitude" undermined the lofty ideals they used to promote it.

Northern Manhattan was still largely agrarian, with steep, natural rock masses that made housing construction costly and difficult. Out of this land, the city created a total of four parks north of 59th Street— Central, running through the center of northern Manhattan, Morningside to the west, St. Nicholas to the north, and Mt. Morris to the east. Central Park was by far the largest, spanning 843 acres. According to city documents, the land cleared for Central Park was "wasteland" inhabited only by "squatters" living in "shanties." This was all the justification needed to decimate Seneca Village, the city's largest settlement of free blacks. Spanning six square blocks, the agrarian settlement housed 264 individuals, three churches, two schools and three cemeteries. Two-thirds of its population were African Americans. The remaining one-third consisted mostly of Irish and a few German immigrants.[9] Historians also believe that Native Americans likely lived on what became park land, although to date they have not found material evidence of their settlements.[10]

While the construction of the park removed certain populations, it attracted others. One by one, iconic, industrial-era families like the Astors, the Vanderbilts, the Fricks, and the Carnegies built mansions along the border of Central Park. Paradoxically, access to the park's natural beauty came courtesy of industries that were polluting natural resources in other places. Although Olmstead fought to keep all parts of the park public, he was also a proponent of the English model where parks generated enough property tax revenue to pay for themselves.[11] As mansions began to appear along Fifth Avenue, Olmstead kept track of property sales. His was the country's first data set on green space's effect on the real estate market. Sure enough, between 1856 and 1873, the tax base of the three wards around Central Park increased from $26.4 million to $236.1 million.[12] Relying on property values to sustain the park was one thing. Creating a truly populist park was another.

Mansion-dwellers did not necessarily want to share their park—no matter how civilizing an influence it was meant to be—with "the rabble." Already, traveling to the park from the Lower East Side, where the city's working classes lived, was a challenge. The trek uptown required either an expensive streetcar ride or a private vehicle. In addition, affluent families pressured the city to institute stringent rules prohibiting the commercial wagons that working-class families would have used for such a drive. They also banned picnics, ball playing on the meadows, and other activities enjoyed by non-elites.[13] As a result, the park's wide paths mainly carried the horse-drawn carriages of the affluent from one end of the park to the other. Even a Saturday concert series was unavailable to most of the working-class population, whose only day off was Sunday. It was not until the late nineteenth century that working-class New Yorkers launched a successful campaign to hold park concerts on Sundays as well.

These exclusions mirrored the biases of the national environmental movement. In addition to wanting to preserve nature as a sanctuary for well-heeled elites, early environmental organizations like the Sierra Club excluded Jews, blacks, Hispanics, and Asians.[14] Mid-to-late-nineteenth-century elites' anxieties and neuroses about urbanization and immigration were thus transfigured into an idealization of the anti-urban. While nature's uplift was theoretically available to all, in reality, only the wealthy had the opportunity to access it. Communing with nature then bestowed the upper classes with superior qualities that conveniently justified their privilege.

## Harlem Strut: The Great Migration (1910–1920s)

While the avenues around Central Park became uptown outposts of white affluence and privilege, the area's waterfronts became bustling industrial zones. In western Harlem, new dairies, meatpacking plants, warehouses, and other businesses set up shop along the Hudson River. An influx of new jobs brought large communities of Jews and Italians to central and eastern Harlem, respectively.[15] Other European immigrants soon joined them.[16] During World War I, however, many of these workers returned to their home countries to enlist in the military.[17] To replace them, industrial owners recruited blacks who were leaving the south in droves, fleeing repressive and racist post-Reconstruction regimes.[18] Between 1910 and 1920, the area's black population grew from approximately 10 percent to 32 percent. By 1930 it was 70 percent.[19] Elsewhere in the city, owners commonly refused to rent to black tenants. Well aware of the limited housing options for black tenants, Harlem landlords charged them more than double the rent they charged white tenants. In 1920, the average "white" rent on a one-room apartment in central Harlem was $40/month. For blacks, it was $100–$125/month.[20]

Nevertheless, plentiful industrial jobs allowed some Harlem families to save enough money to buy their own properties. They were encouraged by Marcus Garvey and other religious leaders who preached the gospel of self-sufficiency. Attracted by its growing reputation as the "Mecca for the new Negro,"[21] migrants from across Africa began moving to Harlem.[22] Poet James Weldon Johnson described the neighborhood in 1925:

In the make-up of New York, Harlem is not merely a Negro colony or community, it is a city within a city, the greatest Negro city in the world. It is not a slum or a fringe, it is located in the heart of Manhattan and occupies one of the most beautiful and healthful sections of the city. It is

not a "quarter" of dilapidated tenements but is made up of new-law apartments and handsome dwellings, with well-paved and well-lighted streets.
It has its own churches, social and civic centers, shops, theaters and other
places of amusement. And it contains more Negroes to the square mile
than any other spot on earth.[23]

As Johnson's utopic vision suggests, Harlem represented the hope that
African Americans could establish and maintain relatively autonomous
enclaves. And it represented the hope that they could inhabit a full range
of occupations and social strata.

In his zeal for promoting Harlem, however, Johnson glossed over
some of its grimmer realities. Hundreds of thousands of its residents
still lived in extreme poverty. As Henry Louis Gates, Jr. points out,

The death rate was 42 percent higher than in other parts of the city. The
infant mortality rate in 1928 was twice as high as in the rest of New York.
Four times as many people died from tuberculosis as in the white population. The unemployment rate, according to Adam Clayton Powell, Jr.,
was 50 percent.[24]

Once again, the geography of these class differences lined up with public green space. Morningside, Marcus Garvey, and St. Nicholas Parks
became physical markers of class distinctions. Duke Ellington, Joe Louis,
Adam Clayton Powell, and Ralph Ellison all owned properties that bordered St. Nicholas Park. Other black-owned mansions clustered around
Mt. Morris and Morningside Parks. As mansions surrounded uptown
parks, they also sealed them off from the lower classes. In "The Negro
Artist and the Racial Mountain," Langston Hughes criticized these class
separations, especially for mimicking white practices.[25] In Harlem as
elsewhere, access to urban nature became a privilege afforded to the
wealthy. Green space thus became a paradox that did more to reinforce
inequality than it did to promote the health of the populace.

The Great Depression disrupted the ordered classism that infused city
parks. Long bread lines now snaked through certain corners of Central
Park, and the Great Lawn became the site of a large "Hooverville," or
squatter settlement. Perversely, it took a massive financial crisis to finally
realize Olmstead's populist vision for city parks.

## "Urban Renewal Means Negro Removal": The Moses Era (1930s–1960s)[26]

The Depression might have democratized the city's parks, but it also left them in terrible shape. With no money for maintenance or repairs, grass was overgrown and covered with trash. Railings, playground equipment, and fountains were in pieces. In 1934, New York City's new Parks Commissioner, Robert Moses, took advantage of New Deal programs like the Works Progress and Civil Works Administrations and launched a massive, federally funded effort to restore the city's parks. Like Olmstead, Moses championed the idea that all city residents should have access to nature. For Moses, however, parks were places of play and recreation rather than places for gazing upon pristine natural beauty. In addition to Jones Beach and other public seashores, Moses constructed public ball fields, tennis courts, swimming pools, and playgrounds throughout Central Park and the city at large. By the time he left office, Moses had created 658 playgrounds in New York City alone and three public beaches. He also built 416 miles of parkways and thirteen bridges that enabled New Yorkers to reach those beaches and other state parks—if they owned cars.[27] While his parkways offered drivers picturesque views of the rivers, they cut off pedestrian access. In addition, Moses's beaches were not oriented to public transportation (with the exception of Jacob Riis Park in the Rockaways, which was originally intended to be served by the IRT and local buses).[28] Although he created an elaborate pool and recreation center in northern Harlem (now known as Jackie Robinson Park), less than a quarter of Moses's park and infrastructure improvements reached northern Manhattan.[29] Indeed, Moses's Harlem legacy has much less to do with the creation of new recreation areas, and much more to do with the discriminatory effects of his urban renewal programs.

During the height of Moses's power (roughly 1934 to 1960), Harlem, especially, needed public investment. Ongoing labor discrimination from employers and unions, along with countless other forms of racism, prevented Harlemites from recovering from the Depression. Meanwhile, the district was becoming even more crowded. 211,200 black southerners migrated to New York City in the 1940s, and by the early part of the decade, two-thirds of all black New Yorkers lived in Harlem.[30] Writer Ralph Ellison eloquently described an overcrowded Harlem in 1948:

Harlem is a ruin—many of its ordinary aspects (its crimes, its casual violence, its crumbling buildings with littered areaways, ill-smelling halls,
and vermin-invaded rooms) are indistinguishable from the distorted
images that appear in dreams and, like muggers haunting a lonely hall,
quiver in the waking mind with hidden and threatening significance.[31]

Moses's answer to these impoverished conditions was to take advantage
of funds provided by the 1949 Federal Housing Act, designed to facilitate
"slum clearance," otherwise known as urban renewal.

As chairman of the New York City Slum Clearance Committee,
Moses used the power of eminent domain to clear black, Hispanic, and
low-income neighborhoods to make way for more expressways and
housing complexes. Far from "slums," many of these neighborhoods
were vibrant, close-knit communities. Harlem's Manhattantown development, for instance, spanned two blocks on the west side of Central
Park. Built in 1905 by black real estate entrepreneur Philip Payton Jr.,
the community housed many of Harlem's biggest artists and scholars,
including Billie Holiday, Arthur A. Schomburg, Rosa Guy, and Robert
Earl Jones, and Butterfly McQueen. In 1951, Moses announced that he
would raze six blocks in southwest Harlem, including Manhattantown,
to make way for a massive, middle-class apartment complex.[32] After
losing a protracted fight against the project, Manhattantown residents
scattered. Many of them found new homes in one of the many public
housing projects Moses was building. Between 1949 and 1961, Moses
built approximately sixteen of these projects in Harlem, making it the
neighborhood with the highest number of public housing units per
capita in Manhattan. Ironically, this density would buffer Harlem from
gentrification and displacement well into the 2000s.

Moses's infrastructure projects also negatively affected Harlem's environmental health. His design for the Triborough Bridge let traffic out
onto 125th Street, rather than onto the more affluent Upper East Side.
In addition, Moses opened the Marine Transfer Station (MTS) on the
Harlem Piers at 135th Street in 1955. Garbage trucks going to and from
the MTS spewed exhaust and noise onto the surrounding community.
The MTS operated twenty-four hours a day, processing more than 1,000
tons of NYC's residential and commercial garbage before transferring it
to barges that sailed it down the Hudson, to Staten Island's Fresh Kills

Landfill.[33] Adding to this burden, in 1962, Moses convinced city leaders to locate a sewage treatment plant on 137th Street in West Harlem. The plant's original location was in the west sixties, near one of Moses's largest urban renewal projects, the massive Lincoln Center complex.[34]

Harlem residents organized to oppose this plant, as they did to oppose the Manhattantown project. Indeed, they had a long legacy to draw on. Many of Harlem's historic activist organizations were on the forefront of national and international movements for racial justice. During the Depression, the Communist Party helped form the Upper Harlem Council of the Unemployed, which organized rent strikes and anti-eviction protests, among other actions.[35] During World War II, employment discrimination in wartime industries inspired Harlem residents to organize citywide protests. Though Marcus Garvey's Universal Negro Improvement Association and African Communities League disbanded in the early 1920s, a resurgence of black national and pan-national movements in the 1950s carried on its legacy. Harlem headquartered two of the most prominent movements of this era, the Universal African Nationalist Movement and the African Nationalist Pioneer Movement. The Nation of Islam also gained steam during the 1950s, especially after Malcolm X became minister of Temple No. 7 on 116th and Lenox Avenue.

Robert Moses and other mid-century power brokers ensured that racial segregation was deeply engraved into Harlem's built and the natural environments (as well as the rest of the city). But that segregation also helped foster a growing infrastructure of opposition.[36] During the 1960s, this infrastructure blossomed into full-blown civil rights struggles.

## "I Can't Walk through the Park Cause It's Crazy after Dark": Harlem's Black Power Movement (1960s)[37]

The 1960s were hard on Harlem. In addition to regressive urban renewal policies, the neighborhood suffered under the impact of the Harlem Riot of 1964, the assassination of Malcolm X in 1965, and the riots that followed Martin Luther King Jr.'s death in 1968. As the city moved closer to fiscal crisis, public services shrank and crime rates rose. Planned shrinkage and similar policies cut funding for city parks, especially in low-income areas. A maintenance man reported replacing basketball backboards nightly in Harlem's playgrounds, and a city engineer described the old Polo grounds in northern Manhattan's Highbridge Park as "a chamber of horrors."[38] But Harlemites were also organized and politicized, and their civil rights activism was ongoing. Green spaces became stages on which tense dramas of social change played out.

In 1968, Columbia University was about to break ground on a new student gymnasium in Morningside Park. For the past few years, the university had been on the move. In an effort to expand, it was purchasing buildings near campus and evicting low-income tenants, who were mostly African Americans and Puerto Ricans. They sometimes withheld heat and hot water to force tenants out. Now, they wanted to encroach on Morningside, a public park, to build a new gym. Although Columbia intended to allow community members to use the gym, it planned to restrict them to a small portion of the gym's facilities, and to a separate entrance. In addition, it would be Columbia, not the community, that would control the gym.[39] For several days, student activists occupied five campus buildings demanding that the university abandon all of its construction plans.[40] Four days later, H. Rap Brown and Stokely Carmichael led 200 junior and high school students on a march down Amsterdam Avenue and onto the campus. On arrival, Brown announced, "the black community is taking over."[41] For six weeks, students and Harlemites worked together to barricade the construction site.[42] Eventually, Columbia administrators backed down and agreed to locate the gym elsewhere. For protestors, Columbia's attempt to take over part of the Park symbolized decades of exploitation and disregard.

About a half mile east of Morningside, another of Harlem's major parks became the site of a very different kind of protest. Mount Morris Park (renamed Marcus Garvey Park in 1973) had become a dangerous hub for drug dealing and other types of crime during the late 1960s. Community members avoided the park, leaving them with no place to recreate. In a neighborhood where many people lived in crowded, substandard housing, access to outdoor spaces is especially crucial. In 1969, community leaders decided to organize "Black Woodstock," a free cultural festival that would bring residents back to the park. The festival was a huge success thanks to a list of performers that included the Fifth Dimension, Sly and the Family Stone, Stevie Wonder, the Staples Singers, Nina Simone, and B. B. King. One group of performers was inspired to start a regular drum circle. Drumming for up to ten hours

Harlem Cultural Festival, 1969. Credit: CBS Photo Archive

every weekend, the musicians discouraged drug dealers and made the park a safe space for children to play and adults to mingle.[43] Over the years, the drums continued to attract local residents, as well as tourists, who joined in, danced, or sat nearby, tapping their feet

That same year, another kind of movement took off in the neighborhood of East Harlem, also known as "El Barrio" or "Spanish Harlem." This area, which ran from Mount Morris Park to the East River and south to 96th Street, saw a major influx of Puerto Ricans following World War I. The migration intensified after World War II, as Puerto Ricans left the island to pursue jobs in the booming mainland economy. Federal programs during that era favored white ethnic groups, allowing them to leave affordable neighborhoods like East Harlem and the Lower East Side. As Jewish, Italian, and Irish families moved to the suburbs, Puerto Rican families took their place. Starting in the late 1950s and 1960s, Robert Moses used those same federal programs to try to keep middle-class families in the city. Moses especially targeted East Harlem for urban renewal, leveling large sections of the area and channeling low-income families into public housing projects. As in Central and West Harlem, segregation, racism, and general economic decline left East Harlem in dire straits by the late 1960s.

Like black Harlemites at the time, El Barrio's young people had come of age during civil rights struggles and were familiar with leftist theory and politics.[44] In the summer of 1969, a group of recent college graduates, mostly of Puerto Rican descent, stood in Tompkins Square Park in the Lower East Side and announced that they were starting a New York City branch of the Chicago-based Young Lords.[45] Styled after the Black Panther Party, the Young Lords were nationalistic in that they fought for self-determination for Puerto Rico and Latinx communities in the United States. Like the Panthers, they, too, started free breakfast and community-based healthcare programs. After surveying residents in East Harlem, the Young Lords agreed that the garbage situation was a priority concern.[46] Drastic cuts to sanitation services in East Harlem had left bags of garbage piling up and rotting on sidewalks and streets. In October of 1969, the Young Lords staged the Garbage Offensive. They piled the garbage bags into five-foot-tall barricades and blocked traffic on Third Avenue before setting the garbage on fire.[47] Later that year, thirty Young Lords staged a sit-in at the City Department of Health and secured 200 lead detection kits for a door-to-door screening campaign. Teaming up with radical doctors from Metropolitan Hospital, the Young Lords found that twenty of the sixty children they screened had lead poisoning.[48] The "Lead Offensive" made the local news, and the city eventually passed provisions for lead paint removal in public housing and established a Bureau of Lead Poisoning Control.[49] The Young Lords went on to initiate a variety of other "offensives" to call attention to the lack of healthcare, education, and other services for East Harlem residents.

Although they had disbanded by 1972, the Young Lords left a lasting legacy of social justice activism in New York City and beyond. By taking over public spaces (whether Third Avenue, the City Health Department, or the sidewalks of East Harlem) the Young Lords forced New Yorkers to acknowledge the environmental hazards facing low-income Hispanic communities. They compelled Hispanic communities and others to look beyond the boundaries of traditional organizing practices and to envision environmental resources as part of a broader constellation of social justice and community development issues. It is no surprise that Luis Garden Acosta, a founding member of NYC's Young Lords, went on to establish El Puente, one of the country's first environmental justice organizations. Long before the term "environmental justice" entered popular lexicons, the Young Lords had protested the unfair distribution of environmental burdens and fought for access to environmental benefits.

Although the fiscal crisis of the 1970s caused widespread suffering in Harlem and other communities of color, it also created unexpected opportunities for neighborhood autonomy and self-determination.

## Flower Power: Guerrilla Greening on the Lower East Side (1970s)

About 100 blocks south of East Harlem, in another predominantly Puerto Rican neighborhood, known as the Lower East Side[50] or "Loisaida," community activists also launched a radical campaign to reclaim urban green space. In order to fully understand its centrality to green gentrification, this section focuses on the community garden movement in the Lower East Side and the pivotal role it plays in the history of green space and redevelopment.

New York City's earliest organized gardening initiatives date back to the recession of the 1890s, when city leaders instituted vacant lot gardening programs to address growing poverty. These garden programs reappeared at the onset of the Great Depression, providing important sources of nutrition. During the First World War, slogans like "Food will win the war" compelled Americans to eat fruits and vegetables in lieu of groceries that could be shipped to troops overseas. This inspired a national movement to grow "liberty gardens," which appeared throughout New York City. Such gardens resurfaced during World War II, through the National Victory Garden Program.[51] Some thirty years later, urban gardens also responded to hard financial times, but in this case they symbolized anti-establishment values.

In the 1970s, New York City's Lower East Side, as in Harlem and other poor neighborhoods, was peppered with abandoned lots. In 1973, Liz Christy, a local artist and activist, grew tired of walking past trash-strewn vacant lots every day. According to local lore,[52] Christy began tossing "seed bombs" packed with fertilizer, seed, and water over the chain link fences surrounding these abandoned properties.[53] After spotting a boy playing alone inside a discarded refrigerator, Christy decided to take her beautification attempts even further. She and a group of friends spent over six months hauling out the trash and gravel from the lot. They then collected horse manure from the nearby police station to supplement the soil and planted seedlings in raised beds. Christy also lobbied the city for a lease on the lot, and in 1974, the city granted it to her for one dollar a month. By that time, Christy had formalized her efforts into a nonprofit organization known as the Green Guerrillas.

News of the Green Guerrillas spread throughout the five boroughs. In areas where arson, neglect and financial hardship had left a glut of vacant lots and valueless property, community members invested sweat equity and created their own gardens.[54] Most of these were in Hispanic and African American neighborhoods, where white flight, planned shrinkage, and other policies had devalued properties in neighborhoods of color and made property ownership untenable.[55] In 1978, the city established the Green Thumb program, which offered plants, tools, horticultural expertise, and dollar-a-year leases to community groups that wanted to cultivate abandoned lots.[56] Over the next decade, the number of city-hosted community gardens grew to more than eight hundred.[57] More than half of those were located in Harlem neighborhoods, above all in East Harlem.[58]

Gardens held intense meaning for Harlem's African American and Hispanic communities. For recent migrants and long-term residents alike, they provided a sense of connection to rural pasts. The "casita" gardens of East Harlem, for instance, replicated Puerto Rican gardens by including chickens, roosters, small shacks (or casitas), religious icons and Puerto Rican Flags.[59] For African Americans, gardens provided a bittersweet link to the brutal history of slavery and sharecropping, as well as the small gardens that slaves and sharecroppers sometimes carved out of the plots of land they tended.[60] Early urban gardens provided a similar modicum of autonomy for members of low-income communities of color.

While gardens held special symbolism for minority communities, they also captured a longing for nature that is common to city dwellers of all stripes. As I have shown, city leaders and property owners historically capitalized on this longing, making access to natural spaces a valuable commodity. The Green Guerrillas turned this profit-minded approach on its head by transforming vacant lots and re-valuing them in non-monetary terms. Yet, as the real estate market rebounded from recession, community gardeners found themselves occupying a far more ambiguous spaces.

## Gentrification Takes Root: Greening Loisaida (1980s)

On the Lower East Side, policies like planned shrinkage lowered the already sinking value of land, driving landlords to stop paying their property taxes. As owners went into arrears, the city took ownership of their properties. By the early 1980s, the city owned much of the vacant land and property on the Lower East Side (as well as in Harlem and the South Bronx). The Koch administration (1978–1989) began selling much of this property to real estate speculators, who banked on the neighborhood's redevelopment potential. For geographer Neil Smith, municipal governments engineer the "rent gap" (the gap between current and potential property values) by first divesting from particular neighborhoods and then, once land values have bottomed out, reinvesting in them.[61]

Also in the early 1980s, Mayor Koch established several subsidized housing projects specifically targeted to those working in the creative arts, who were being displaced from other downtown neighborhoods like SoHo and Tribeca. Soon, makeshift art galleries, bars, and clubs began to flourish alongside the community gardens. This fertility drew media "buzz," which in turn attracted adventurous, upwardly mobile professionals. Once considered a dangerous slum, the Lower East Side now became a hip destination where more and more people wanted to live. Speculators now sold their land to developers, who began to erect new apartment buildings and demolish old ones.

At the same time, however, the community garden movement had seeded homesteader and squatter movements in which collectivities occupied and often renovated abandoned properties.[62] Homeless people had also created a large encampment in Tompkins Square Park. As property values on the Lower East Side rose, so did the tensions surrounding these spatial occupations. In the summer of 1988, police began to enforce a 1:00 a.m. park curfew, confining the homeless to one quadrant of the park and evicting them on a nightly basis. Some long-term residents, including groups of punk and anarchist squatters, organized a protest that devolved into a clash with police. A week later, protestors returned with a banner that read, "GENTRIFICATION IS CLASS WAR!" This time, the police were already in the park in riot gear and, as the conflict escalated, they charged the crowd.[63] In the aftermath of what became known as the Tompkins Square Park riot, Mayor Koch lifted the curfew. Several months later, however, he reestablished it and resumed his aggressive redevelopment agenda. The battle over Tompkins Square demonstrates how market values tend to dictate the publicness of urban spaces, especially those that were green.

The rent gap created by community gardens was especially pronounced. Gardeners had already cleared them of debris, so they were essentially construction-ready.[64] With gardens increasingly under threat from the city's efforts to sell them to developers, Lower East Side gardeners banded together, holding protests and rallies throughout the mid-1990s.[65] In 1998, however, Mayor Rudolph W. Giuliani announced his intention to make all seven hundred of the city's community gardens available to private interests. "This is a free market economy," he announced. "Welcome to the era after communism."[66] Community gardeners, along with hundreds of allies, raised a great hue and cry, organizing further demonstrations and filing lawsuits. When the city held an auction to sell several Lower East Side garden lots, protesters released 10,000 crickets into the room.[67] Gardeners also sought help from the Trust for Public Land and the New York Restoration Project (a nonprofit started by actress Bette Midler in 1995) purchased fifty-nine and fifty-five gardens, respectively.[68] A few years later, the city agreed to preserve 198 gardens holding Green Thumb leases. They classified another 110 as being "subject to development," while thirty-eight were slated for immediate closure, to be replaced by new housing structures. Non-lease holding gardens could remain in place until the land under them was sold or claimed.[69]

As irate as gardeners were at the city, some also recognized how they had become their own worst enemies. That is, gardens beautified blocks and neighborhoods, making them more desirable and gentrifiable. In 1998, a local activist, Henry George, wrote on his website:

Do we see, people, do we understand how the sweat and love of the creators of the Lower East Side Community Gardens were turned (inevitably, because that's how the system works) to their undoing? What made the neighborhood into that funky place that the gentrifiers wanted to

gentrify? The people who lived there, and cared about their neighborhood enough to work to reclaim it from drugs, crime, and hopelessness.

It would be overly simplistic to argue that community gardens alone
caused the gentrification of the Lower East Side. Rather, a complexity of
factors—from its growing cultural cachet, to neighborhood disinvestment and the devaluing of land, to municipal incentives, to a growing
availability of global capital for real estate financing—combined with
community improvements to gentrify the area.[70]
At the same time, recent studies find strong associations between
proximity to community gardens and gentrification. NYU's Furman
Center found a substantial gain in property tax revenues within a 1,000-
foot ring of a community garden. The more disadvantaged the neighborhood, the greater that impact. In poor neighborhoods, a garden raised
neighboring property values by as much as 9.4 percentage points within
five years of the garden's opening.[71] A second study, based in Brooklyn,
found that income levels of people living within a quarter mile of a community garden increased significantly over a five-year period. In other
words, over time, gardens were being surrounded by increasingly affluent households.[72]
Community gardens continued to generate controversy in the sustainaphrenic city as they took on even greater symbolic value, which
was often at odds with their market value. Gardens evoked a sense of
community-mindedness, concern for the environment, and progressive,
liberal values (including colorblindness) that appealed to new gentrifiers.[73] As sociologist Sharon Zukin observes,

> Over successive decades, the meaning of urban community gardening
> changed from a grassroots movement that contested the state, to repre-
> sent ethnic identity, to secular culture, and finally to sustainability ideals
> of urban food production. Each of these forms is the outcome of a differ-
> ent ethnic group and social class arriving at the gardens.[74]

Every few years, a mayoral administration would take over a new spate
of gardens and institute a new set of regulations on the rest. And each
time, gardeners from across the city joined forces to protest those

takeovers in the name of community and sustainability. Yet considering the degree to which gardens helped drive up the price of property and to fuel uneven development, what they sustained is subject to question.

## Hour of Chaos: Harlem and the Crack Epidemic in the 1980s

Harlem's redevelopment in the 1980s was meant to keep pace with the Lower East Side's. Burdened with a similar number of vacant properties, the Koch administration worked to transfer abandoned Harlem buildings to private owners.[75] In *The Revanchist City*, Neil Smith describes how Dennis Cogsville, president of the Harlem Urban Development Corporation, plotted out a gentrification plan in 1984:

> "That's going to be a tough project," [Cogsville] said, looking out at the tenements below: But here's how we're going to do it. Starting from 110th Street, we will make a first beachhead on 112th Street. You know, some anchor condominium conversions. Then a second beachhead up on 116th Street. That'll be a hell of a job. There's drugs, crime, everything up there. But we're going to do it. Essentially the plan is to circle the wagons around and move into Central Harlem from the outskirts.[76]

Cosgsville's principle foe was the crack epidemic, which hit Harlem with a vengeance in the 1980s.[77] Vacant buildings provided shelter for drug dealers and their customers, while crack's highly addictive qualities and low price made for a thriving industry.

Nonetheless, Koch announced that lots would be auctioned off for anywhere from $5,000 to $35,000. Prospective buyers could submit applications and enter a lottery for a chance to participate in the auction. Although the lottery would be weighted toward Harlem residents, only 262 African American households in Harlem earned more than $50,000, according to the 1980 Census. In the end, 80 percent of applicants for the lottery were middle-class African Americans from outside the area earning between $50,000 and $187,500.[78] One by one, these new owners removed the tattered wooden boards crisscrossing the soft brown stones, rounded windows, and ornate trim of Harlem's finest homes.[79] With so much invested, owners had the motivation and resources to begin lobbying for quality-of-life improvements. Their successes, in turn, attracted more African American homeowners.

A brief recession at the end of the 1980s brought much of Harlem's redevelopment to a halt. In response, Mayor David Dinkins successfully applied for federal "Empowerment Zone" funds to help trigger commercial development along 125th Street.[80] Old Navy, Modell's Sporting Goods and other chain stores arrived, as did HarlemUSA, a shopping center that included a nine-screen movie theater partly owned by basketball star Magic Johnson.[81] And at the end of his second presidential term, William J. Clinton announced that he intended to locate the offices of the Clinton Global Initiative on 125th Street.

Despite such efforts, Harlem's gentrification nonetheless continued to stutter along in fits and starts, for several reasons. First, the area still contained more public housing projects per square block than any other Manhattan neighborhood. East Harlem alone had the second highest concentration of public housing in the city and the nation. Not only did projects occupy a lot of space, but crime rates also tended to be higher around public housing projects, which deterred potential gentrifiers. Second, although several large condominium projects now appeared along Cogsville's "beachheads," and renovated brownstones were scattered throughout the neighborhood, dilapidated and vacant buildings still comprised much of Harlem's housing stock. Finally, Harlem housed the largest number of industrial sites and contaminated properties in Manhattan (for reasons I explain in the next chapter). Just as urban green space enhanced property values, the opposite was true of "brown" spaces.

The slow pace of gentrification meant that local activists faced the same conundrum as early gardeners. If they supported the city's redevelopment initiatives and pushed forward some of their own, they would bring the neighborhood improvements that accompanied reinvestment. But those improvements also made the neighborhood more marketable and less affordable. As Smith writes,

It is difficult to avoid the conclusion that for Central Harlem residents, gentrification is a "Catch-22." Without private rehabilitation and redevelopment, the neighborhood's housing stock will remain severely dilapidated; with it, a large number of Central Harlem residents will ultimately be displaced and will not benefit from the better and more expensive housing. They will be victims rather than beneficiaries of gentrification.[82]

For environmental justice activists in the 1980s, the choice was clear. Harlem's contaminated and toxic environment threatened their health and well-being, and something had to be done.

## Uptown Funk: Environmental Justice Comes of Age in the 1990s

In 1971, Peggy Shepard left her position at the *Indianapolis News* (where she was its first black reporter) and moved to New York to take a job with Time Life Books. Shepard then took a job as a speech writer and eventually became the public relations director for Jesse Jackson's presidential campaign. Shepard next decided to run for office herself—she owned a townhome in West Harlem and decided to enter the race for Leader of her Democratic district in 1985.[83] As she campaigned, Shepard kept hearing from constituents about the North River Sewage Treatment Plant (NRSTP), a newly opened sewage treatment facility at 135th Street and the West Side Highway. Most people wanted the facility to hire locally. Shepard won her campaign, and managed to secure about a dozen jobs for local residents. Soon after, however, nearby residents realized that they faced much bigger problems—the sewage treatment plant emitted a continuous, noxious stench, adding to already high levels of both noise and air pollution.[84] Shepard and her neighbors realized that a dozen local jobs did not come close to making up for the environmental risks the new project imposed.

At 7:00 a.m. on Martin Luther King Day in 1988, Shepard, along with Chuck Sutton, State Senator David Paterson and four others, who later became known as "The Sewage Seven," led a team of Harlem residents to the West Side Highway. Wearing gas masks and holding signs that said, "Breathing in this Neighborhood is Hazardous to Our Health" and "Our Community is Dying," protestors blocked traffic for several hours. In addition to the NRSTP, protestors also opposed the 137th Street Marine Transfer Station which sat just two blocks away. Together, the two facilities treated most of Manhattan's solid waste. For these Harlem activists, the neighborhood's racial composition had everything to do with its numerous environmental burdens. They realized that creating more environmental equity would require a sustained effort. A few months after the protest, its organizers formed the West Harlem Environmental Action Coalition (WEACT) and sued the New York City Department of Environmental Protection, charging that the NRSTP was a public and private nuisance.

Just a year before, in 1987, the United Church of Christ's Civil Rights Commission had published "Toxic Wastes and Race," a landmark study that decisively determined that race (rather than income, land values, or other factors) was the most significant variable in the siting of hazardous waste facilities.[85] The report ignited a grassroots movement that was building steam around the country. WEACT brought attention to environmental injustices in Harlem and elsewhere. The organization called on city leaders to factor race into future siting and planning decisions, especially those that involved harmful facilities.[86] In 1993, the City of New York settled the sewer treatment plant lawsuit for $1.1 million. WEACT did not have any paid staff at the time, so it used settlement funds to hire three full-time staff members. The organization then set out to address a broader range of environmental justice concerns.[87] One of its top priorities was to lobby the EPA for an assessment of Northern Manhattan's air quality. That assessment found harmful particulates that exceeded acceptable air quality standards by more than 200 percent.[88]

Harlem also housed five of Manhattan's seven bus depots, and the Department of Transportation intended to construct a sixth in the neighborhood. Almost all of the depots were located next to schools, hospitals, and housing projects, and during the winter, buses would sometimes idle all night to prepare for the morning commute.[89] To challenge this situation, WEACT filed a complaint under Title VI of the Civil Rights Amendment[90] charging the Metropolitan Transportation Authority (MTA) with "siting diesel bus depots and parking lots disproportionately in minority neighborhoods in Northern Manhattan."[91] Four years later, the Federal Transportation Authority ruled that while the MTA had complied with Title VI on the whole, it needed to improve its efforts to consider environmental justice in the future. In the meantime, WEACT worked with the MTA and the governor's office to develop a plan for switching MTA buses to cleaner fuels. In

addition to working on outdoor air quality, WEACT also made indoor air quality a priority. The organization was instrumental in the
creation and passage of Local Law 1, a lead poisoning prevention bill.
And, along with the National Resources Defense Council, WEACT
successfully sued the EPA for inadequately protecting children from
rat poison exposure.[92]

WEACT also fought for more equitable access to green spaces. About
a decade after its founding, the organization asked the city to create a
new, two-acre park on an abandoned pier at 135th Street and the Hudson
River. The site was adjacent to the 135th Street Marine Transfer Station
(MTS). A few years later, however, Mayor Michael Bloomberg decided
to reopen the MTS so that Manhattan's garbage could be barged to landfills in other states. Once again, WEACT organized community members in protest, and Bloomberg quickly backed down. Determined to
keep the MTS permanently closed, WEACT expanded its waterfront
park proposal to include repurposing the MTS site. It also proposed a
participatory planning process to determine a new use for the site.[93] In
2007, just in time for the release of PlaNYC 2030, the Mayor's office ac-
cepted WEACT's proposal and commissioned the organization to lead
the planning process.

A year later, I sat in the small, cramped office of Cecil Corbin-Mark,
WEACT's deputy director. A tall, African American man with a soft
voice and an easy laugh, Corbin-Mark reached behind his desk and
pulled out a booklet entitled "Harlem-on-the-River: Making a Community Vision Real." On the back cover, a multiracial group of about twenty
people stand at the water's edge raising their fists in victory. Beneath
them, bold yellow letters read "Ten years in the making." Corbin-Mark
chuckled and shook his head, "It must have been the longest planning
process ever." He and WEACT staff had worked hard to ensure that
the planning process was truly inclusive. Even more difficult was their
struggle to protect the park from private investors. Corbin-Mark explained that the planning group repeatedly fought off developers who
offered project funding in exchange for the rights to build a luxury hotel,
a high-rise condominium, a dinner theater, and a concert band shell.[94]
Their decision to keep the space public was a trade-off. While private investment would significantly expand the park's amenities, it would also
exclude the very people the park was meant to benefit.

## Build It and They Will Come: Parks in the Bloomberg Era (2002–14)

Private investors' offers to fund the West Piers Park signaled important shifts in the way the city maintained its public parks. Up until the 1960s, the city relied on Olmstead's model of using property tax revenues to finance park upkeep. But in an effort to stem white flight in the 1960s and 1970s, city and state legislators reduced taxes on prewar townhouses, co-ops, and condos.[95] They also capped annual property taxes increases, decoupling them from property values. After the fiscal crisis, Mayor Koch offered tax breaks to incentivize development in neighborhoods suffering from disinvestment. An eroding tax base combined with budget reductions left the city's parks in severe disarray. This not only affected local residents, it also deterred desperately needed tourists. Former Mayor Ed Koch came up with a solution. He created the Central Park Conservancy (CPC), a nonprofit entity that could raise private donations.[96] Right away, the CPC raised enough money to complete a number of capital projects, while the city continued to pay for basic park upkeep. The Conservancy continued to do so well that it hired its own staff to work alongside the city's civic employees. In 1998, the Giuliani administration took things a step further and formalized an agreement to pay the Conservancy four million dollars a year to manage the park, including its capital projects, maintenance, and staffing. The city would continue to control major policy decisions and to police it. Eventually, all of the city's major parks adopted the Conservancy model, which proved to be far more effective at raising funds than Olmstead's property tax model. By 2011, the CPC was running a surplus—it was bringing in approximately $47 million and spending only $40 million.[97]

In "The Central Park Effect," an assessment of the park's economic benefits to the tourism and real estate industries, researchers estimated that the park added "more than $26.0 billion to the market value of properties on the blocks closest to [it]."[98] Donors to the CPC and other conservancies could thus raise the value of their properties and use their contributions as a tax deduction. This was not only a win-win for owners and developers, it was a win for the city budget as well. Even with tax breaks, property still generated revenue for the city, which also saved money by outsourcing part of the parks budget. Such public/private partnerships were a favorite of Mayor Michael Bloomberg who made the Central Park effect a cornerstone of his luxury city strategy. Shortly after taking office, Bloomberg penned the foreword to a design study for the High Line Park. In it, he wrote:

> Any brick put down or any tree planted must recharge the urban economy; it must attract new businesses, residents and visitors by creating appealing, healthful, safe work and home environments; it must spark financial activity, raise property values and generate tax revenues.[99]

To execute this utilitarian vision, Bloomberg appointed wealthy socialite and urban planner Amanda Burden as his Planning Commissioner.

Burden was known for transforming Battery Park City (BPC) from a barren, sandy landfill to an award-winning, 92-acre planned community. In a 2014 Ted Talk, Burden explained that the secret to BPC's success was her "radical" idea to carve out one-third of the land allotted to BPC to create an expansive, lushly landscaped waterfront. "Instead of building a park as a complement to future development," she recalled, "why don't we reverse that equation and build a small but very high-quality public open space first, and see if that made a difference?"[100] Burden's gamble paid off. The park attracted plenty of investment and the rest fell into place.

Bloomberg gave Burden full reign to expand her "build it and they will come" strategy. Instead of waiting for development to take off before creating a park, green space planning now *generated* development. In a 2011 interview with the Urban Land Institute, Burden expounded on the importance of "well-designed, well-used public open spaces . . . for the economic and social well-being of a city." Such spaces serve as "an amazing catalyst" for economic development, Burden explained, often changing the entire perception of a city. "They can be very transformative in how people feel about making a private investment," she concluded.[101] With high-end parks anchoring new, luxury developments, the Bloomberg-Doctoroff-Burden team rezoned 40 percent of New York City, including 730 acres of new parkland. In most cases, formerly industrial waterfronts were rezoned to allow for high-end residential and commercial developments. To attract that development, abandoned waterfronts and industrial infrastructures were reborn as state-of-the-art, sustainable spaces with native plants, self-watering systems, and other low-impact features.

But high-design spaces like the High Line, Brooklyn Bridge Park, and the Williamsburg/Greenpoint esplanades did not come cheap.[102] Each new park was accompanied by a not-for-profit entity that solicited donations from private individuals and developers. Tax incentives supplemented these donations. For instance, the city allowed developers along the High Line to expand building heights in exchange for donations to a special High Line Improvement Fund.[103] With Brooklyn Bridge Park, the city paid for the construction of the park. It then drew a boundary around the park's footprint and made it into a special tax improvement district. This funneled taxes collected from individual property owners directly to the park's budget for maintenance and operations. In addition, the city lifted common charge restrictions for developers within the footprint, allowing them to charge a few extra dollars for park maintenance. Between extra common charges and tax breaks, developer payoffs were huge. A 2017 study of the Highline's "halo effect" showed that resale values of nearby properties rose a cumulative ten percentage points faster than areas only a few blocks farther away.[104]

The halo's glow was limited, however. Private developers, as well as individual and corporate donors, had an unprecedented level of control over the design, security, and operations of the parks to which they donated. The High Line's major donors, for instance, wanted the park to retain an air of sophistication, so they made sure its design did not include spaces for children to play, or for the types of recreation typically found in parks. The Highline included relatively scant places to sit or linger, and its vendors catered mainly to the tastes of affluent tourists and visitors.[105] Brooklyn Bridge Park's private donors also asserted control over the space. In 2017, residents living within the footprint sued the city to block it from constructing a new residential project that included affordable housing. The suit argued that revenue from existing residential projects was exceeding revenue projections and had already created a generous endowment to maintain the park. This obviated the need for more housing.[106] Finally, Gould and Lewis found a strong correlation between the restoration of Brooklyn's Prospect Park and the construction of nearby luxury housing. Simultaneously, they saw a decrease in the number of residents of color living in those same neighborhoods.[107]

In other words, they found that "the 'greening' of urban areas became code for the 'whitening' of urban areas."[108]

While Central Park and other major conservancies had money to burn, people in poor neighborhoods did not have extra money to donate to local parks. At the same time, the conservancy model rationalized major cuts to the parks budget. By the end of the Bloomberg era, the polarization was palpable. In rich neighborhoods, parks had never been more lush and serene, while in poor neighborhoods, the bathrooms were unkempt and the grounds were strewn with hypodermic needles, condom wrappers, and litter.[109] During his campaign, Mayor Bill de Blasio supported a plan to force conservancies to give up to a fifth of their budgets to underserved parks. Although that idea failed, de Blasio convinced the eight largest conservancies to provide services to thirty-five parks in the South Bronx, East Harlem, and central Brooklyn.[110] In response to a *New York Times* article about this plan, one reader commented, "Haven't seen the full list, but 'Ranaqua Park in Mott Haven in the Bronx. Saratoga Ballfields in Brownsville, Brooklyn. Luther Gulick Park on the Lower East Side of Manhattan' are in neighborhoods where the Gentrification assault is in full gear."[111] While it is too soon to verify these claims, the commenter's skepticism about the consequences of green space improvements is clear. To take a closer look at how low-income communities of color experienced and expressed this skepticism, we return to Harlem.

## Harlem Shakedown: Resisting Green Gentrification

Back in Marcus Garvey Park, the drum circle from Black Woodstock was still going. For nearly four decades, good weekend weather brought African American, Caribbean, African, and white musicians to the park's southeast corner. As the sound of trumpets, cowbells, tambourines, flutes—and, of course, drums filled the park with sound, children, tourists, and colorfully clad West African women moved to the beat. While the drum circle remained consistent, the area surrounding the park was changing. On Fifth Avenue, a new luxury co-op, with apartments priced at a million dollars on average, overlooked the park. Co-op residents complained that noise from the drum circle penetrated their apartments and prevented them from speaking on the phone, watching

TV, or sleeping. Other nearby residents would sometimes grumble about the noise. In such cases, they would speak to the drummers, and the drummers would usually shift to another spot. In the summer of 2006, however, new condo owners took their complaints straight to the police.

On the popular blog, "Harlem Fur: Dogs, Cats and Petrification,"[112] a discussion about the fate of the drum circle quickly turned into an acerbic debate over gentrification. Eventually, a supporter of the drumming threatened: "There will be severe backlash against you newcomers who complain about noise in Harlem. Adapt or perish you fucks." To this, a co-op-supporter retorted, "no matter how many good things are happening up here, things will never truly raise [sic] up to the Manhattan standard unless these MASSIVE projects are destroyed." For this commenter, the public housing projects that provided thousands of Harlem's poor residents with affordable shelter stood in the way of the neighborhood's potential to become as exclusive as the rest of Manhattan. Eventually the conversation turned from economic diversity to racial diversity.

The co-op's residents were predominantly white professionals, and Harlem's public housing populations were predominantly African American and Latinx. By fall, the racial tensions simmering beneath the Marcus Garvey Park controversy rose to the surface. A racist message circulated on the co-op listserv and was leaked to a reporter from the *New York Times*. It read,

> Why don't we just get nooses for every one of those lowlifes and hang them from a tree? They're used to that kind of treatment anyway! I hope you all agree that the best thing that has happened to Harlem is gentrification. Let's get rid of these "people" and improve the neighborhood once and for all.[113]

The message got the attention of the New Black Panther Party (founded in 1996 to revive the ideals and goals of the original group), which organized a march in support of the drummers.[114]

In the end, the Parks Department negotiated a compromise. It dedicated a small area in the middle of the park to the drum circle. Marked with a small plaque that read "Drummer's Circle," the area included about six benches arranged in a U-shape. On Saturday (and sometimes Sunday) afternoons in good weather, those benches still fill with a wide

Drummers' circle, 2007. Credit: James Nova

array of musicians, and around them, an eclectic assortment of people listened to the music, tapped their feet, danced, and shot videos with their phones.

Controversies also revisited Morningside Park in 2006. The Parks Department had just completed an extensive renovation. In addition to a 20-story luxury high-rise on the park's southwest corner, the restoration brought new park rules and enforcement efforts. Like all city parks, Morningside was officially open only from dawn to dusk. Nonetheless, residents frequently walked their dogs or cut through the park after dark. Park police began fining them for this practice. In addition, new park rules limited barbeques to designated areas and restricted the number that could be held on any one day. Parties of twenty or more had to obtain special-events permits via an online system, at a cost of $25.[115] Some parks had always charged fees for such events, but they were rarely enforced. Now, police routinely asked to see barbeque permits.

Harlem's social life had always spilled onto its stoops, sidewalks, and other open spaces. In summer, tenants of cramped, hot apartments turned gritty sidewalks into ad-hoc party rooms, setting up boom boxes, folding chairs, and coolers in front of portable grills. Every weekend, the smell of charcoal and the sound of old soul flowed through Harlem's narrow side streets. In public parks, much larger groups gathered for birthdays, family reunions, holidays, and anniversaries, almost year-round. Changes to barbeque rules thus seemed like a deliberate affront to those who had spent their lives celebrating milestones, large and small, in the neighborhood's parks. Accordingly, in June 2006, long-term Harlem residents crowded into an angry town hall meeting. "We have been barbequing for years. We have a Father's Day event that's been going on for over thirty years and now they want to stop us from doing it. You want us to enjoy the park and the park is for the community; we *are* the community," one woman exclaimed.[116]

But newer community members welcomed the rules. In Yelp reviews and comments on popular online media sites, newcomers commonly complained about the trash and noise generated by picnics and barbeques. On a Yelp review of Morningside Park, for instance, a reviewer wrote, "The bad part—it's so full of garbage come Monday morning from the weekend's BBQs and picnics. It can be really gross."[117] Similarly, negative comments about picnics, BBQs, and teenagers "hanging out" in the park often circulated on neighborhood listservs, and newcomers were quick to complain to local police about noisy barbeques. As time and gentrification moved forward, the controversies continued. One early June evening in 2013, a round of shots was fired in Morningside Park. Two weeks later, the local police precinct held a public forum to discuss park safety. After a brief discussion of increased police patrols in and around the park, a heated debate about barbecues overtook the meeting. Although some tried to steer the conversation back to gun violence, issues surrounding barbeques stubbornly dominated the rest of the meeting.[118]

The Bloomberg administration's aggressive redevelopment agenda, combined with its privatized approach to parks funding, allowed afflu-ent, mostly white property owners to assume a new kind of control over public parks. This enabled park rules to privilege certain kinds of cul-tural expression while suppressing others. No wonder low-income Har-lem residents increasingly believed that the neighborhood's new green spaces were not for them.

## A Place to "Shoot the Shit": Selective Sustainability (2000s)

On a mild evening in early January 2010, I climbed the smooth, marble steps of the New York Public Library's 115th Street branch. Built in a "rusticated Italian palazzo style" and funded by Andrew Carnegie, the library first opened its stately doors in 1908.[119] A few hundred yards

Philip Randolph Square, 2019. Credit: Melissa Checker

from the library, 115th intersected with Adam Clayton Powell Boulevard and St. Nicholas Avenue, which ran on a diagonal. The three streets created a tiny triangle that was filled in with a tree, some shrubs, and a placard that read, "Samuel Marx Park." A block up, St. Nicholas formed a larger triangle that contained a few benches, several trees, and a placard that read "Randolph Park." The Parks Department purchased the first park in 1896 and the second in 1923, both from private owners. The bedraggled triangle parks were a testament to ongoing cuts to the Parks Department budget—both appeared tattered, dusty, and unkempt. But they were rarely empty: smokers, homeless people, and various others often sat and chatted in the fresh air.

Around them, this part of Harlem bustled. Known as "Little Senegal" (for its large population of West African migrants), men wearing loose caftans and knitted caps and women in bright purple, yellow, or green printed dresses and matching head scarves, went in and out of shops selling African soaps, incense, lotions, and food. Interspersed among these were bodegas, hair and nail salons, liquor stores, and small groceries. Every few blocks, a newly renovated apartment building advertised one, two, and three bedroom units, a new restaurant offered some kind of fusion cuisine, or a new coffee shop served oat milk lattes and vegan muffins. The triangle parks sat squarely in the middle of these eclectic—and transitional—spaces.

I was headed to the library that night to attend a public meeting about the fate of the parks. Inside, the library's high-ceilinged meeting room was full. A cross section of people representing multiple generations, ethnicities, and income levels were milling around, examining poster boards displayed with colorful drawings and photos. Titled "Green X:Change," the posters depicted both triangle parks transformed into one lush expanse filled with bright flowers, romping children, and grinning adults. The Harlem Community Development Corporation (HCDC) and the Department of Transportation (DOT) were proposing to join the parks and create one large green space— the Green X:Change. According to meeting materials, the aim of the Green X:Change meeting was to "engage the Harlem community in a discussion of how to improve our lives as pedestrians in an era of green awareness."[120] Based on a conservancy model, the DOT would pay for the park's construction, and a local nonprofit organization would maintain the park and oversee its programming. Expanding the parks, materials promised, would provide central Harlem with improved green space and quality of life, as well as "color St. Nicholas Avenue a more prosperous shade of green" by promoting sustainable economic development and community revitalization.[121] Notably, "sustainable" economic development consisted of any commercial and real estate enterprises that the new park might attract.

Harlem residents immediately questioned this version of sustainability. One woman asked, "Is this going to be like Morningside? Now you need permission to get in to picnic there." Others complained that the project would take away too many parking spaces, especially from local churches. Indeed, a large number of suburbanites traveled back to Harlem on Sundays to attend their "home" church. The parking space discussion led one man to ask, "Won't closing off streets add to traffic congestion? Seems like that will make the air quality worse instead of better."

"We've been asking the city to improve those parks for years," said one woman. "Why is the city only doing something about it now, with those new condos going up on 116?" A woman who introduced herself as a member of Community Board 10 remembered a similar proposal from a few years back. "Then," she said, "it was about commercial space zoning— now they're saying it's about 'green.' Why?" This question prompted several people to ask who really stood to profit from this project.

A tall man who represented a local community garden asked whether they could locate a large greenhouse on the new space. They hoped to grow heirloom vegetables that homeless people could sell for profit. City planners responded that they wanted to keep the space open and free of enclosed structures. This prompted a woman who looked to be in her thirties to stand and question the Green X:Change's most basic assumptions: "Kids have plenty of places to play around here. We already have three parks nearby. We need an adult park. I need a place to go and smoke a cigarette and hang out and shoot the shit . . . This is retarded."

Suddenly, meeting attendees wanted to know who was looking out for the "winos" and homeless people that currently populated the park. Green X:Change organizers seemed surprised—many of these same people routinely complained that the city neglected those triangle parks. Why were they now dead set against the Green X:Change plan?

Finally, "William," a WEACT staff person, stood to address them. He began by politely but firmly stating that WEACT was not interested in becoming a project partner as it had too many other issues to address. He then acknowledged community members' questions and suggested a compromise: planners could reduce the size of the parks and remove fewer parking spaces in exchange for residents' support of the project. He also reminded everyone that the purpose of the meeting was for community members to provide their input, and he pleaded for them to continue to participate in the planning process.

By that point, however, it seemed clear that most residents in attendance wholly rejected the Green X:Change and favored the status quo. As the meeting wrapped up, a staff person from the Department of Transportation shook his head and said, "If the community wants parking over taking back space, then we will go to other communities with this project." In the end, Harlem residents ran headlong into the paradox of profit-driven sustainability. This left them the painful choice of either resisting environmental improvements altogether or of being priced out of their neighborhoods.

## Conclusion

The lofty ideals associated with urban nature developed in a dialectical relationship with industrialism. As the latter brought noise, pollution, hordes of people, and hard-driving capitalists, nature was valorized for representing the opposite—its immaterial value involved social and moral uplift, repose, and respite from all things urban and capitalistic. Paradoxically, these same qualities turned urban nature into a valuable commodity. Once green space became a mechanism for generating revenue, it also became a mechanism for uneven development, separating wealthy, white residents from low-income neighborhoods and communities of color. Accordingly, affluence provided greater access to public parks and squares. Economic downturns temporarily reversed these trends as devalued green spaces provided opportunities for low-income communities to reclaim public space.

In its resilience, however, capitalism co-opted these opportunities and interventions. As the real estate industry became increasingly central to the city's economy in the late twentieth and early twenty-first centuries, the value of green space also ramped up. Not only did it raise the market value of surrounding properties, but it also helped to brand certain neighborhoods as livable and sustainable. This combination of material and symbolic value dovetailed nicely with a move toward privatizing public resources. In fact, green space became the perfect darling of the sustainable, neoliberal city. It came prewrapped in longstanding ideals of uplift, morality, and democracy. Sustainability doubled down on these positive ideals, adding to them concern for the environment, political neutrality, and colorblindness. Undergirded by such ideas and bolstered by new funding structures that empowered individual and corporate donors, green spaces became luxury amenities. In this way, sustainability ultimately perverted environmental justice by cloaking an aggressive, growth-driven agenda in bright, green cloth.

3

# "Dirty Deeds Done Dirt Cheap"

*Industrial Gentrification and the Geography of Sacrifice and Gain*

"I don't want to end up wearing cement shoes!" joked Victoria Gillen, crooking a finger against the side of her nose. It was late spring of 2011, and Gillen was presiding over a meeting of the North Shore Community Coalition for Environmental Justice (NSCCEJ). With straight brown hair and a subtle splash of freckles, Gillen lived with her family in Elm Park, a small North Shore neighborhood alongside the Bayonne Bridge. In 2006, she began working for a local architecture/urban planning firm and became increasingly active in the Elm Park Civic Association. An avid kayaker, Gillen grew especially concerned with the high levels of contaminants in the Kill Van Kull and with the pollution surrounding Elm Park, a predominately working-class neighborhood, with a large number of Polish American and Hispanic families.[1]

That night, about ten NSCCEJ members, sat around a large folding table in the basement community room of the Parkside Senior Citizen Apartments. Behind us, well-worn book shelves and scattered vases of plastic flowers softened the room's institutional linoleum floors and cinderblock walls. Our purpose that evening was to plan an anti-idling campaign targeting trucks traveling to and from New York's port on the northwest tip of Staten Island. Known as the New York Container Terminal, the port hosted an estimated seven thousand diesel trucks per day. Beginning around 4:00 a.m., drivers would begin lining up to access the port as soon as it opened. As they waited, often on residential side streets, the drivers would idle their engines to keep their trucks' refrigeration and heating systems running. They also often turned around in private driveways, shining headlights in people's windows. In addition to the diesel spewing from the trucks, the vast amounts of fuel required to power container ships contained high amounts of sulfur, a potent green-

Container ship on the Kill Van Kull, 2010. Credit: Melissa Checker

house gas and pollutant. Some experts estimated that each ship visiting the port emitted as much sulfur as fifty million cars.[2]

The anti-idling campaign sought to cut down the number of trucks idling on residential streets. The plan was as follows: First, members would stake out certain corners for a few hours a week and record the number of trucks they observed idling their engines. Second, they would send this information to the New York State Department of Environmental Conservation (DEC), which was sponsoring the campaign. The DEC would identify idling "hotspots." Finally, DEC enforcement agents would set aside a day to issue tickets to trucks that were violating its idling policies. Tension had been building during the meeting, and Gillen's comment about cement shoes expressed a common concern. Some local trucking companies were connected to organized crime. As people chuckled at Gillen's joke, Pete, a sixty-something activist from St. George said, "Remember the waterfront cleanups? They found bags of drugs, a gun . . ."

"Twice they found guns," Gillen interrupted. "And stacks of money." I nodded—these stories were recited often. Activists also frequently pointed out that many waterfront properties were bought outright with cash. No financing meant that they were not subject to environmental reviews. These properties also tended to be surrounded by opaque fencing. "No one knows what goes on behind those fences," they would say, in ominous tones. To be sure, the North Shore waterfront was an opportune place for illegal activity. Shrouded by the watery shadows of container ships and industries lined up along the Kill Van Kull, the area appeared to exist under the radar of the media, politicians, and most New Yorkers.

This chapter traces New York City's long and sometimes fraught relationship with industrial spaces. Allocating these spaces was a tricky matter. City planners had to maximize industrial productivity while also protecting affluent residents, who were constantly on the run from industrial encroachment. Zoning codes became the answer to protecting these residents while charting out a course for economic development. But as economic priorities began to shift in the early 1960s, industrial businesses were sidelined to the geographic margins of the city. The North Shore was on those margins, and as an especially out-of-the-way locale, it became a repository for industrial facilities. Zoning decisions both mapped out a path for the city's shifting economic agendas and structured the kinds of opportunities available to different groups of people. They dictated whether neighborhoods would be adjacent to a waste transfer station or factory, to a park, or to a commercial area. Zoning decisions set property values, transportation options, the quality of schools, and health outcomes. In short—they demarcated which parts of the city would be protected from environmental harms, and which would be sacrificed to them.

If North Shore was a zone of sacrifice, then Manhattan and eventually most of Brooklyn, became zones of gain. This is the story of how urban planning strategies guided those dynamics through the medium of space. Popular narratives about deindustrialization cast it as an inevitable outcome of globalization, technology, and the rise of private capital. This history debunks that narrative by revealing political and corporate leaders' deliberate efforts to drive industry from the city. Zoning regulations provided an important tool for implementing this agenda. Just as the institution of zoning in 1916 helped establish New York as an industrial city, in 1961 zoning reforms rearranged urban space and recreated itself as a worldwide center of the new finance and real estate-based global economy.

In this chapter, to trace a comprehensive history of how zones of privilege developed in relation to zones of sacrifice (and vice versa), I tack back and forth between the North Shore, Manhattan, and parts of Brooklyn. We begin on the North Shore with the advent of the industrial era, then travel to Manhattan to discuss how the city's precedent-setting 1916 zoning codes charted an economic blueprint for the next forty-five years. At the city's economic core, spatial arrangements continued to radiate out from Manhattan until at least the early 2000s.

## City Meets Industry

When Henry Hudson sailed into the New York Bay in the early 1600s, he spotted the northern edge of an island he later named "Staaten Eylandt." Like most of the region, the Island was inhabited by Lenape Indians. After three attempts, European settlers drove the Lenape from their lands and planted their own farms, which would supply food to the rest of the city for several centuries.[3] By the early 1800s, the Island's quiet coasts had become a vacation destination for the city's hoi pol-loi, and several private and publicly funded institutions served the city's poor, infirm, mentally ill, and developmentally disabled citizens.[4] In the 1830s, architect Minard Lafever built Snug Harbor, a collection of Greek Revival buildings that offered a haven for "aged, decrepit, and worn-out sailors."[5] From its origins, Staten Island supported other parts of New York City by supplying necessities like fresh food, vacation spots, and housing for disabled citizens.

As the industrial era took hold, the North Shore's geographic position became critical to New York City's economic future. The Kill Van Kull provided a passage for marine traffic traveling down the East Coast and, starting in 1860, a new local rail system linked the North Shore to the B&O railway, which sent products and raw materials to manufacturers and merchants throughout the mid-Atlantic region. When the Panama Canal opened in 1914, it provided passage for ships traveling from the Pacific Oceans to East Coast ports. The opening of this route, along with Europe's entrance into a war, almost tripled import/export traffic to the Staten Island port.[6] By this time, the waterfront housed some of the city's largest manufacturers, including the Jewett White Lead Company, US Gypsum, Proctor and Gamble, and Archer Daniels Midland (ADM) linseed oil factory.[7] A steady stream of European migrants also arrived, seeking work in those factories. By the early twentieth century, the North Shore comprised only one-third of Staten Island's land mass, but was twice as populated as the rest.[8]

In addition to the North Shore, ports in lower Manhattan and southern Brooklyn also did a bustling business. Ship repair yards, various factories, warehouses, and small commercial establishments also proliferated in these areas. Merchants, middlemen, industrialists and low-wage workers from other countries and from other states flooded into neighborhoods that fanned out from the waterfronts. Pretty soon, it seemed that the city was bursting at the seams.

## Order Amid Chaos

In 1909, the Equitable Life Assurance Company, headquartered at 120 Broadway in downtown Manhattan, became the first skyscraper to have passenger elevators. Equitable's president was not satisfied with that accomplishment, so he decided to demolish the building and reconstruct it as the tallest office building in the world—except that, before demolition could begin, a fire destroyed the current building. Fearing the damage that a fire could do to an even taller building, Equitable changed course and created a sprawling, 1,200,000 square foot structure that was serviced by more than fifty elevators.[9] The scale of the Equitable project raised a good deal of public ire. Historian Sally Kit Chappell summarizes the complaints it drew:

> It was said that the Equitable blocked ventilation, dumped 13,000 users onto nearby sidewalks, choked the local transit facilities, and created potential problems for firemen. The Equitable's noon shadow, someone complained, enveloped six times its own area. Stretching almost a fifth of a mile, it cut off direct sunlight from the Broadway fronts of buildings as tall as twenty-one stories. The darkened area extended four blocks to the north. Most of the surrounding property owners claimed a loss of rental income because so much light and air had been

deflected by the massive new building, and they filed for a reduction in the assessed valuations of their properties.[10]

Manhattanites' complaints about the city's building boom had been mounting for some time, and the Equitable building became a tipping point.

Along Fifth Avenue, merchants were lobbying to regulate signage, which they worried was becoming too garish. In addition, the Manhattan sky was disappearing into an ever-expanding number of buildings, each taller than the next.[11] Historian William Fischel explains that trucks "liberated heavy industry from close proximity to downtown railroad stations and docks.[12] This meant that some manufacturers could move to cheaper areas on the outskirts of the city, which happened to be in residential districts. At the same time, motorized passenger buses and subway lines made it easier for some middle and working-class New Yorkers to move to these same areas. Wealthy families had just fled the crowds of downtown for these more pristine environs on the city's outskirts. Now they worried that workers would infiltrate those environs. Now they feared being chased out again.

All of these issues got channeled into public opposition to the Equitable building, and city leaders were pressed to take action. In 1916, they established the nation's first set of zoning codes. Tall buildings now had to begin narrowing at a certain height and continue to narrow as they climbed. This "wedding cake" design (made famous by the Chrysler and Empire State Buildings) mitigated skyscrapers' blocking of light. Zoning regulations also divided the city into three types of use districts: residential, commercial and unrestricted. In the first two, new properties had to fall within certain height and width restrictions. The third, unrestricted districts, contained both industrial businesses and housing for factory workers.[13]

Manhattan's scarcity of space and high rental costs generated an eclectic industrial sector that specialized in small-scale production of items such as fine jewelry, small machinery, blouses, stock certificates, and other printed items. By setting aside districts specifically for these businesses, the zoning codes offered them stability. For printing, fashion, and food manufacturers that needed to be closer to their customers, this was especially critical.[14] In other cities, the advent of trucking enabled manufacturers to leave urban confines. New York's unrestricted zones encouraged them to stay and densify.

Also in 1916, sixteen immigrant families from Finland pooled their money and built a co-op apartment building in a new unrestricted zone in Sunset Park, Brooklyn. More Finnish families followed suit, as did a number of leftist Jewish worker alliances. Eventually, New York City joined in, creating a Housing Authority which built one of the first public housing projects in the nation, First Houses on the Lower East Side. Housing for factory workers was not just affordable, it was located in the heart of unrestricted zones, so its residents could have "advantageous opportunities for walking to work."[15] This proximity was critical for garment workers, who made up nearly half of Manhattan's entire workforce, and of whom more than 70 percent were women.[16] On top of working twelve to fourteen hours per day, seven days a week, female factory workers had childcare and domestic duties, which made long-distance commutes impossible.[17]

A lack of zoning restrictions also preserved the vibrant ethnic enclaves that migrants had already formed. In some neighborhoods, like the Lower East Side, developers built higher-end apartments for upwardly mobile workers who wanted to remain close to extended families and friends. Unrestricted districts thus filled with both working and middle-class residents. By the 1940s, over half of the city's inhabitants lived in one of these zones.[18]

At the same time, the designation of strict residential and commercial zones codes stemmed the exodus of affluent residents. In Midtown's posh Murray Hill district, for instance, elite families had been moving out as housing for workers expanded towards their neighborhood. The new zoning codes protected Murray Hill as a low-density residential district, and set up a large commercial district on Fifth Avenue for expensive clothing and food shops. This not only prevented more Murray Hill residents from fleeing, it also enticed people to move back in. A headline in the *New York Times*, dated three months after the enactment of the 1916 zoning code, reads: "Home-Coming Season in Murray Hill—Interesting Changes in Old Center; Many Former Residents Moving Back from Uptown—Zoning Act Removes Fear of Business Invasion. . . ."[19] In the outer boroughs, lower-end commercial and residential districts like Sunnyside and Jackson Heights in Queens similarly catered to skilled laborers, clerical workers and other residents with "light blue"-collar jobs.

New arrangements of industrial, residential, and commercial space thus mapped the city into well-defined zones that dictated the value of the properties within them. In this way, zoning codes set up an almost caste-like system whereby affluent residents lived in quiet, low-density neighborhoods. Commercial zones and sometimes higher-density residential zones buffered them from industrial areas. Moreover, the codes protected industrial spaces from being taken over by commercial or residential development, which in turn maintained low property values for manufacturers and their workers. This complex jigsaw puzzle became much more than a spatial blueprint—it also set up which New Yorkers had access to transportation, to parks, to schools and to clean, healthy air. Spatial configurations would change over time, but the impacts of these initial zoning arrangements would last for generations.

## City "Loses" Industry

Manufacturing in New York City reached an all-time high at the end of World War II. But after 1947, it began to decline sharply.[20] Refrigerated trucks made it less necessary for industries to locate close to rail lines and shipping ports, which allowed businesses to relocate to cheaper environs. Advances in containerization—and later, communications and technology—made it easier for companies to move manufacturing and assembly operations overseas. These factors alone, however, cannot account for the deindustrialization of New York City; rather, they were part of a complex and unique set of circumstances that were both deliberate and unanticipated.

New York City housed one-fourth of all clothing factories in the United States in 1964, and they continued to employ more workers than any other industry. Despite the long hours demanded of these workers, rates of productivity remained at a standstill. Finally, the federal government stepped in and offered subsidies for new machinery. Yet upgrading to larger and more sophisticated machines required bigger and more up-to-date spaces than New York's manufacturing buildings could accommodate. Large manufacturers could not refuse the subsidies—they needed automation to remain competitive. At the same time, New York City was reducing tax incentives and loans to manufacturers.[21] Faced with opposing pressures both to expand and to downsize, garment and printing companies began leaving the city.

This exodus was part of a new economic strategy. By mid-century, New York City headquartered nearly one-third of the nation's 500 largest corporations. "New York was the site of unprecedented economic power," writes labor historian Josh Freeman. "The leading local businessmen were the most important economic decision-makers in the world. What they decided, and what happened on local financial and commodity markets, affected the lives of billions of people."[22] Courting this influence and nurturing corporate growth now became the basis of New York's economic development initiatives.

In 1958, David Rockefeller (whose brother was elected New York's governor later that year) convened the Downtown-Lower Manhattan Association (D-LMA), an organization of powerful corporate leaders who lobbied for a city planning agenda that favored the burgeoning finance economy. The D-LMA's first priority was to rearrange some urban space. They released an 80-page master plan for traffic improvements, new housing, office buildings, and recreational facilities that would make lower Manhattan more attractive to corporations and the white-collar professionals moving to the city to work in them.[23] The plan singled out an unrestricted district close to Wall Street, later known as "Soho," (which stood for "south of Houston") as a prime location for housing those professionals.

South of SoHo and north of Wall Street, the D-LMA also proposed replacing Manhattan's port with a new exhibition-and-office complex that would become a center of world trade. Containerization had radically transformed the shipping industry making it possible to ship massive amounts of goods around the world for only fractions of the previous cost.[24] Most of New York City's ports were too shallow for these advanced container ships, but just across the Hudson River, the new port of Newark sat ashore deeper waters.[25] New York City's dock workers' unions demanded that the Port Authority of New York and New Jersey (PANYNJ) expand and deepen the city's ports so they could compete with Newark. The union and its allies, which included small businesses and other manufacturers along the waterfront, organized picket lines and protests at the proposed site for the new World Trade Center. None-theless, Mayor Lindsay and the D-LMA moved the plan forward and shut down Manhattan's docks. By 1970, the number of longshoremen in New York City was down to 21,600 from 35,000 in 1954.[26]

The World Trade Center decision made it clear that city and cor-porate leaders were now in dogged pursuit of a new economic future. Their vision was to create a city that relied almost exclusively on finance, insurance, and real estate (aka "FIRE") sectors, along with "producer services" (law, accounting, advertising). Starting in the late 1950s, as historian Robert Fitch argues, "New York rid itself of everything that blocked its potential to become the biggest and best FIRE and producer services city in the world."[27]

## Deindustrialization by Design

The 1916 zoning codes presented one major obstacle to this new agenda. Unrestricted zones were now taking up much-needed space that could be used to grow FIRE industries. In 1961, the City Council passed a new zoning resolution which divided New York City into residential, commercial, and manufacturing areas. The codes offered more flexibil-ity in building heights by allowing developers to add extra floor space in exchange for incorporating public plazas into their projects.[28] With a few assorted exceptions, most of Manhattan was rezoned for com-mercial and residential uses, while light manufacturing businesses were placed along its edges. All heavy manufacturing, or "M-zones," were moved to the outer boroughs and subdivided into "light," "heavy," and "mixed-use" designations.

As a still-thriving manufacturing center, SoHo maintained its M-zone designation, contrary to the D-LMA's plans to make it a residential zone. Not to be stopped, the D-LMA lobbied to have SoHo declared a blighted area, full of vacant and abandoned properties, crime, and general eco-nomic decline. Blight would trigger federal funds for urban renewal, which in turn would force the removal of manufacturing businesses and their replacement with residential and commercial uses. In 1963, the city conducted an evaluation of SoHo's manufacturing sector and declared that it was not a candidate for urban renewal because the neighborhood still contained a large number of viable local industries.[29]

But SoHo was actually in flux. Most of its manufacturing businesses rented floors in large factory buildings. Not all of these businesses were spared problems associated with automation, rising rents and labor costs, and changes in transportation. As some of them moved out, landlords allowed local artists to move into their spaces. Although artist live/work studios did not technically comply with zoning codes, city officials tended to look the other way.[30] Recognizing the potential of these conversions, the D-LMA now played the long game. They partnered with community groups and commercial businesses to foster a coffee house culture in SoHo, encouraging bars, restaurants, and galleries. SoHo became funkier, as Wall Street expanded. This drove up residential and commercial demand for factory spaces and sent rents climbing. Soon it was more profitable for landlords to convert their buildings to residential uses than to rent them to factories. By 1969, conversions reached a critical mass, prompting city officials to change SoHo's zoning to allow live-work spaces.[31]

Once the new zoning was in place, city policies continued to encourage residential conversions. Strict noise constraints that made it impossible for manufacturing firms to conduct their day-to-day operations, as well as landmark status, tax breaks, and housing subsidies, made it easy for developers to take over their spaces.[32] Eventually, fines and high rents forced out most of SoHo's industrial tenants.[33] But these businesses were not forgotten—SoHo's industrial chic became a popular urban aesthetic that eventually overtook most of the city's manufacturing neighborhoods.[34]

With zoning revisions paving the way, New York City's manufacturing sector continued to dwindle. Between 1967 and 1976, the city lost a fourth of its factories and one-third of its manufacturing jobs.[35] But those industries did not go down without a fight.

## Zoned In

When city leaders instituted zoning codes in 1916, nearly every square foot of available land was already accounted for in Manhattan, Brooklyn, Queens, and the Bronx. Staten Island, however, still had hundreds of acres of vacant land beyond its northern waterfront. Zoning maps left much of the Island up for grabs, designating nearly half (40 percent) of it

as "unrestricted."[36] Initially, much of that area was too swampy for development. Advances in building technologies over the next few decades,
however, made it possible to build on that swampland. Residential, commercial, and industrial properties began to fill in wetland areas on the
southern and eastern shores. Because these were still designated unrestricted zones, multifamily dwellings went up alongside townhouses,
single-family homes, factories, automobile establishments, wholesale
stores, and junk yards.[37]

Over time, one factory replaced another without concern for the contaminants left behind. For instance, the Jewett White Lead Paint works
became Sedutto's Ice Cream factory; an oil tank storage facility became the Port Richmond Sewer Treatment Plant; and soap production
facilities at Port Ivory were acquired by the Port Authority. For many
decades, layers of contaminants accumulated, along with the environmental health risks facing local residents.[38]

The reforms of 1961 promised to bring more order to land use while
charting a course forward for the borough's economic future. But that
future was subject to heated debate. Once it issued a set of proposed
zoning changes, the Department of City Planning held a series of public
hearings. Several scathing editorials, published during the hearings, re-
veal a borough deeply divided over its fate. On one hand, "industrialists"
sought to protect the interests of existing industrial businesses. They opposed the proposed changes, which would rezone a number of manufacturing districts for residential uses. Existing properties could remain in
place for at least ten years, but then they would be forced to move. Need-
less to say, in these areas, industrial expansions were out of the question.
Industrialists believed that such directives struck at the heart of the Island's economy. "Residentialists," on the other hand, supported the way
the proposal favored residential development and restricted industrial
growth. Unsurprisingly, residentialists included real estate professionals,
commercial business owners, and many civic associations interested in
raising their property values.

At one public hearing, local architect Albert Melniker spoke on behalf of the industrial economy:

We have large industrial establishments and we feel that it is necessary
to have the proposed zoning retain these uses and give them room to

grow . . . . It is an established fact that industrial and commercial uses are the heaviest taxpayers in any community.[39]

For Melniker, restricting these businesses was like biting the hand that fed the borough. Going even further, he quoted an editorial from the *Staten Island Advance* that insisted:

> There must be industry in the borough. It's hardly conceivable that our transportation system, still mostly dependent upon ferry boats, can handle thousands of new commuters to Manhattan. The answer is for the new home owners to find work near home.[40]

The editorial went on to comment that the depletion of industrial jobs would send both new and old residents off the Island.

At the public hearing, Harold E. Witteman, President of the Emerson Hill Association, expressed the residentialist perspective:

> Staten Island in these areas needs and wants and can support these [builders] bringing many thousands of residents to the Island, because of its [sic] many present advantages and nearness to Manhattan and Brooklyn. This is the bolster we need for our economy and yapping [sic] about heavy industry which we cannot get and may lose what little we have, this will bring Staten Island from a status of existence to a status of maintenance and growth.
>
> Today we have over fifty stores vacant in Stapleton, more in Tompkinsville, New Brighton and etc. because the economy is weak, what we need is more good people to live and spend on the Island . . . What difference does it make where they work?

From Witteman's perspective, the borough's economic future turned on its becoming a bedroom community within a city.

Indeed, Staten Island had an edge over the nearby suburbs that were luring away so many white New Yorkers. As mentioned, at the time, federal programs like the GI Bill and the Federal Homeowners Association were making homeownership possible for working and middle class, white families.[41] Unlike suburban townships, Staten Island was within the city's jurisdiction, which meant that houses could be built on smaller lots, making them even more affordable. Also in 1961, construction on Robert Moses's most ambitious project, the Verrazano Bridge, was well underway. By the time it was completed in 1964, it would be the longest suspension bridge in the world, connecting Staten Island's East Shore to Bay Ridge, Brooklyn. At the time, young, white, ethnic families were fleeing neighborhoods in Brooklyn, Queens, and upper Manhattan as African American and Latinx families moved in.[42] Finally, Moses' Staten Island Expressway (SIE) would soon cut across the Island, connecting the Verrazano, to the Goethals Bridge to Elizabeth, New Jersey. In short, Staten Island potentially offered white, ethnic families all of the of single-family homes, driveways, shopping malls, and homogeneity that the suburbs offered without having to leave the boundaries of New York City.

The 1961 zoning changes were key to creating this suburbatopia. South of the SIE, low-density zones would feature single-family homes surrounded by small lots, a miniature version of the suburbs complete with picket fences. At the public hearing, impassioned testimonies pleaded for these low-density districts. In the following excerpt, a local resident, whose neighborhood of Emerson Hill was already low-density, begs city officials not to up-zone the neighborhood *adjacent* to his:

> If you take it [R-2 zoning] away, if you build an apartment on Emerson Hill, the people on Emerson are going to disappear. . . . They are going to join the trek away from the City of New York into the suburbs and elsewhere, and they are going to be replaced by apartment-house dwellers, who have their right in the sun without a doubt, but people who do not contribute so substantially to the soundness of the area.

The speaker argues that the entire Island was threatened by high-density zoning. Once installed on Emerson Hill, "apartment-house dwellers"— that is, racial minorities and low-income families—would drive away current residents. More apartment-house dwellers would take their place and before anyone knew, the entire Island would become "unsound." This language of invasion and pathology also rationalized planning decisions that positioned "apartment-house dwellings" as buffers that insulated affluent communities from hazardous facilities.

In the end, the residentialist perspective held sway. South of the expressway, two-thirds of Staten Island became the city's answer to a bedroom community. North of the expressway, the remaining third became a mix of residential, manufacturing and mixed-use districts. For the most part, heavy manufacturing zones along the waterfront were bordered by mixed-use and high-density areas. Beyond these mixed-use areas, low-density residential zones reached all the way to the expressway.

## Zoned Out

As zoning reforms cut a path for the growth of the FIRE economy and pushed manufacturing businesses away from New York, tens of thousands of blue-collar workers lost their jobs. The mixed-use zones where these workers lived were now beset by widespread unemployment, which in turn led to multiple vacant and abandoned properties. As city leaders divested from these neighborhoods, their problems of crime, arson, and dilapidated housing only worsened. It was easier for white residents, including ethnic groups of European descent, to take advantage of federal mortgage and insurance programs to purchase homes in suburban areas. Meanwhile, during the 1960s, African Americans left the South in droves to settle in northeastern and midwestern cities.[43] In the aftermath of Civil Rights-era reforms, the federal government instituted measures to address some of the cumulative harms caused by residential segregation. Among other things, they mandated school integration through bussing. The idea of integrated schools drove even more white families out of inner-city areas. During the 1970s, New York City lost more than eight hundred thousand people.[44]

Only a small portion of those who left were black or brown. Redlining, a practice by which banks declared mixed-race neighborhoods to be bad investments, justified the denial of mortgages and housing insurance to people of color. In addition, neighborhood covenants as well as inequalities in employment, education, healthcare, and criminal justice multiplied the effects of residential segregation, making it even more unlikely that families of color could move out of inner-city, mixed-use zones.[45] While some proportion of working-class, white families stayed in such areas, overlapping systems of discrimination made it nearly impossible for communities of color to leave.

Postindustrial or not, every city requires space for municipal facilities and for surviving industrial businesses—hence the ongoing need for mixed-use and manufacturing zones. But where those facilities go is another matter. Environmental reforms like the 1970 Clean Air Act included opportunities for local communities to oppose the siting of new facilities in or near their neighborhoods. While these opportunities were open to any community, such oppositions took time, money, and political clout.[46] This meant that wealthy areas like Manhattan's Upper West Side blocked hazardous facilities (such as waste treatment plants and transfer stations, incinerators, and waste storage facilities), which then clustered in poor, minority neighborhoods.

In addition, the new zoning regulations contained an "as of right" clause that allowed owners of M-zone properties to expand their facilities without City Planning approvals, as long as they continued to comply with zoning restrictions. An owner could also sell his or her property to another industrial facility without seeking zoning approvals.

Economist Yale Rabin refers to zoning codes that allowed, and even encouraged, the clustering of industrial facilities in neighborhoods of color as "expulsive zoning." For Rabin, this term refers to zoning decisions that "permit—even promote—the intrusion into black neighborhoods of disruptive, incompatible uses that have diminished the quality and undermined the stability of those neighborhoods."[47] Rabin's formula emphasizes the degree to which industrial facilities can be a cause, and not just a symptom, of neighborhood degradation.

In some ways, the North Shore stood as an exception to Rabin's formulation. While multifamily apartment buildings prevailed in the other boroughs, Staten Island's lack of development prior to the 1960s sustained its single family homes. Many white ethnic families had purchased these homes during the early part of the twentieth century when blue-collar jobs on the Island were heavily unionized. These were passed from generation to generation. As industry declined in the 1960s and 1970s, so did the incomes of these working families. While some were able to leave for the suburbs, others stayed to be close to family or because they could not afford to move.[48] Over time, it became more and more expensive to maintain these old homes, even though property values were in decline. On top of that, historic redlining practices marked mixed-race neighborhoods as bad credit risks, making it more difficult to sell homes. The North Shore also housed a number of multifamily apartment buildings, including several large public housing

complexes built in the early 1960s, through federal and state urban renewal programs.

Across the North Shore's approximately fifteen neighborhoods, racial
composition varied widely. In the late 1970s, for instance, large groups
of migrants from Liberia began moving into the neighborhoods of Park
Hill and parts of nearby Stapleton. In such high-density residential
zones, as few as 16 percent of residents were White, non-Hispanic. But
in low-density, residential zones, up to 72 percent of households were
White, non-Hispanic.[49] Regardless of racial background or income levels, North Shore neighborhoods shared one important trait: they were
all located on the most forgotten part of the forgotten borough. Here,
the shadows cast by expulsive zoning and arrangements of industrial
space would linger for decades to come.

## "You Too Can Glow in the Dark"

One contaminated site in particular demonstrates the perniciousness—
and invisibility—of this toxic legacy. In 1940, Archer Daniels Midlands
(ADM), which operated a linseed oil plant on the North Shore, built a
warehouse at the foot of the Bayonne Bridge. It sat on a small, triangular
piece of waterfront property bordered by the Kill Van Kull, an adjacent property and Richmond Terrace, the two-lane road that separated
waterfront industries from residential neighborhoods. As the US geared
up to enter World War II in 1940, ADM decided to lease its warehouse.
Its tenant was Edgar Sengier, the Belgian owner of a Congolese uranium
mine reputed to produce the world's richest ore. Sengier anticipated the
Nazi invasion of Belgium and wanted to secure his uranium by moving
most of it offsite. After storing it on the North Shore for two years, a
United States army Colonel purchased it, along with the rest of the ore
from Sengier's mine. Once the ore was all together at the ADM warehouse, Sengier planned to ship it to locations across the country, where
scientists were working on a top-secret government project.[50] This was,
of course, the infamous "Manhattan Project," so named for its headquarters in Manhattan.[51]

But a significant portion of Sengier's uranium never made it off of
Staten Island. At some point, approximately 1,250 tons of it spilled, either
from leaky barrels or during a ship-to-shore transfer. The spill, which

covered the northwest corner of the site, was covered with topsoil and later surrounded by a chain link fence.[52] And thus it remained, even after ADM sold the parcel. Subsequent owners leased the property on the opposite side of the fence. The Metropolitan Transportation Authority stored its buses there for a period of time; then a private transportation company used it for truck storage. Finally, it was bought jointly by Apple Towing and Margarella Asphalt & Concrete.

The site was also in an area zoned for mixed uses, so it was quite close to residential properties. Those who grew up nearby remember being warned away from the site. "My mother used to tell me, 'You'll get cancer if you play over there, and your kids will have six fingers and toes,'" Terrence McCarthy, a 56-year-old truck driver, told the Daily News.[53] Activist Dee Vandenburg once told me, "we like to call it 'you too can glow in the dark.'"

In 1980, the Department of Energy (DOE) began evaluating radioactivity at all of the sites used for the Manhattan Project. At the ADM site (now officially known as the "Staten Island Warehouse Site," investigators found residual radioactivity in the soil that exceeded regulatory limits.[54] Yet the site was not prioritized for cleanup. Twelve years later, the New York State Department of Environmental Conservation (DEC) conducted another assessment, this time of subsurface soil. The department found that soil below the ground was far more radioactive than the surface samples studied by the energy department. Still, no action was taken.[55]

In 2007, Beryl Thurman was in the middle of her project of compiling historic information on the North Shore's twenty-one contaminated sites. Thurman had heard the rumors about the warehouse site, so she dug deep and found the two reports confirming its radioactivity. Alarmed that the site flooded during heavy rains, and that it sat just across the road from residential properties, she began calling the DEC and the EPA. She continued to call them for the next twelve months until the EPA agreed to test the property. This time, the agency found levels of radium and uranium approximately two orders of magnitude greater than the levels initially reported in 1980.[56] After another year of sustained pressure from local activists and negotiation with the Department of Energy, the EPA agreed to clean the site, subject to a Congressional funding allocation. While funding for that allocation

Flooding at the corner of Nicholas Avenue and Richmond Terrace, 2011. (The corner is approximately 400 feet from the former State Island Warehouse radioactive site.) Credit: Beryl Thurman.

lingered, Nicholas Avenue flooded regularly. After Hurricane Sandy in 2012, Thurman and other activists became especially concerned about the radioactive site and lobbied hard to get city agencies to include its remediation in their plans for resiliency—to no avail. To this date, the remediation has yet to begin.

Elected officials might have ignored the warehouse site, but international groups of nuclear activists knew that it was part of a constellation of radioactive sites. In 2009, a Japanese film crew traveled to the North Shore to film part of a documentary about the legacy of the atomic bomb, and every so often European journalists or filmmakers would contact Beryl Thurman for an interview about "the Manhattan Project site." In August 2011, to mark the sixty-sixth anniversary of the dropping of atomic bombs on Hiroshima and Nagasaki, the Unitarian Church of Staten Island planned a memorial service which included Japanese musicians and Native American drummers. It also appeared in numerous books and articles about the legacy of the nuclear era.

Locally, however, planners and state agencies seemed unconcerned about the site's potential risks. In 2013, the Port Authority of New York and New Jersey (PANYNJ) began a multiyear construction project to raise the Bayonne Bridge. To create a staging area for the project, the PANYNJ cleared a small parcel of land at the foot of the bridge. Learning that the parcel was a few feet from the radioactive site, local residents raised alarms. At a public meeting, the PANYNJ assured residents that samples of debris and dust from the area would be tested nightly for contaminants. Residents were in no way satisfied with this answer, but the project proceeded regardless. About a year later, the City Council approved permits for "Nicholas Estates," an 83-unit duplex housing development targeted to middle-income families and located less than half a mile from the warehouse site. Alarmed, North Shore environmental justice activists lobbied hard to stop the development, claiming that its proximity to the radiation would endanger new residents. The area tended to flood, and the proposed development, itself, sat on two or three small, natural wetlands. Their efforts were unsuccessful, however. In 2015, the Facebook sales page for Nicholas Estates went live.

In 2017, the Staten Island Economic Development Corporation (an arm of the NYCEDC) announced a design competition for the North Shore High Line. Modeled after Manhattan's highly successful High Line Park, the agency intended to repurpose part of an old rail line that ran for a half mile along the Kill Van Kull between Herberton and Nicholas Avenues. The park would end at Nicholas Estates, now a popular development that was already set to expand. Redevelopment policies and plans have shifted the contours of sacrifice zones, but they have consistently put low-income communities and communities of color on the front lines of environmental risk.

## Reindustrialization: City Wins Industry Back

For nearly fifty years, city leaders favored real estate over manufacturing development. None have been more vocal about it than Michael Bloomberg, who, on taking office, immediately set to work building a high-end real estate economy. A year into his first term, Bloomberg famously told a reporter from the *Financial Times*, "If you are a pharmaceutical company or a steel company, you do not need to be here . . . New York City should not waste its time with manufacturing."[57] In order to put manufacturing spaces to uses that better served his vision of a luxury economy, the Bloomberg administration began converting industrial districts into other uses.[58] One by one, former manufacturing zones like Hunters Point in Queens, Melrose in the South Bronx, Manhattanville in upper Manhattan, and large swaths of Greenpoint and Williamsburg in Brooklyn gave way to residential and commercial districts. Between 2002 and 2010, the city lost over 20 percent of its industrial lands to rezoning.[59]

Most of this rezoning was underway when Bloomberg rhetorically reversed course. Running for his second term in 2005, Bloomberg announced that the city would welcome and make room for industrial businesses through the Industrial Business Zone (IBZ) program. The IBZ set aside sixteen safe havens that protected industrial areas from being rezoned for residential uses, and it created a tax credit for the one-time relocation of businesses—many coming from rezoned areas. Additionally, the city would dedicate several of its publicly owned properties to manufacturing.[60] In a press release describing the new industrial incentives, Bloomberg said, "Over the past half century, the City's industrial base has declined, along with many other American cities, but industry remains a powerful engine of our economy and its 500,000 jobs represent about 15 percent of our workforce."[61] Within four years, Bloomberg's rhetoric about industry had gone from seeing it as "a waste of time" to celebrating it as "a powerful engine of [the] economy." Behind this shift was a recategorization of what constituted the industrial sector, and who it served.

It was around this time that Bloomberg began to promote New York City as a future leader in the technology and innovation sectors. During the 2005 campaign, he also launched the "Made in NYC" program, which provided 5-percent tax credits on production costs for qualifying film and television productions filmed in New York City.[62] Using similar tax credits as well as small business loans and subsidies for office space and broadband, Bloomberg courted technology startups and giants like Google, Yahoo, and LinkedIn. According to a report commissioned by Bloomberg Philanthropies, by 2013 the tech/information sector (which included businesses that produced software, hardware, information, entertainment, media services, and fashion) had become "the second-largest engine of the New York City economy, supporting 262,000 jobs in the city."[63]

To expand on this new industrial base, the NYCEDC unveiled a set of initiatives called "Manufacturing 2.0" in 2011. This time, it focused on small manufacturing businesses, including local crafters, woodworkers, artisans, food and beverage manufacturers, technology startups, film studios, visual artists, and fashion designers. Manufacturing 2.0 monies would be used to update vacant or underused industrial properties and rent them to small manufacturers at affordable rates.[64] According to the NYCEDC, New Yorkers' recent consumption patterns showed they favored locally sourced, specialty products and high-end, hand-crafted items, especially furniture and clothing.[65] Of course, these trends were also associated with green consumption patterns and pro-environmental attitudes. In other words, Manufacturing 2.0 targeted a particular subset of New York City residents/consumers—affluent, upwardly mobile denizens of a luxury city.

## The Rise of the Making Class

In 2014, Rick and Michael Mast, co-founders of Mast Brothers, an artisanal chocolate company, moved the bulk of their production to a new factory at the edge of the Brooklyn Navy Yard. Known for their long, Mennonite-style beards, the Iowa-born brothers leaned into a burgeoning rage for all things organic and handcrafted. They hand-sourced, roasted, and ground their cacao beans (they used a bean-husking machine especially designed by a friend who was an aerospace engineer). Then they ground, melted, and mixed the beans into $10-per-piece bars covered in custom wrapping paper. The Masts were also known for their commitment to being "oil free." A 2010 video produced by the website "coolhunting," details how they hand-retrofitted a 70-foot cargo ship into a three-masted shipping schooner and sailed it to the Dominican Republic. There, they loaded the ship with nearly twenty tons of organic cocoa beans and returned to Brooklyn.[66] The Mast Brothers may have flown too close to the sun, however. In late 2015, rumors began circulating that when they started out, the Mast Brothers used other people's chocolate but represented it as their own. While some foodies defended the Masts, others took aim at the entire Mast mystique, alleging that they were "the Milli Vanilli of chocolate."[67]

The Mast Brothers' saga and the national attention it received provides a window into New York's twenty-first-century industrial renaissance. The company rose to prominence in the wake of the 2008 fiscal crisis, in the midst of an extremely tight job market, Occupy Wall Street, and mounting concerns about sustainability and climate change.

Indeed, the Masts are considered to be among the founding fathers of the "Maker" movement. Especially popular with millennials, Makers collectively responded to the rampant corporatization of the previous several decades by eschewing mass production, chain stores, and multinational corporations. Instead, they combined open-source learning, contemporary design tools, social media, and technology like 3D printers with a do-it-yourself production model.[68] In 2014, *Adweek* described the movement as "the convergence of computer hackers and traditional artisans."[69]

The movement took Brooklyn by storm. Soon, rooftop gardens, backyard chicken coops, and beekeepers were appearing in the borough's trendiest neighborhoods, along with popular spots like Brooklyn Flea, Smorgasburg and By Brooklyn, which sold locally made food and other goods. By 2014, "Made in Brooklyn" artisanal pickles, kimchi, rhubarb jams, green tea cookies, beard oil, spectacles, clogs, and more could be found in stores and markets across the globe.[70] In 2015, the *New York Daily News* reported that Brooklyn had fifteen licensed distilleries, the highest number in New York State (Buffalo, the second highest, had only five). But hand-made, small-batch, sustainably sourced products did not come cheap. Jars of hand-made pickles cost fourteen dollars; bags of Brooklyn-based granola cost nine dollars and a travel-size bottle of Brooklyn-made beard oil would set you back fifteen dollars. The Maker movement signaled the gentrification of manufacturing itself.

Makers knew their target market, because they *were* their target market—urban sophisticates invested in taking care of their own health as well as the health of the environment. Paying a premium for locally sourced, hand-produced goods marked consumers as environmentally concerned citizens. Moreover, as sociologists have noted, green products acted as an imaginary buffer against environmental dangers that are beyond individual control.[71] A second way Makers expressed fears about environmental risks and the consequences of industrial capitalism was by romanticizing preindustrial times. Long, Mennonite beards appeared on the faces of many twenty- and thirty-something Brooklynites, and women began knitting their own dresses, scarves, and hats. In the *Daily News* article cited above, Brooklyn-based rum distiller Bridget Firtle commented on this aesthetic:

I think a lot of that romanticism has been lost over the years with big conglomerates and corporations . . . The people consuming our goods really find nostalgia a powerful selling tool and I think they like things that are real and authentic and not trying to brand themselves from an image perspective but just being what they are.[72]

Of course, as Firtle's statement suggests, both nostalgia and authenticity are inherently contradictory categories. Makers relied on all kinds of contemporary technologies to produce, market, and buy their authentically homemade products. And, while the movement venerated a preindustrial, pre-consumerist period, it was itself based on consumerism. Finally, as anthropologist Kim Humphery notes, this nostalgia for a pastoral past also accompanies a distinctly bourgeois focus on gastronomic pleasures and culinary knowledge.[73]

Indeed, despite their generally liberal and inclusive politics, Makers were a socio-economically homogenous bunch. In 2012, *Make Magazine* (considered the movement's flagship publication) surveyed its 300,000 readers and found that their median household income averaged $106,000. Moreover, 97 percent had attended college, and 80 percent had a postgraduate education.[74] Clearly, these manufacturers were not the low-income or working-class New Yorkers who once had formed the city's industrial labor force. Rather, they were part of Richard Florida's "creative class"—highly educated, upper middle-class, creative professionals who, according to Florida, are crucial to the economic success of contemporary cities.[75] It was these individuals who populated the environmentally gentrifying neighborhoods of the sustainaphrenic city.

## Industrial Gentrification

In 2014, the Mast Brothers moved into a brand-new factory at the edge of the Brooklyn Navy Yard. Located between DUMBO and Williamsburg, the Navy Yard was at the epicenter of hipster Brooklyn. Initially owned and operated by the Department of Defense, the Navy Yard employed 70,000 people at its peak in the early 1940s. In 1996, the Department of Defense closed the site and, three years later, the city reopened it as an industrial park. During the 1970s and 1980s, the

Navy Yard faltered, especially after its two major tenants, maritime businesses both, moved out. During the late 1990s economic boom, the Yard rebounded, providing space to 200 small to mid-sized businesses and employing approximately 3,000 people.[76] With the launch of the Industrial Business Zones in 2005, the City pledged $200 million to expand and update the Navy Yard. To oversee this development, the NYCEDC installed as CEO Andrew Kimball, a rising, young urban planner who had just spent three years trying to bring the Olympic Games to New York City. From the get-go, Kimball made sustainability integral to the Navy Yard's new brand. Its website devoted an entire page to listing the green manufacturers who leased space at the site. Another highlighted environmental initiatives undertaken at the Yard, including LEED-certified buildings, hybrid vehicles, the largest rooftop farm in New York City, solar-powered trash compactors, and solar and wind-powered street lamps.[77] This emphasis was in keeping with Bloomberg's PlaNYC 2030, and it certainly appealed to prospective new tenants who clamored to move in.[78]

Key to the Navy Yard's success was its location between two neighborhoods that had rapidly upscaled in the early 2000s. In 2015, DUMBO became Brooklyn's most expensive neighborhood for sales.[79] Indeed, the Navy Yard became the centerpiece of a much larger development plan known as the "Brooklyn Tech Triangle." Between 2005 and 2015, the EDC invested over 5.2 billion dollars in the Tech Triangle area, creating 1.5 million square feet of retail space, 332,000 square feet of office space, and 12.8 million square feet of development. This redevelopment also coincided with the creation of the state-of-the-art Brooklyn Bridge Park, which ran along part of the East River, as well as the Barclays Center, a massive arena in downtown Brooklyn. All of these projects combined to install Brooklyn as a major worldwide brand.

Unlike the industrial facilities that once degraded M-zoned neighborhoods, the Navy Yard set the stage for a host of development projects designed to upscale this part of Brooklyn. For instance, Navy Green, a $146 million housing complex consisting of four multifamily, mixed-rate high-rises and twenty-three single-family, luxury townhouses, opened in 2015.[80] On the opposite side of the yard in an area known as Vinegar Hill, several luxury condominiums were under construction in 2015. To accommodate these new residents, developers also built a

74,000-square-foot high-end supermarket and a row of storefronts filled with "quirky, weird mom-and-pop Brooklyn shops."[81] Conveniently, Makers would be able to live, create, and sell their wares without ever having to leave downtown Brooklyn.

Which is not to say that Manufacturing 2.0 developments were limited to a single borough. Nine out of nineteen new spaces were located in Manhattan. Each was located in a neighborhood undergoing high-end redevelopment, including Kips Bay, the Garment District, Hudson Square, Harlem, and Washington Heights. Four of the largest spaces (the Navy Yard, the Made in New York Media Center, the DUMBO Incubator, and the NYC Urban Futures Lab) clustered in and around the Brooklyn Tech Triangle. Long Island City, Queens got a business incubator, as did the South Bronx. The last space was in Staten Island's St. George, in a newly rezoned strip of waterfront that was within walking distance of the ferry terminal. Indeed, all but one of these projects were located in neighborhoods where gentrification was already underway. This proximity was no accident. Like green space, trendy, small-scale, "green" manufacturing businesses had become an amenity that helped fuel neighborhood gentrification.

The de Blasio administration extended Bloomberg's industrial makeover. In November 2015, Mayor de Blasio unveiled the "Industrial Action Plan" (IAP), promising to invest more than $115 million in the City's industrial sector. "Manufacturing isn't just part of New York City's past—it is a thriving part of our twenty-first-century economy," he declared. As part of the IAP, de Blasio closed a loophole in the Industrial Business Zone (IBZ) program, which allowed hotels and mini-storage facilities to locate within them. Hotels raised property values, and mini-storage facilities provided a convenient way for speculators to purchase land and hold it until a neighborhood began to gentrify. Then they would convert the storage into high-end commercial or residential properties.[82] In addition, de Blasio and others conjured rosy images of an updated, green manufacturing sector that would provide thousands of well-paying, secure jobs to unskilled, non-college educated workers. In a press release for the IAP, de Blasio said, "These investments are going to generate tens of thousands of good jobs for New York City families."[83] But the reunion between the twenty-first-century city and its estranged industrial sector was freighted with the baggage of sustainaphrenia. Jobs in the new manufacturing sector were as dramatically different from unionized jobs in the old manufacturing sector as the twenty-first city was different from the city of early twentieth century.

## The Other Makers

Between 2001 and 2012, the total number of manufacturing *jobs* in New York City decreased by nearly 50 percent. Yet, after 2006, the average number of manufacturing *businesses* stabilized. During the same period, industrial output declined at a far slower rate than industrial jobs.[84] These numbers indicate that manufacturing businesses were hiring fewer workers and relying heavily on technology. Manufacturing 2.0's high-tech and small-scale businesses follow this trend. In 2014, for instance, the 330 companies at the Navy Yard averaged nineteen people per business. The Brooklyn Army Terminal in Sunset Park averaged thirty-four workers per company. A report by the City of New York's Independent Budget Office found that industrial subsectors such as biotech, computer, and electronics manufacturing, broadcasting, and motion picture and sound hired relatively small numbers of workers, especially without college degrees, relative to traditional industrial firms. Moreover, the report found that "many of the industrial subsectors that did employ a large number of workers without college degrees, like food manufacturing or warehousing, pay wages that are comparable to the average wages for workers in *non*industrial sectors."[85] These statistics demonstrate that in practice, small-scale manufacturers provided few opportunities for low-skilled workers.

Traditional manufacturing jobs had also undergone irrevocable change. Automation and technology dramatically altered the scale and type of jobs available to industrial workers, demanding highly specialized and skilled expertise. Only some of those jobs offered the livable wages and benefits attributed to them. Anti-union legislation, globalization, and outsourcing had all diminished the power of unions, which lowered both wages and benefits. In 2013, only 10.1 percent of US manufacturing workers belonged to labor unions.[86] Industrial manufacturers increasingly turned to informalized, or "day" labor, often preferring to fill low-tech jobs with undocumented workers.[87]

Privatization and the rise of the "gig," or contract economy radically reduced the number of full-time workers in all employment sectors, worldwide. A 2015 study by two Princeton economists found that nearly 16 percent of workers in the United States were engaged as independent contractors, up from 10 percent a decade before.[88] Blue-collar workers were not immune to the effects of this shift. In addition to being replaced by subcontracted, undocumented or ununionized laborers, the privatization of certain industries turned union jobs into contract work. The trucking industry exemplifies this point. After the federal deregulation of the trucking industry in the 1980s, truckers were reclassified as independent contractors. Truckers were now paid by the load (rather than hourly), and they owned their own trucks. In 1977, the median annual wage for truck drivers hovered around $96,552 in today's dollars. In 2018, that wage was $43,680.89 On top of lower wages, truckers were responsible for all of their expenses, including fuel, taxes, insurance, maintenance, and repair costs. With scant resources, truckers were often unable to update and maintain their trucks, which, in turn, led to higher emissions and more pollution.[90] Even state-sponsored Clean Truck Programs, which offered low-cost loans for cleaner-fueled trucks, pushed drivers into debt.[91]

The call for a return to manufacturing crosses the political spectrum—from de Blasio to Bernie Sanders to Barack Obama to Donald Trump. Purportedly, creating more manufacturing jobs will revive an unsteady economy and a sinking middle class.[92] For those on the left, it will also help the environment by emphasizing cleaner and greener technologies. This rhetoric not only elides the new realities of manufacturing jobs, but it also facilitates industrial gentrification and uneven development. As light, green industries cluster in gentrifying neighborhoods, heavy, dirty industries further consolidate in non-gentrifying neighborhoods.

## While You Were Out

On a Thursday morning in July 2012, Victoria Gillen happened to be reading through *The City Record*, a publication that compiled public notices. To her surprise, she found a notice for a public hearing to discuss amendments to Industrial Business Zone (IBZ) boundaries. The meeting was scheduled for the following Friday. As mentioned above, IBZs offered tax incentives and other forms of assistance to industrial businesses within the zone. In 2012, the city convened a special commission to redraw the boundaries of four IBZs, and to discuss the addition of a new IBZ on Staten Island's North Shore. Gillen quickly emailed Thurman and some other environmental activists. Collectively, they hit the roof. The buried public notice, not to mention scheduling the hearing in the middle of a Friday *in the summer*, was infuriating. Clearly, Gillen told me, the city was trying to avoid their opposition. Nevertheless, five North Shore activists rearranged their schedules to appear at the public hearing. Each of them offered passionate testimonies about why the North Shore did not need an industrial business incentive zone. Several months later, the EDC issued a press release announcing the creation of a new IBZ on Staten Island.

Gentrification had its limits as an economic strategy—the city also needed to maintain some kind of heavy manufacturing economy. Even more importantly, like any city, New York needed to house industrial facilities like waste transfer stations, sewage treatment plants, truck and bus depots, and power stations within municipal boundaries. In 2012, these ongoing imperatives collided on the North Shore, one of the only remaining working waterfronts left in New York City.[93] Even without the IBZ, activists had recently challenged the expansion of a waste transfer station to include a dredged soils facility, as well as the creation of a new cement manufacturing plant, a natural gas pipeline, a port expansion, and the raising of the Bayonne Bridge. They were also still fighting to remediate existing contamination, like the uranium polluting the radioactive warehouse site.

Another IBZ in Brooklyn's Sunset Park offers an important contrast. Like the North Shore, Sunset Park was a predominantly low-income and working-class Latinx and Asian American neighborhood, and it included a large industrial waterfront that once hosted one of the city's busiest ports. United Puerto Rico Organization of Sunset Park (UP-ROSE), a local environmental justice group, fought for many years to transform four of those piers into a waterfront park. In 2014, their efforts came to fruition when the Parks Department opened Bush Terminal Park. A few blocks away, within the expanded boundaries of Sunset Park's IBZ, the city had also opened Industry City, a Brooklyn Navy

Bayonne Bridge protest, 2013. Credit: Marie Wausnock

Yard-style development. In fact, the EDC installed Andrew Kimball from the Navy Yard as the project's CEO. Kimball quickly established a set of maker spaces (subsidized through Manufacturing 2.0) and a set of artisanal shops. He also rented a large space to the Brooklyn Nets basketball team to use for practices. Early in his first term, Mayor Bill de Blasio proposed designating Industry City as a special "innovation district" which permitted developers to build within the IBZ a hotel, a university facility, a conference center, and expanded retail.[94]

UPROSE and other activists were furious. For years, they had lobbied the city to build Bush Terminal park alongside their own detailed vision for a set of green industrial spaces that would employ members of the community. As a nod to UPROSE's plans, Industry City included a publicly funded job training and placement program to serve Sunset Park's immigrant, non-English-speaking labor force. However, many of the jobs offered to local residents were in retail services.[95] Allowing for hotels, more retail and academic space would only increase the number of service jobs, rather adding the kinds of skilled manufacturing opportunities UPROSE called for. As UPROSE battled it out with Kimball and Industry City developers, other parts of the project moved forward. By 2019, Industry City had become a hipster hub, with dozens of new artisanal spaces and coffee shops, outdoor film screenings, sunset yoga classes, and co-working spaces. That year, the Lonely Planet travel guide named Sunset Park one of the "coolest neighborhoods" to visit in the world.[96]

The reinvention of industrial areas like Sunset Park and the Brooklyn Navy Yard, and the ongoing accumulation of polluting industries on the North Shore epitomize sustainaphrenia's dynamics of sacrifice and gain. None of this was lost on North Shore activists.

## Conclusion

Nostalgia for the manufacturing-based, industrial economy glosses over certain factual details. While this economy provided white workers with stable jobs and the wages and benefits needed to achieve middle-class lifestyles, the nostalgia downplays the fact that racist policies excluded people of color from those benefits. Similarly, narratives about deindustrialization cast it as an inevitable outcome of globalization, technology and the rise of private capital. This chapter, however, reveals how political and corporate leaders used zoning regulations to attract, and then repel, manufacturing businesses. In 1916, the institution of zoning codes drew protective boundaries around wealthy areas, insulating them from industries and immigrant workers. Simultaneously, the elite players protected industrial zones from the commercial and residential real estate market. In 1961, zoning reforms rearranged urban space to recreate New York City as a worldwide center for the new finance and real estate-based global economy. In both cases, low-income communities and communities of color were relegated to living near and among industrial facilities, serving as human buffers for the waste they generated.

Rather than correcting the systemic inequities of industrial and real estate capitalism, the twenty-first-century reboot of the industrial economy remained embedded in those very same inequities. High-tech and small-scale, trendy manufacturing businesses raised the cultural capital of a neighborhood and emitted significantly fewer pollutants. In so doing, they shifted the burden for all of the city's heavy manufacturing industries onto the shoulders of neighborhoods that were not slated for revitalization and that were already saturated with polluting facilities. Like other forms of environmental gentrification, industrial gentrification thus greened certain neighborhoods while sacrificing the environmental health and safety of others.

Shortly after the IBZ hearing, Victoria Gillen wrote an eloquent letter to the editor of a website that covered architecture news:

> Wonderful Hipster Havens are created; Water-front parks offer diversion to the residents of new "luxury" units. Where do the displaced heavy industrial firms go? Bottom line: the areas with people of color, people without tremendous economic resources, are paying the price for Bloomberg's projects—while our taxes support these changes, we do not share in the benefits, and find ourselves, here on Staten Island, once again a dumping ground for the City's unwanted garbage.[97]

4

# Brown Spots on the Apple

*Brown Gentrification and the Repurposing of Polluted Properties*

On a damp Thursday night in February, 2012, I shifted restlessly on a metal folding chair. It was about 9:00 p.m., and the public meeting I was attending was starting to get rowdy. Along with about forty North Shore residents I had gathered in the drafty, basement community room of the Reformed Church of Staten Island for a presentation on the Port Richmond Brownfield Opportunity Area (BOA). On the face of it, the BOA seemed like just what Port Richmond, the North Shore's most industrialized neighborhood, had been waiting for—the program targeted low-income communities where industrial contamination inhibited neighborhood revitalization. Residents had arrived at the church that night with lots of ideas about how the BOA grant could clean up and repurpose its many contaminated properties. But presenters revealed a prepackaged set of strategies that had little to do with residents' priorities. Victoria Gillen scraped her chair back and stood up, half facing the presenters and half facing the crowd. "Initially, I heard about this and thought, oh Brownfield, yeah great. We need that. But now," Gillen sighed and shook her head. "Now, I'm just stunned."

Bordered by West Brighton and the Bayonne Bridge, Port Richmond contained a wastewater treatment plant, two private waste transfer stations, transit depots for MTA buses, Access-a-Ride vehicles, and DEP garbage trucks. The Staten Island port was also located there, as well as a number of ship repair yards, auto body shops, and salvage yards. But those industries had not employed local residents for decades and 25.6% of Port Richmond's population fell below the federal poverty line.[1] About 20 percent of residents identified as African American and about 40 percent as Hispanic.[2] One local nonprofit estimated that the income for a Port Richmond family of three averaged approximately $19,000 in 2010.[3] In addition to a surfeit of unwanted industrial uses, drug treatment and mental health facilities, homeless shelters, and other residential programs were also clustered in Port Richmond.

This chapter examines a third subset of environmental gentrification, which I refer to as "brown gentrification." Like other urban sustainability initiatives, brown gentrification seemed to offer a win-win scenario. Rather than relying on public funds to pay for expensive cleanups, brownfield programs used tax breaks and other incentives to entice private developers to clean up and repurpose contaminated properties. For funding-strapped agencies, brownfields thus offered "the best hope for cleaning up the toxic land and water [by improving] each site as it develops."[4] What's more, brownfield programs generated a small set of subsidiary businesses, such as environmental consultants, inspection services, and remediation experts. The BOA program targeted entire neighborhoods that contained a large number of contaminated sites. Thus, on the face of it, brownfields offered a solution to some of the most pernicious environmental problems facing low-income communities of color.

I argue, however, that in practice, brownfield cleanups undermined the very environmental improvements that they promised to deliver. Because the program was based on private investment, it favored neighborhoods where property values were set to rise. Conversely, in neighborhoods that had less potential to gentrify, developers were less likely to use the program. This meant that there was no mechanism for cleaning contaminated properties in those neighborhoods. The term "brown gentrification" describes the close connection between brownfield cleanups and high-end redevelopment. Like green and industrial gentrification, brown gentrification displaced unwanted land uses from redeveloping neighborhoods and allowed them to accrue in low-income communities of color. At the end of the day, I contend, this privatized model for environmental cleanup compromises the health and safety of all urban residents.

## Port Richmond Can't Breathe

Two small graveyards dating back to 1665 flanked either side of the Reformed Church of Staten Island in Port Richmond. On my way to NSWC meetings, usually held at the church, I almost always stopped

Reformed Church of Staten Island, 2017. Credit: Robert Cluesman

to peer through the black, wrought-iron fence and eye the weathered stones inside. They stood surprisingly straight, as if paying homage to the stalwart Dutch colonists whose remains lay beneath—although centuries of East Coast weather had long since smoothed away their names.[5] In 2010, elder Warren MacKenzie (who also happened to be NSWC's treasurer) had the church listed on the National Register of Historic Places and as a New York City Designated Landmark. Even so, the church was constantly on the verge of closing. Although its centuries-old structure evoked a certain quietude and reverence, it had no air conditioning, stuck windows, and a noisy, expensive heating system. Upkeep was expensive to say the least, and congregants came and went. In recent years, the church has appeared in the odd film or TV show (it was featured in HBO's *Boardwalk Empire*), which helped replenish some of its coffers. Yet its existence remained fragile at best.

The church's tenuousness was part of a larger motif in Port Richmond. In some ways, walking along its narrow streets was like stepping back in time, or into another city. Enormous oak trees swung over the roofs of colorful, gingerbread Victorians and turreted, Queen Anne houses built by robber barons in the late 1800 and 1900s. NSWC President Beryl Thurman, registered her house (built circa 1861) as a city land-mark. With broad gables, bay windows, and a wide veranda, the house caught the eye of *Boardwalk Empire* location scouts and also appeared in the penultimate season of the show. Thurman and other owners of Port Richmond's historic homes took enormous pride in their houses. But they struggled mightily to keep them up. Close inspection of the neighborhood's ancient, fanciful, and picturesque homes often revealed peeling paint, broken steps, and cracked sidewalks.

The struggles of Port Richmond's homeowners were deeply tied to the economic struggles of the North Shore more generally. As the North Shore's oldest neighborhood, and one of its largest, Port Richmond played a central role in the waterfront's industrial heyday. At its peak in 1922, Port Richmond contained 175 industrial plants that employed 35,000 workers, according to its Board of Trade.[6] These industries gave rise to a bustling commercial district, centered on Port Richmond Av-

Beryl Thurman's house, 2017. Credit: Robert Cluesman

enue, which served communities from across the Island. But, in the 1970s, factory downsizing, automation, and closures wreaked havoc on the restaurants, repair shops, and other businesses that relied on those factories. In the same decade, two new shopping centers—Forest Avenue Shoppers Town, just south of Port Richmond, and the Staten Island Mall in New Springville—lured shoppers away from Port Richmond's small business district. Port Richmond sagged under the weight of these closures, its dilapidated housing stock, and an accumulating number of municipal waste facilities.

Low rents attracted large populations of migrants throughout the 1990s and early 2000s, which in turn fostered ethnic-related businesses, selling *leche* and *pan*, rosary beads, phone cards, and Mexican candies. Between 2000 and 2010, Port Richmond's foreign-born population increased by 90 percent, with the majority of migrants hailing from Mexico (Dominicans were the second largest group, followed by Central Americans and Puerto Ricans). All told, according to the 2010 US Census, approximately 41 percent of Port Richmond's population identified as Hispanic, with whites comprising about 49 percent, blacks 21 percent, and Asians 4 percent.[7] Importantly, these numbers reflect only residents who filled out census forms; the actual number of recent immigrants to the area is likely higher. Official poverty rates in the area also rose by nearly 17 percent during this period.[8] In many cases, tentative immigration status made migrants especially vulnerable to exploitation by landlords, and Port Richmond was also known for its substandard housing stock and illegal housing conversions.[9] It was here that Eric Garner lived until an NYPD Officer choked him to death in 2014 for selling "loosie" cigarettes.

Demographic shifts gave rise to interracial tensions, which boiled over in 2010. Over a period of four months, eleven Hispanic day laborers were attacked and robbed by bands of black youths. Several Hispanic community groups joined with local nonprofits, politicians, and other residents from around Staten Island and New York City to rally against racially motivated violence. Black communities also condemned the violence of the attacks, but they refused to characterize them as racially motivated. Rather, they noted that day laborers were paid in cash, making them vulnerable to robberies.[10] They also linked such "crimes of opportunity" to larger structural problems like massive unemployment among young black men and police harassment. A national media pile-on only escalated the tensions. With all eyes on Port Richmond, things got uglier. In May, Bronx State Senator Ruben Diaz arrived in Port Richmond along with a busload of fifty Bronx clergy members and residents. They planned to march through the streets of Port Richmond in the name of unity and to meet with local clergy. Instead, however, they were met by state senator Diane Savino and Assemblyman Matthew Titone, who dangled a black wig, a red high heel shoe, and a black lace glove. "If they are going to act like media whores, they should at least dress the part," said Titone, "They are looking to exploit Staten Island for their own purposes."[11]

Environmental justice activists on the North Shore believed that the media oversimplified interethnic relationships and exaggerated tensions. Historically, Hispanic, black, and white residents had participated in environmental justice meetings and events in fairly equal numbers. About a year before the attacks, the EPA found unsafe levels of lead in the soil around the former Sedutto's Ice Cream Factory/Jewett White Lead Company and declared it a Superfund site. Further testing revealed that high levels of lead, as well as arsenic, extended to nearby Veteran's Park, which fell under the jurisdiction of the City of New York's Parks and Health Departments. When the agencies announced their plan to cover contaminated "hot spots" with extra soil, burlap, and gravel, large contingents of Hispanic, African American and White community members joined forces to oppose the city's remediation measures and push them to develop a more thorough plan.

But the race-based controversies of 2010 continued haunt media representations of Port Richmond and local memories. Wikipedia's "Port Richmond" page contained a large subsection entitled "Racial Tensions between Blacks and Hispanics," and urban planning reports and studies usually included a paragraph or two on racial tensions in Port Richmond.[12] For Port Richmond residents whose everyday experiences of interracial cooperation belied such representations, the events of 2010 symbolized another form of collective victimization. In 2015, for instance, Beryl Thurman got into an email dispute with State Senator Diane Savino about the siting of a medical marijuana facility in Port Richmond. For Thurman, local opposition to the facility was tied to residents' lasting sense of betrayal. She wrote to Savino:

I have asked people when was the last time they have seen your face here? And the area committee meeting was the first time since the alleged Bias Attacks, which were nothing more than a farce to further target American Black men and continue to make them into villains. And to cruelly and falsely label Port Richmond as a racist community nationwide on TV. We are sure that there were those who benefited from that, but it deeply hurt the people of this community who were never allowed to come to their own defense. None of that has been forgotten nor forgiven.

For Port Richmond residents, what lingered after 2010 had far less to do with interracial relations than it did with local resentment of media and political opportunism.

## Shelter in Place

Thurman and Savino's heated email exchange made reference to a brewing controversy concerning land uses on the North Shore. In addition to contaminated sites, Port Richmond and the North Shore more generally, hosted a disproportionate numbers of social service agencies. In 2015, Port Richmond housed over fifty immigrant rights and service organizations, day laborer centers, drug treatment and mental health facilities, subsidized housing developments, homeless shelters, and other social services. A geographic study of Staten Island's social service facilities found that Port Richmond contained approximately twenty more facilities than the next most saturated area, St. George.

For North Shore activists, the accumulation of social services followed an all-too-familiar pattern. Warren MacKenzie explained the problem at an NSWC meeting: "They don't have room for [their clients] at the shelters or halfway houses in other boroughs, so they ship them over here and just drop them off. Most of them have never even been to this area." MacKenzie and other NSWC activists consistently pointed out that their beef was not with social service provision per se, but with the fact that recipients of those services had no allegiance to the neighborhood and therefore did not invest in its well-being.

In an email blast, Thurman reiterated the gist of the community's frustration (the emphasis is hers):

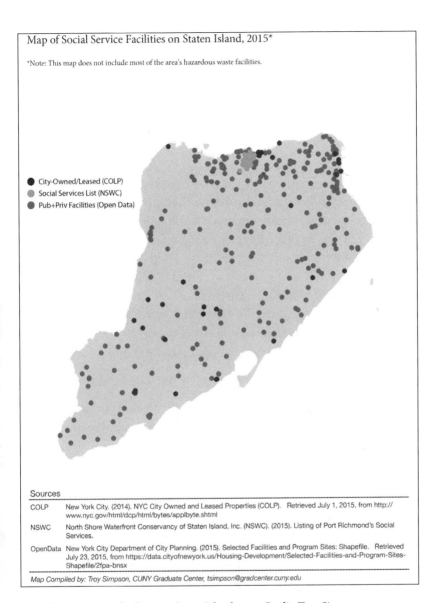

Map of Social Service Facilities on Staten Island, 2015*

*Note: This map does not include most of the area's hazardous waste facilities.

● City-Owned/Leased (COLP)
◉ Social Services List (NSWC)
● Pub+Priv Facilities (Open Data)

Sources

COLP      New York City. (2014). NYC City Owned and Leased Properties (COLP). Retrieved July 1, 2015, from http://www.nyc.gov/html/dcp/html/bytes/applbyte.shtml

NSWC      North Shore Waterfront Conservancy of Staten Island, Inc. (NSWC). (2015). Listing of Port Richmond's Social Services.

OpenData  New York City Department of City Planning. (2015). Selected Facilities and Program Sites: Shapefile. Retrieved July 23, 2015, from https://data.cityofnewyork.us/Housing-Development/Selected-Facilities-and-Program-Sites-Shapefile/2fpa-bnsx

*Map Compiled by: Troy Simpson, CUNY Graduate Center, tsimpson@gradcenter.cuny.edu*

Map of social service facilities on Staten Island, 2015. Credit: Troy Simpson

Apparently, we cannot say it long enough, loud enough, or often enough. IT HAS LITTLE TO DO WITH WHAT KIND OF SOCIAL SERVICE IT IS. OUR GRIEVANCE HAS TO DO WITH THE NUMBER OF THEM THAT ARE LOCATED WITHIN A 1.5 TO 2 MILE RADIUS OF EACH OTHER IN THE ENVIRONMENTAL JUSTICE COMMUNITY OF PORT RICHMOND! IT'S THE NUMBER OF THEM WHICH IS TOO MANY!

During the same time period, the national opioid crisis was hitting Staten Island especially hard. Rates of heroin and prescription drug overdoses were higher in Staten Island than in any other borough. In March 2016 New York State expanded funding for addiction treatment and awarded a $1 million grant to a residential drug treatment center to expand its in- and outpatient services in Port Richmond, despite the fact that almost all overdose deaths occurred in Staten Island's more suburban districts. In addition, because the rehabilitation facility already complied with zoning codes, the expansion was considered "as of right," and did not require public review.

Infuriated North Shore residents discussed their opposition on Facebook. One man wrote:

[It is] Apparent that most of the Drug & Heroin problems are in the Mid-Island & South Shore. . . . Politicians in other Districts are acknowledging there is a problem, but, NONE are embracing the problem in their own Districts.

This comment received a number of likes and several people affirmed their suspicion of the nonprofit organization that ran the facility. Alice,[13] a longtime activist and local resident, commented,

I saw them renovating and was fearing the worst! Just, "as of right," I guess? if its affiliated with [the nonprofit organization], that just means big salaries . . . enough is enough! Protest anyone:)??

Another commenter clarified that it was the organization's executives, not its case workers, who received these "big salaries." A man named Jason, who later revealed himself to be one of the nonprofit's clients, defended the need for social service agencies, but agreed that Port

Richmond as a whole suffered under the weight of too many facilities, and he questioned the motives of those who ran them.

The de Blasio administration shared these concerns. Early in his first term, de Blasio proposed creating ninety new facilities that would be spread evenly throughout the five boroughs. Unsurprisingly, the plan met with fierce resistance. From low-income neighborhoods in Crown Heights to wealthy households on East 58th Street in Manhattan (aka "Billionaires' Row") to working-class residents in Ozone Park, Queens, local communities rallied, protested, and threatened the de Blasio administration with lawsuits.[14]

The distribution of homeless shelters was only one part of the problem, however. New York City's "right to shelter" law mandated the provision of shelter to individuals and families who needed it. Since the early 1980s, the city had been shifting to a privatized system of social service provision, including homeless shelters. As options for affordable housing dwindled decade after decade, the rate of homelessness expanded, as did the shelter industry. In its scramble to comply with right-to-shelter laws, the city relied more and more heavily on private companies and non-profits. For some of these, the affordable housing shortage became an opportunity to overcharge the city for rent on the temporary apartments and hotel rooms being made available to homeless residents. A 2015 Department of Investigation report, for instance, showed that the city paid an average of $2,451 a month in rent in areas where market-rate rents ranged from $528 to $1,200.[15] A second report by the New York City Comptroller's Office investigated the purchase of 468 privately owned apartments in the Bronx and Brooklyn for $173 million. An independent appraisal commissioned for the investigation valued the units approximately $30 million below their purchase price.[16]

Privatized management and operation of homeless facilities similarly led to profiteering. In 2019, New York City officials found that one of the city's top not-for-profit homeless-shelter operators was subcontracting its security services to a for-profit company owned by the nonprofit's CEO.[17] While controversies over these ethical violations raged, the rehabilitation center in Port Richmond received state monies for two more expansions. In 2017, a new recovery center opened in St. George, and, in 2019, the city announced a new 200-bed homeless facility in the North Shore neighborhood of Tompkinsville.

Brownfield of Dreams

Brownfield programs present a slightly more complex case of privatization. Initiated in 1995 by the Clinton administration, the federal Brownfields Program sought to address an unintended consequence of environmental regulation. In urban areas, owners of contaminated properties chose to abandon them rather than assume the cost of remediating them to regulatory standards. Potential new owners refused to take on the costs and liabilities associated with these properties. Unused, vacant, and abandoned, these "brownfield" sites often stood in the way of large-scale redevelopment efforts. To address the problem, the Clinton EPA offered seed money to local governments that wanted to inventory their brownfield sites, to assess their contamination levels and to develop plans for redeveloping them. Within a decade, nearly all fifty states had funded their own brownfield programs, with enthusiastic support from environmental justice activists, real estate professionals, and municipal governments.

New York State established its brownfield program in 1996, offering tax credits and certificates of limited liability to developers willing to purchase, clean, and redevelop contaminated properties that qualified as brownfield sites.[18] In 2003, the state broadened the program, directing funds to larger swaths of land contained multiple contaminated sites. Known as Brownfield Opportunity Areas (BOAs), these districts were also marked by disinvestment and disrepair. Those purchasing contaminated sites within the BOA were eligible for a "BOA bump-up" a bonus of up to 5 percent on their brownfield tax credits. In an effort to encourage community participation in the program, the state offered competitive grants to local organizations that wanted to develop their own plans and guidelines for BOA revitalization.[19]

Even so, as time wore on, the state's brownfield programs began to look a little tainted. First, eligibility for brownfield incentives required developers to demonstrate a certain level of financial, legal, and insurance resources, including staffs of at least twenty-five full-time employees.[20] Second, because tax credits were of no use to nonprofit developers, which already had tax-exempt status, the vast majority of New York State's brownfield incentives went to wealthy developers and landowners. Moreover, funds were targeted to New York City and other areas

with "robust real estate markets," even though former industrial properties were spread throughout the state.[21] Finally, the program disproportionately benefitted wealthy New Yorkers: over one third of the value
of brownfield tax credits served market-rate residential development.[22]

In 2015, New York State responded to these criticisms by revamping
its eligibility guidelines. The idea was to direct tax credits away from
high-profit projects and toward those that benefitted low-income communities. In cities with over one million people (i.e., NYC), developers had to prove that site contaminants exceeded the state's acceptable
threshold, and it had to meet at least one of the following criteria: (1)
75 percent "Upside Down" financing (which meant that cleanup costs
amounted to at least 75 percent of the clean property value); (2) 50 percent of the property had to be located in a census tract with high poverty
and unemployment rates; (3) the site would be redeveloped to provide
affordable housing; or (4) the site was currently being underutilized.[23]
The state also stopped accepting new BOA applications.

With the launch of PlaNYC 2030 in 2007, Mayor Michael Bloomberg
promised to clean up more than 7,000 acres of brownfield sites. To accomplish that goal, he established the country's first municipally funded
brownfield cleanup program.[24] Participants could deduct cleanup costs
from federal taxes, and the city also granted protection from future liability to both owners and their lenders. In addition, enrollees could
apply for "Brownfield Incentive Grants," which helped offset the cost
of actual cleanups.[25] Finally, the city's new Office of Environmental
Remediation (OER) offered developers close guidance and assistance
throughout the assessment and remediation, or cleanup, process.[26] In
keeping with Bloomberg's managerial approach to bureaucratic services,
the brownfield process was streamlined and speedy. Project approval
required authorization only by the OER, bypassing lengthy City Council
or Community Board approvals. For private developers, the time from
application to the start of remediation often took less than a year.

To encourage development in disadvantaged areas, the city's brownfield program provided bonus grants to for-profit and nonprofit developers for "Preferred Community Development" projects that would
provide public benefits such as open space, affordable housing, or community health care facilities. The OER required applicants for the program to submit letters of support from community-based entities. From

there, the agency determined whether a project merited "Preferred" status. It did not take long for controversy to ensue. In one example, the
OER granted preferred status to the developer of a new, for-profit hotel
near the recently rebuilt Yankee Stadium. While the developer claimed
that the hotel would bring dozens of new jobs to the area and had substantial community support,[27] the local community board challenged
that idea that a hotel would address the community's needs and maintained that the developer had never notified them of its plans.[28] Another
Preferred project in the Bronx converted a former industrial site into
ninety-one units of affordable housing. Here again, the local community
board opposed the project, citing concerns about already overstrained
infrastructure and schools. Some local residents also worried that the
developer had left the definition of "affordability" vague. Would the
project target middle-class or low-income families?[29] Importantly, in
both cases, community boards' opposition came too late. According to
the OER's timeline, developers released site information to the public
thirty days prior to beginning cleanup. By that point, plans for redevelopment were already approved and underway.

Despite these issues, New York City's brownfield program was widely
hailed as a success. In 2015, Harvard's Kennedy School of Government
selected it as one of five finalists for its Innovations in American Government Award. That same year, the brownfield program enrolled its
375th project, leveraging an estimated total of $10 billion in new pri-
vate investment. According to the OER's website, approximately 20 percent of these projects provided affordable or supportive housing, and
"over 70% of these properties, were located in historically disadvantaged
neighborhoods—such as Harlem, Washington Heights, the South Bronx,
north and central Brooklyn, and the North Shore of Staten Island."[30]

## From Brown to Green

A closer look at the geography of New York City's brownfield projects
puts a slightly different slant on the OER's narrative. Forty-eight percent
of VCP sites were clustered around Brooklyn waterfronts, and almost
a quarter of the city's total brownfield projects were in Williamsburg/
Greenpoint, two of the city's most rapidly gentrifying neighborhoods.[31]
Most of Greenpoint's industrial waterfront had been designated as a

BOA and in 2012, a local community organization published a report detailing its vision for revitalizing the space. The report emphasized the importance of encouraging new industrial uses for the waterfront, especially those that emphasized both production and recycling, or a "cradle to cradle" approach.[32] To be sure, change was afoot in Greenpoint. In 2013, just west of the BOA area, real estate developers broke ground on "Greenpoint Landing." Comprised of ten residential towers rising thirty to forty stories high, the development also included a pedestrian bridge over the creek, a new marina, and a seasonal putting green/ice skating rink. Each tower, according to project developers, would be capped with a green roof, and a scattering of brand-new public parks would provide local residents with prime recreational space. According to the de Blasio administration's mandate, 20 percent of the complex's apartments (three of its towers) would be made affordable to low-income tenants. The other seven towers would be marketed to high income earners, who could enjoy a large deck with a swimming pool, hot tub, and barbecue area, and indoor amenities such as concierge and valet service, a fitness center and spa, a racquetball court, a golf simulator, a children's playroom, and a movie room. These lavish amenities and the project's eco-friendly features contradicted the realities of Greenpoint's postindustrial environs.

Once a busy industrial waterfront, Greenpoint contained dozens of brownfield sites, including some of the locations for Greenpoint Landing's towers. Moreover, Newtown Creek, which cuts through the area, was the site of one of the largest oil spills in US history. In 2010, the EPA designated it as a Superfund site and as construction began on Greenpoint Landing, the agency was preparing for one of its most extensive—and expensive—cleanups to date. Nonetheless, Greenpoint Landing set off a building boom, and approximately eighteen nearby sites received either state or municipal brownfield funding to build mostly market-rate residential developments. In 2010 the median household income in this area was ranked thirty-fourth among the city's fifty-nine community districts. By 2017, it had jumped to number sixteen.[33]

Environmental justice activists became concerned about the link between brownfield development and gentrification as early as 2006. The National Environmental Justice Advisory Council (an entity established by Clinton in 1993), issued a white paper entitled "Unintended Impacts

## Map of Completed Brownfield Cleanup Projects, 2015

● NYC Remediation Sites (PROJ TEAM)
● NY State Remediation Sites (NYS DEC)
▦ Parks, Post-2002 (PROJ TEAM)
▦ Parks (NYC DPR)
▦ EG Index Census Tracts (PROJ TEAM)
  -6 -4 -2 0 2 4 6

▦ Post-2002 Rezoning (NYC DCP 4)
▦ Census Tracts (NYC DCP 2)
▦ Borough Boundaries (NYC DCP 1)

N

▲

Miles
0 0.250.5    1    1.5    2

Map of Completed Brownfield Cleanup Projects, 2015. Credit: Troy Simpson of Redevelopment and Revitalization Efforts in Five Environmental Justice Communities." According to NEJAC, the report "examined concerns that EPA's Brownfields Program may unintentionally exacerbate historical gentrification and displacement of low-income and minority communities through the cleanup of brownfields."[34] Since then, a handful of scholars have conducted both qualitative and quantitative studies which similarly find a relationship between gentrification and brownfield development.[35]

My own quantitative study (conducted in conjunction with Queens College's Office of Community Studies and the City University of New York School of Public Health) found that the majority of sites receiving brownfield funding were located in gentrifying neighborhoods, where incomes, rents, and property values had dramatically increased in the past several years. Only a scattering of sites in non-gentrifying neighborhoods received brownfield funding even though these areas contained numerous toxic sites. The program's bias toward gentrifying neighborhoods should not be surprising. Providing a tool for private, profit-minded development was the whole point of the Brownfield Program.

## Storage Wars

In the spring of 2012, Joelle Morrison and her husband moved their belongings to Devon Self-Storage, a two-year-old facility on Staten Island's North Shore, not far from the Kill Van Kull. The Morrisons were in transit. They had just sold their house and were staying in an apartment while they finished work on a new home. And then Sandy hit. The storage facility, which sat on a former wetland, filled with water, submerging its entire first floor. "About 20 percent [of our belongings] are left," Morrison told me a few weeks after the storm, "and it all has to be cleaned . . . It smells terrible." At the time, Morrison attributed the smell to mold and to discharge from the nearby sewage treatment plant. But North Shore activists also wondered whether, and to what degree, Sandy's coursing waters had dislodged local contaminants.

Devon Self-Storage was located on a former shipbuilding and maintenance yard. After discovering soil vapors containing high levels of trichloroethylene (TCE) and perchloroethylene (PCE) during construction, property owners enrolled in New York City's Voluntary Brownfield Cleanup Program. TCEs and PCEs are chlorinated hydrocarbons often used as industrial solvents. Long-term exposure to them is associated with disorders of the central nervous system and several types of cancers in humans, especially of the kidney, liver, cervix, and lymphatic system. Importantly, vapor levels were low enough to allow storage operations to go forward, but they were high enough to impede the future reuse of the site for residential or certain commercial purposes.

Devon was a national chain headquartered in Northern California and a subsidiary of Equitec Financial Group, a real estate assets firm. And indeed, self-storage facilities offered strategic investments for real estate speculators on several levels. Although these were commercial properties and generated few jobs, the city historically permitted them for light industrial zones. This allowed self-storage facilities to cluster on the edges of newly gentrifying neighborhoods where they could make new customers of new residents. Not only were the facilities inexpensive to build and maintain, they could be easily repurposed for residential or commercial uses, should their locations be rezoned. In other words, they made lucrative placeholders while speculators kept an eye on nearby property values.[36] In this case, Devon's owners also leveraged brownfield monies to offset the cost of remediating the property to a commercial standard, thus enhancing the property's marketability.

Ostensibly, this scenario set Devon's owners up for financial gain while remediating one of Port Richmond's many contaminated sites. Since the remediation was a public health matter, the OER posted Devon's project documents (site assessments, work plans, reports, and analyses) on its website and established a six-week public comment period. The documents contained highly technical and expert language, but environmental justice activists quickly become fluent in environmental engineering.

Both Beryl Thurman and Victoria Gillen read through all of the Devon documents, and learned that the company planned to remediate the site by capping the contamination and covering it with a hard surface. For both Gillen and Thurman, this level of cleanup (known as a partial remediation) was far too risky. The comment that Gillen submitted emphasized the storage facility's proximity to a residential area.

Noting the presence of residential property within several hundred feet of the clean-up site, and being exquisitely aware of the preponderant historic disregard for residential interests on Staten Island's North Shore, we hereby request, as is our right, an assessment of proposed remedies by a professional in the environmental remediation field.

Gillen makes several important points here. According the rule that established the OER, its mission was "to promote community participation in the remediation and redevelopment of brownfields" and "to facilitate the remediation of brownfields."[37] The OER also had sole jurisdiction for certifying that brownfield work plans adhered to applicable regulatory standards. There was no process by which members of the public could request an independent assessment if they believed that the remediation plan involved risky shortcuts.

In her comment, Thurman took a different tack, arguing that because the waterfront property was built on landfill, increasing storm surges could displace the containment:

This property like many of the waterfront properties on Staten Island's North Shore is vulnerable to sea level rising, storm surges and flooding from the Kill Van Kull. In such an event it is highly likely that even paved, or black topped properties would be damaged, causing any contaminants that were below the hard surface to become exposed during a storm and then swept toward the residential communities and then back into the nearby waterways such as in the case with New Orleans' Ninth Ward and Hurricane Katrina in 2005.

This reference to New Orleans was well taken. Research conducted in the aftermath of Hurricane Katrina demonstrates that, indeed, flood waters dislodged and distributed heavy metals.[38] Other research shows that storm surges have breached retaining walls and other barriers meant to seal in toxic contaminants.[39]

In 2014, the OER itself acknowledged this risk and issued an amendment to program rules. The rule change states, "it has become clear that flooding and coastal erosion have the potential to disperse contaminants located on coastal properties to neighboring properties."[40] The new requirements tightened cleanup standards for waterfront properties in light of their susceptibility to coastal erosion from severe storms. The Devon storage facility's remediation, however, occurred in 2012, two years prior to this rule change. Although the OER's director met separately with Thurman and Gillen to discuss their comments, the final version of the work plan remained unchanged from the original.[41]

As if emphasizing its determination to gloss over activists' concerns, the OER website erroneously stated that the Devon project had elicited no public comments.[42] The closing of the comment period also ended the citizen participation portion of the brownfield project. While the OER required Devon to implement a Citizen Participation Plan, this plan was never made publicly available. Thus, the only opportunity for public comment occurred *after* the OER approved the project's work plan. There were no mechanisms for ongoing public accountability.

Bypassing a meaningful public input process was key to streamlining the City's brownfield cleanup process, which advertised a permit-free, one-stop shop. To this end, the OER kept a list of "Brownfield Cleanup Program-certified" firms and offered property owners free environmental assessments (including estimates for cleanup costs) if they used the consultants on that list. Most of these firms coordinated site cleanups as well. The assessment thus became an opportunity to provide an estimate on a much more lucrative contract. Usually, these estimates emphasized cost-saving measures such as partial remediations like the one Devon was using.[43]

In sum, the case of Devon Self-Storage demonstrates how the brownfield program was shot through with priorities that emphasized profits rather than public health risks. Indeed, developer interests dictated almost the entire process, from remediation to reuse.[44]

Accordingly, the cleanup process foreclosed any opportunity for meaningful public input and circumvented any mechanisms for ongoing public accountability. In the following section, I further describe how brownfield redevelopment used public monies to accomplish predetermined planning goals that did not necessarily take local residents' needs into account.

North Shore 2030

Between 2006 and 2016, city agencies produced half a dozen planning studies for redeveloping the North Shore. By far, the most
influential of these was the Staten Island North Shore—Land Use
and Transportation Study, or "North Shore 2030." Released in 2010
by the Department of City Planning (DCP) and the NYC Economic
Development Corporation (NYCEDC), this study outlined a comprehensive set of planning goals that became the basis for subsequent
development initiatives. In November 2009, I attended an "open
house" designed to present a draft of the study and solicit public
feedback from North Shore residents. I arrived as the sun was setting
over the Snug Harbor Cultural Center, a sprawling 83-acre park interspersed with nineteenth-century brick and Italianate buildings. Built
as a charity home for retired sailors, Snug Harbor was purchased by
the City of New York in 1976 and reopened as a cultural center.[45] In
2009, it included three museums, a botanical garden, an urban farm,
a Center for Contemporary Art, an art school, and a music hall. It
was located on Richmond Terrace, about halfway between St. George
and Port Richmond. After wandering the grounds for twenty minutes, I found my way to the faded brick edifice of Building P. On the
ground floor, a capacious ballroom with high, painted ceilings and
ornate moldings stood empty, as if waiting for revelers to fill it. A
couple of maintenance personnel were just finishing their shifts, and
they pointed me to the building's staircase. Two floors up, I entered a
large meeting room with creaky wooden floors and pale-yellow walls.
The rooms were flanked by two folding tables laden with coffee, tea,
hot chocolate, and pink boxes of pastries from a local Italian bakery.
About fifty people filled six circular tables.

The meeting was dominated by middle-aged and senior residents
who had lived on the North Shore for a long time and who regularly engaged in civic meetings, as well as six or seven 20-something newcomers
who lived in St. George. Residents were joined by staff members from
the EDC, the City Planning Department, the Staten Island Economic
Development Corporation, and at least two of the five consulting firms
hired to contribute to the plan. A cheerful brunette named Susan[46] stood
in front of a large screen and ran through a PowerPoint presentation of

the study's preliminary findings. When I arrived, she was explaining a slide titled "What Have We Heard?" which summarized feedback from the two previous listening sessions. According to the slide, major community "wants" included "improved access to the ferry and region, quality jobs and workplaces, improved access to the waterfront, and new waterfront open space." A few spaces below this list, a single bullet point read, "We are planned out!"

This last sentence was a familiar refrain that I heard over and over throughout my fieldwork. It seemed that every few weeks, city planners were inviting North Shore residents to attend a workshop, visioning or listening session, or presentation. The North Shore 2030 open house illustrates why, despite ample opportunities to provide input into planning strategies, residents remained frustrated with the process and felt "planned out."

Moving on to a slide titled "Emerging North Shore Themes," Susan read out four categories that structured the rest of the presentation, and the final study. For each theme, a set of slides depicted the North Shore's assets and challenges as well as the study's ideas for moving forward. Under the first theme, "Improve Mobility," Susan explained that North Shore residents had some of the worst commute times in the country. Nearly half of all commuters spent over forty-five minutes traveling to work.[47] This information elicited a round of vigorous nods and affirmative comments. In response, the study proposed a fast ferry service, something Staten Island residents had demanded for a long time. The second theme, "Create and Retain Jobs," involved a "lack of predictability in the environmental permitting process." According to the study, an overly bureaucratic and drawn-out process delayed and sometimes prevented developers from investing on the North Shore. This slide received a round of audible grumbles and mutters. Many of those in the room had spent hours working to oppose those very same permits on the grounds that new development projects added to local pollution and/or threatened natural flood protections. "Revitalize Commercial Centers," the third theme, provoked more eye rolls than ire. Residents had been discussing mechanisms for bringing tourists and shoppers to the area for decades, to little avail.

The final theme, "Restore & Provide Waterfront Access & Open Space," emphasized new public spaces like waterfront access through bike paths and lanes, kayak launches, and promenades. While the newcomers greeted this theme with enthusiasm, long-term residents seemed irritated. One slide read, "Visual barriers block waterfront views" and showed a photo of an opaque fence encircling a waterfront business. The next slide suggested a solution, "Work with business owners to provide views of the working waterfront." Susan commented, "It's wonderful to celebrate the waterfront and be able to see down to the water."

One woman's hand shot up. "We've been trying that for years. The property owners won't take down their fencing." Residents nodded in agreement.

"We're considering granting tax incentives to owners willing to take down or open up their fencing," Susan replied.

"Good luck with that," laughed another woman and a few people chuckled sardonically. North Shore lore held that waterfront businesses used opaque fencing to hide less than legal operations.[48] Such businesses were unlikely to pay taxes let alone be enticed by tax incentives.

From the back of the room, a heavyset man in a polo shirt demanded, "What's the point of creating green space, waterfront access, and bike paths while ignoring flooding problems and toxic sites?" This question summed up long-term residents' own themes—that planners were disconnected from the everyday realities of life on the North Shore, and that the need to address environmental problems superseded the need for economic development.

## The Budget Games

Susan reached the end of her PowerPoint and turned the meeting over to "Mary," a planner who worked for the EDC. "We're going to play the Mock Budget Game," Mary announced, passing around a handout. On it, each of the four themes outlined in the PowerPoint was subdivided into specific budget items and some extra space for "other projects not listed." Each budget item was also assigned a cost. Mary told us to rank the budget items by priority, cutting those we did not think deserved any funding at all.

Most of the budget items were taken from the PowerPoint, which meant they no more responded to residents' priorities than the slides

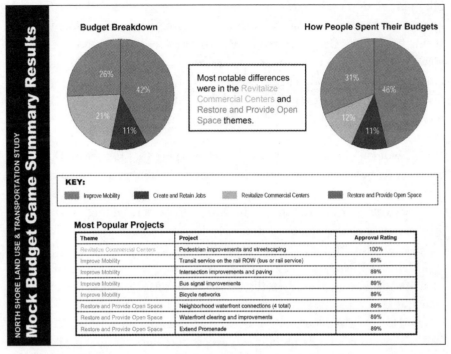

Sample of mock budget game, 2009. Credit: North Shore—Land Use and Transportation Study

had. For example, bicycle infrastructure appeared under two different themes, but toxic remediation and flood protections did not appear at all.

After taking about ten minutes to fill out our individual worksheets, we worked with our tablemates to create a consensus budget. Now the room's yellow walls reverberated with the buzz of debate. At my table, two twenty-something artists who had recently moved to St. George wanted to prioritize bicycle infrastructure, farmer's markets, food co-ops, and kayak launches. The rest of our table disagreed. They were long-term North Shore residents and wanted to prioritize faster ferry service. After much discussion, they decided to write in the rest of their priorities—the cleanup of contaminated properties, air pollution, and flood protections including better storm drainage. In the end, the most popular items involved improving transportation infrastructure, and the second most popular involved open space. Although the EDC devoted one sixth of its budget to projects designed to bolster maritime businesses, almost no one in the room prioritized them, much to planners' surprise.

The next morning, Beryl Thurman sent a long email to the EDC in which she tried to explain residents' reactions:

> There was some confusion over why people didn't want more money to go to maritime businesses. They are permitted by law to discharge into the Kill Van Kull and Arthur Kill and never look to the right or left of their shores and notice the fishermen and women who are catching the fish to take home to feed their families. So, when you say that Staten Island's North Shore is a working waterfront, why would you think that any person living near it, as it is, would continue to want to support it as it is?

Thurman notes that maritime businesses made poor neighbors. In addition to discharging waste into the local water body, she alleges that they were unconcerned about the health effects of that waste. For that reason, residents refused to get behind planners' call for more maritime businesses. Instead, Thurman's email proposed, residents would prefer to bolster local infrastructure, especially if new populations were on the way. She wrote:

> At no point and time did EDC mention sewers and clean water systems, or schools. So, you are basically encouraging a population of people who will not be able to flush their toilets. There was no mention of land banking for schools, hospitals, or something as simple as park-and-rides for residents that live outside of a 3-block walking distance of commercial streets.
>
> I think that the city is unrealistic in its expectations and spends a great deal of its time in search of money and contradicting itself in the process. Our waterfront is a huge contradiction to the City's claim of going green, the New York City Waterfront Revitalization Plan, and PlanNYC 2030.

For Thurman, planning to attract new residents without first improving the sewer system, or expanding the capacity of local schools, hospitals, or transportation was unrealistic and short-sited. More generally, she noted that the heavily contaminated and under-protected North Shore waterfront itself contradicted the city's sustainability goals.

The final version of North Shore 2030 was released a few months later. Organized around the same four goals as the Open House, the report included long lists of action items and recommendations that looked similar or identical to the budget items provided in our Mock Budget Game. Importantly, planners *did* incorporate some of the environmental concerns that residents raised that evening. In particular, a section of the report entitled "Community Priorities" listed "brownfields and the need to enforce environmental standards for existing and expanded industry." The action item for this priority tasked city planners and industrial and maritime businesses with working together to improve performance standards, bulkhead replacement policies, gray water discharge, the management of dredged materials, and to modernize their operations. A final action item involved taking advantage of state and municipal brownfield clean-up programs.

Two things are notable here. First, "environmental standards" on the Community Priority list became "performance standards" in the action items. This shift was significant in that environmental standards are enforced by regulatory agencies, while performance standards are typically enforced by businesses themselves. Second, the Port Richmond BOA became the DCP's answer to North Shore 2030's call to take advantage of brownfield funding.

## Constricted by the BOA

Two years after the release of North Shore 2030, the Northfield Local Community Development Corporation (NCLDC), a nonprofit based in Port Richmond, received a BOA grant to create a community-based strategic plan for brownfield redevelopment. The meeting at the Reformed Church, where I began this chapter, marked the first step in that process. NCLDC's Executive Director, "Emily," began the meeting by announcing that NCLDC had already taken its first step on the grant—hiring a consultant to coordinate the strategic plan. After interviewing several candidates, NCLDC decided to hire the New York City Department of City Planning (DCP) as its consultant. Those of us in the audience looked at each other, mouthing our surprise. The woman next to me mumbled, "Is that legal?" Emily hurriedly explained NCLDC's reasoning. In creating the North Shore 2030 plan, the DCP had already done a lot of the "legwork" for the BOA. In addition, the planning agency had suggested that NCLDC apply for the BOA in the first place. The whole thing seemed fishy. The city's planning agency would be paid to consult on a project that it initiated. Moreover, the grant monies were supposed to fund a strategic plan created by and for Port Richmond residents. Residents' experiences with the DCP suggested their inclusion would be minimal. "If it's a community-based plan," someone asked, "then why weren't we included in the hiring process?"

Emily next turned the floor over to Len Garcia Duran, director of the DCP's Staten Island office. Garcia Duran ran through a series of PowerPoint slides that summarized Port Richmond's assets and challenges. Most of these mirrored the slides presented at the North Shore 2030 meeting, including a "challenges" slide that reiterated how the state's cumbersome environmental permitting process hindered redevelopment. Once again, residents muttered their disagreement with this assessment. They were especially galled to hear a representative from the DCP complaining about the regulatory process. They expected to hear this narrative from the EDC, whose entire mission was to promote economic development. But the DCP's mission was to ensure that land use decisions were controlled in way that made "all of New York a better place to live."[49] Taken literally, this would have made the DCP a development-neutral agency whose priorities were trained on protecting human and ecological health. The BOA meeting, however, revealed the blurred boundaries distinguishing these agencies' missions.

Garcia Duran moved on to a slide outlining the game plan for executing the rest of the BOA grant. This included: 1) conducting an assessment of existing conditions; 2) using that information to create a proposal for rezoning part of the waterfront from industrial to commercial and residential uses; 3) conducting an analysis of economic and market trends; and 4) based on these trends, identifying strategic brownfield sites for redevelopment. Assuring meeting-goers that all of these steps would be taken according to consensus. Garcia Duran said, "We know that 100 percent of people won't be happy. We are shooting for 80 percent consensus to go forward with the rezoning. We will need community support." But the community members in the room that evening were not in a supportive mood. They recognized that the nascent BOA plan was a restatement of North Shore 2030, and that neither reflected their needs.

It did not take long for people to speak up. Thurman spoke about upgrades needed at the Port Richmond Sewage Treatment plant. Already, it released approximately thirty million gallons of sewage and storm water overflow into the Kill Van Kull every year, and sewers overflowed with each heavy rain. Although the plant was due to receive a $29 million overhaul, it was one of only two sewage plants on the island. There would be no way for it to keep up with a booming population.[50] The head of Port Richmond's NAACP chapter raised the issue of school crowding. "How dare you talk about drawing in new populations?" he demanded, emphasizing that the district had been violating city rules about limits on school seats for decades.

Another woman asked, "How will this increase traffic on Port Richmond Avenue?"

"It's already at a standstill during rush hour," someone added. These comments launched a lengthy discussion about the heavily trafficked two-lane road that traversed Staten Island from east to west.

Finally, Victoria Gillen brought the conversation back to the issue of contamination. "Brownfield makes it sound like you're going to clean up, but I don't see where cleanup comes into this," she said.

"That's down the road," responded Garcia Duran. "This is about economic development. Remediation is down the road. . . ." He explained that the first order of business was to develop a rezoning proposal and get it passed. The rezoning would then inspire investment interest in Port Richmond. Prospective property owners would be directed to those brownfield sites that the trend analysis marked as being strategic for redevelopment.

"Shouldn't we define [strategic sites] based on which sites are the most contaminated?" someone asked. A loud, collective rumble of dissent followed this question.

Speaking over the noise, Emily from NCLDC repeated, "If the community decides not to do this, then we won't do this." This was the point when Victoria Gillen scraped her chair back and said "I am stunned!" The intrusion of market-based priorities into a grant that residents believed would clean up contamination was a crushing blow. It seemed clear that the BOA was a tool for carrying out the city-planning goals established by North Shore 2030—goals which had never aligned with the community's priorities in the first place.

I was surprised to learn several weeks later that Gillen and Thurman had agreed to join the BOA steering committee. NCLDC had decided to go forward with the planning phase of the BOA. Thurman explained that she joined the steering committee because she "wanted to make sure that if the community was going to get screwed, they [the DCP and NCLDC] would have to work real hard to do it." In short, neither she nor Gillen trusted that those in charge of the BOA had "environmental justice interests at heart."

Many months later, the final BOA plan was released. Most of the plan's "action items" continued to reflect the goals of the DCP and EDC (fostering new residential and commercial uses as well as craft and artisanal manufacturing). Notably, however, the final action item—"address environmental challenges"—no longer referred to the relaxing of environmental regulations. Instead, it specified strategies for testing and cleaning brownfield sites throughout the entire neighborhood. In addition, the plan prioritized the remediation of a city-owned site on the edge of the Kill Van Kull and repurposing it as a public plaza, something for which community members had lobbied for many years.[51]

In the end, however, almost none of the action items in the BOA plan came to fruition. In the next section, I explain how the redevelopment of other New York City waterfronts wound up superseding, and upending, the redevelopment of Port Richmond.

## "The Great Poonami" and the Gentrification of Gowanus

In 2010, a flash flood filled Central Brooklyn's Gowanus Canal with waste water in what became known as the "Great Poonami." Located across the Upper New York Bay and northeast of the St. George Ferry Terminal, the Gowanus Canal already had a storied reputation for being one of the country's most polluted—and putrid—waterways. This section demonstrates how the fates of Gowanus and the North Shore became intertwined in the early 2000s. Both waterfronts grappled with the aftereffects of their industrial histories; however, as I show, their trajectories eventually became mirror images.

Originally a tidal inlet of navigable creeks set inside a saltwater marshland, Gowanus Creek became the site of New York's first mill in 1645. Shortly thereafter, a second mill joined it. As more industries began to locate along the creek's banks, it became a valuable transportation route, carrying materials and goods to and from Upper New York Bay. In the mid-nineteenth century, New York State decided to make the waterway into a canal that could more effectively drain waste water from surrounding Brooklyn neighborhoods as well as from the factories, warehouses, tanneries, coal stores, and manufactured gas refineries that lined it. By World War I, the Gowanus was the nation's busiest commercial canal. But by the 1950s the amount of dredging required to maintain it made it unviable. In addition, the rise of the freight trucking industry diminished the need for water-based transit. Throughout the 1960s and 1970s, industries along the Canal declined, until it became more of a dump site than a waterway.[52] During this period, many of the white working-class Irish and Italian families living near the Gowanus migrated to the suburbs and African American and Puerto Rican families took their place.[53]

As central Brooklyn began to gentrify in the 1990s, the Gowanus's stench and unsightliness turned the neighborhood into an island of underdevelopment. High poverty and crime rates continued to plague the area, and the banks of the Canal became a popular spot for drug and sex trafficking. But, as rising rents displaced Brooklyn's artist communities from other neighborhoods, they found that Gowanus's ample warehouse spaces and low property values outweighed its smells and general noxiousness. Following typical gentrification patterns, these artists opened cafés, music clubs, art galleries, and restaurants. Soon, the neighborhood became a hip destination, and soon after that, more hipsters wanted to live there. Real estate developers caught on to the trend and began to purchase speculative properties in the area.[54] Before long, the DCP issued a proposal to rezone the banks of the Canal for higher density residential and commercial development.

But long-term Gowanus residents had been lobbying the EPA to clean the Canal since the 1970s. In 2009, around the time the DCP was circulating its rezoning proposal, the EPA announced that it was considering designating the Canal as a Superfund site. Then-mayor Michael Bloomberg voiced strong opposition to the designation, arguing that it could scare away developers and stigmatize the area.[55] Instead, the city proposed its own plan, a piecemeal strategy that relied on private development (funded partially through tax incentives) to clean contaminated properties around the Canal, and on federal and state dollars to clean the water. After a protracted series of public meetings and grassroots organizing efforts, the Superfund designation prevailed. While the City's grand rezoning plan was shelved, individual developers could apply for and receive single variances that enabled them to build large, multifamily apartment complexes. Soon, plans were in the works for a 470-residence condominium at the edge of the canal, and a 700-apartment rental compound alongside it.[56]

Fears about Superfund stigma turned out to be unwarranted— the gentrification train had already left Gowanus's station. In 2013, a 56,000-square foot Whole Foods Market opened on a former brownfield site, complete with an in-house record shop, a bike repair station, a rooftop beer garden that overlooked the Canal, and the only commercial rooftop greenhouse in the entire country. The following year, median rent in Gowanus increased by 17.4 percent, twice as much as it increased in Brooklyn as a whole, and the median home value in Gowanus rose to $785,000, up 6.1 percent from the year before.[57] By August 2019, that value was $1,084,600.[58] Developers now banked on the EPA cleanup, reframing it as an amenity. Brochures advertising new apartments featured watercolor renderings of a Canal filled with clear, flowing water and lined with parks, esplanades, and canoe launches even though cleanup had not yet begun and would take a decade to complete.[59]

Notably, these new residential sites were located on the northern end of the Canal. The de Blasio administration designated the southern end as an IBZ in 2013. That same year, the DCP successfully nominated an overlapping part of Gowanus for the state's BOA program.[60] Taking advantage of incentives issued by both programs, two local developers filed plans to construct a *new* light industrial building within the Gowanus IBZ. The development consisted of eight floors of space devoted to boutique manufacturing. "The building will most likely be used by small-scale makers," developers anticipated.[61] With its industrial aesthetic, green future, Whole Foods Market, and high-end, eco-friendly condos, Gowanus encapsulated all three types of environmental gentrification— green, industrial, and brown.

## The Dialectics of Waste

"The Gowanus Canal runs through Carroll Gardens. Put the stuff there!" shouted a third-generation resident of Brooklyn's Red Hook neighborhood.⁶² A round of applause from about 200 fellow Red Hook residents filled the room of a May 2013 public meeting hosted by the EPA. The agency had just released plans to process decontaminated sediment a mile away from Gowanus, just offshore from Red Hook. A barge-based processing plant would mix the sediment with concrete and repurpose it as construction materials.⁶³ But Red Hook was also gentrifying, and a cabal of real estate owners and developers, new residents, and old-timers had shown up at the meeting to express their opposition to any plan that involved their neighborhood. Carrol Gardens residents, meanwhile, joined forces with their neighbors in Gowanus to make sure the materials would be taken well off-site. In the aftermath of the rowdy May meeting, the EPA announced that neither Gowanus nor Red Hook would bear the environmental burden of treating Gowanus sludge. In fact, the agency promised to ship the waste out of Brooklyn entirely.⁶⁴

Just a few months later, I attended another crowded community meeting, this time on the North Shore. First on the agenda was a permit application from Flag Container Service, a local waste transfer station. Flag proposed expanding its operations to process dredged soils from across the five boroughs and repurpose them as concrete mixtures.⁶⁵ Gowanus sludge, it appeared, could be destined for Staten Island's North Shore. Adding insult to this injury, the Flag facility happened to be just across the street from the vacant lot that the BOA committee was planning to turn into a plaza. Now it was North Shore residents' turn to be furious.

"This is right next to where we were going to have cafes and restaurants," a member of the BOA steering committee demanded. "You want us to sip cappuccino right next to this?" Another steering committee member added, "We spent a lot of hours discussing this and everyone agrees. We want waterfront access. We want a nice place. We don't want barges with dredged spoils feet away from there. That's not the future we were hoping to see." .

Finally, an African American woman from Port Richmond turned the conversation toward the bigger picture. "There's all this stuff dumped on us all the time—the Bayonne Bridge, group homes, toxic waste sites, sewage treatment plants—what are our children supposed to breathe?"

The Flag permit application also surprised staffers from the NCLDC and the DCP itself. Flag's expansion clearly worked at cross purposes to the BOA. In addition to ruining plans for the plaza, another industrial facility would undermine the BOA's goal to create light industrial, commercial, and residential spaces. In addition, BOA planning strategies relied on real estate speculation to turn environmental liabilities into assets. What speculator would choose to invest in an area that was browning instead of greening? Most importantly, with no investment, there would be no cleanup or mitigation of the environmental risks facing North Shore residents.

## Conclusion

The pages of the North Shore 2030 planning study are decorated with watercolor renderings of brightly dressed pedestrians strolling along car-free promenades shaded by storefront awnings. In the background, the blue waters of the Kill Van Kull flow gently by, interrupted only by the long necks of industrial cranes rising from the water like graceful dinosaurs. Here, the three aspects of environmental gentrification— green, industrial, and brown—come together in one harmonious vision of a working waterfront that is neither noisy nor noxious, but part of an eclectic, future-oriented, environmentally responsible city.

But this city also catches low-income communities in a double bind. Either succumb to redevelopment pressure, mitigate environmental hazards and face the threat of displacement, or oppose redevelopment and contend with even more unwanted land uses. In short, environmental gentrification subordinates public health to property values.

In a larger sense, using profit incentives and private investment to drive environmental protection rather than regulations endangers all urban residents. For sociologist John Clark, the outsourcing of environmental improvements represents a wider and more systematic divesting of state responsibility for serving and safeguarding its citizens, a process Clark defines as "abandonment." To obscure its abandonment, the state offers multiple opportunities for civic engagement, which offer the appearance of participatory governance but do little to impact predetermined public decisions.[66] More simply, as Beryl Thurman said of the BOA steering committee, "It's called a steering committee because they are steering us in the direction that they want us to go." The next part of this book investigates Thurman's statement by taking an in-depth look at the contradictions of participatory politics.

PART II

The Politics of Sacrifice

5

# "Democracy Has Left the Building"

## *Activist Overload and the Tyranny of Civic Engagement*

I will not be at Thursday's meeting because, like Elvis, democracy has left the building.
—Beryl Thurman, email, July 24, 2012

On a Saturday afternoon in early December, 2016, I pushed open the
gate to the white picket fence enclosing Beryl Thurman's yard and
stepped onto her porch. Across the street, a group of kids kicked a soccer ball across a small patch of dusty grass in Veteran's Park, calling
to each other in Spanish. It was hard to believe that seven years had
passed since the EPA had discovered high levels of lead and arsenic in
Veteran's Park. Seven years since I sat in Port Richmond High School's
auditorium and listened as the NYC Health Department told some 200
confused residents that the contaminants "were not alarming" even
though in some places the level of arsenic was approximately six times
the hazardous threshold.[1] Using a translator (about half the crowd was
Spanish-speaking), a representative from the NYC Parks Department
explained that they had covered all of the "hot spots" with fine mesh,
fresh dirt, plants, and wood chips. I remembered how late one night the
Port Richmond Civic Association posted homemade signs around the
park warning about the contamination. And how the Parks Department
removed the signs almost as soon as they went up. I remembered how
hard community members fought for official warning signs that were
printed in both English and Spanish.

Seven years later, sneakers and soccer balls had loosened most of the
mulch and plant containments in Veteran's Park. Although the EPA had
completed remediation on two Superfund sites on the North Shore, the
radioactive warehouse site remained untouched, save for a new "No
Trespassing" sign on its chain link fence. Just across Richmond Terrace

Signs in Veteran's Park, 2017. Credit: Robert Cluesman

and a couple blocks south, dozens of low-income to middle-income families had purchased homes in Nicholas Avenue Estates. The owners of Flag Container received their permit to treat dredged soils, but had not used it. After several of its employees died on the job, the company had come under heavy scrutiny by the Department of Labor.[2] Construction on the new Bayonne Bridge was well underway. Although the project would not be finished for another few years, superships were already sailing underneath it.

Local environmental justice activists led campaigns to challenge all of these issues, and many more. Although they often met with their city councilmember, state assembly member, the Staten Island borough president, and other local officials, and regularly received media coverage from NY1 and the *Staten Island Advance* and other outlets, grassroots victories seemed few and far between. What activists did win were accolades and awards from other nonprofits, small grants from government agencies, and invitations to sit on innumerable committees. Beryl Thurman, in particular, became a major player in the regional environmental justice scene. Her mantle displayed at least a dozen public service awards. In addition, NSWC had received environmental justice grants sponsored by the city, the state, and various nonprofits, and it partnered on several other grants with nonprofits like the Natural Resources Defense Council and Clean Water Action. As the years wore on, it had become clear that awards and acknowledgements were a double-edged sword. Grants came with byzantine hoops to jump through, which meant that Thurman's time was constantly in demand. Increased recognition meant that government agencies, academics, students, planners, and other nonprofits constantly invited her to participate in (and, in some cases, to lead) visioning sessions, studies, summits, workshops, student presentations, toxic tours, and other events. Notably, these in-

Contamination containment at Veteran's Park, 2017. Credit: Photo by Robert Cluesman

viters often expected Thurman to volunteer her time. Meanwhile, new developments, major construction projects and other calls to action came fast and furiously. Exhausted, frustrated, and often broke, Thurman regularly told me, "Melissa, I am tired. I don't know how much longer I can take this."

This chapter investigates the sources of Thurman and other activists' exhaustion, and explains how activist overload became another symptom of sustainaphrenia. I first noticed this overload when I began researching environmental justice some twenty years ago. In addition to working full-time jobs, grassroots activists had to teach themselves basic environmental engineering and chemistry. They spent hours reading and commenting on four-inch thick environmental impact statements and assessments, as well as Phase I and Phase II reports.[3] In addition to their own environmental justice meetings, they attended meetings with other environmental nonprofits, attorneys, city council hearings, and land use and zoning committees, on top of countless public hearings. Two decades later, visioning sessions, planning charrettes, steering committees, community-driven initiatives, and other forms of public participation had become so ubiquitous, and yet ineffective, that they seemed like empty rituals.

I also noticed that activists were constantly called on to participate in academic rituals such as symposia, conferences, classes, and fieldtrips. While such endeavors seemed like a straightforward way to increase awareness about environmental justice, in this chapter, I show how they were of a piece with participatory politics.

That is, the strings attached to small grants, superficial forms of public participation, and academic outreach co-opted grassroots activism. Just as profit-minded agendas co-opted environmental justice initiatives, processes that appeared to support collective action and citizen engagement actually achieved the opposite. Political philosopher Sheldon Wolin argues (as mentioned earlier) describes this situation as a kind of "inverted totalitarianism" or managed democracy. He writes:

The United States has become the showcase of how democracy can be managed without appearing to be suppressed. This has come about, not through a Leader's imposing his will or the state's forcibly eliminating opposition, but through certain developments, notably in the economy, that promoted integration, rationalization, concentrated wealth, and a faith that virtually any problem—from health care to political crises, even faith itself—could be managed, that is, subjected to control, predictability, and cost-effectiveness in the delivery of the product.[4]

According to Wolin, the long reach of political contributions and lobbyists dominate governmental decisions, replacing political sovereignty with economic sovereignty. Unlike traditional totalitarianism, in which power is exercised directly, the inverted form works subtly, through consent and co-option. For Wolin, "An inverted regime prefers a citizenry that is uncritically complicit rather than involved."[5] Discourses about "shareholder democracy" offer a "sense of participation" that distracts citizens from making real demands. Gone was the protesting, dissenting citizen of the 1960s, only to be replaced by the deferential and dutiful meeting-goer, who valued compromise and consent.[6]

The activists I worked with served as a rejoinder to this depiction. They spoke out and fought back against empty rituals of participation and activist overload. These activists refused to accept the paradoxes of sustainability, even if they could not entirely refuse them. In the end, I argue, it is the push and pull of everyday activism that reveals the gravest dangers of the sustainaphrenic era.

## Democracy is Unpaid Work

Over the past twenty years, as inequality has risen in the United States, funding sources for nonprofit organizations in the United States have shifted considerably. Large nonprofits receive massive grants donations from public agencies, wealthy individuals and donor advised funds, while small, grassroots organizations are left to compete for smaller and smaller grants.[7] This section explores the constant contortions that small nonprofits must perform to win and retain funding. I argue that, over time, these complicated exercises take a heavy toll. Eventually, all the funding hoops that grassroots organizations must jump through land them far from their original goals.[8]

Geographer Jennifer Wolch explains that, after Reagan dismantled the welfare state in the 1980s, private nonprofit organizations were tasked with administering and implementing public service programs.

Competing for ever-fewer public dollars, these nonprofits found themselves conforming to the state's agenda.[9] Wolch writes:

> In the United States, voluntary groups have gained resources and political clout by becoming a shadow state apparatus, but are increasingly subject to state-imposed regulation of their behavior. . . . To the extent that the shadow state is emerging in particular places, there are implications for how voluntary organizations operate. The increasing importance of state funding for many voluntary organizations has been accompanied by deepening penetration by the state into voluntary group organization, management, and goals.[10]

As the federal, state and local dollars budgeted for social services were cut back, trickle-down economic policies cut corporate taxes and relaxed regulations allowing corporate fortunes to accrue. As a further tax break, those fortunes could be sheltered by philanthropic foundations. In a 1997 *Atlantic Monthly* article, journalist Nicolas Lemann found that the total net worth of philanthropic foundations grew by more than 400 percent between 1981 and 1996, reaching over $200 billion.[11] In turn, philanthropies dispensed funding to nonprofit service agencies, many of which worked to undo the consequences of the trickle-down system.[12] As with public service contracts, nonprofit providers had to comply with philanthropic funding agendas.[13] Thus developed the "nonprofit industrial complex" (NPIC), a vast network of relationships between the state, capitalists, foundations, and nonprofit/NGO organizations.[14]

The NPIC reinforced capitalist structures by allowing corporations to mask exploitative practices through philanthropy and by managing and controlling grassroots activism.[15] As Ethnic Studies professor Dylan Rodriguez asserts, "Forms of sustained grassroots social movements that do not rely on the material assets and institutionalized legitimacy of the NPIC have become largely *unimaginable* within the political culture of the current US Left."[16] Without grants and other forms of legitimation from the NPIC, grassroots organizations faced marginalization, alienation, and obscurity.

Wolch forecasts that over time, the shadow state (and by extension the NPIC) will intensify, generating a "dynamic of reduced autonomy" whereby nonprofits are less and less free to execute their long-term goals and missions. This dynamic, she predicted, will have the following consequences (I am paraphrasing):

1. The state will force voluntary groups to plan reactively, in response to new state policies and practices, rather than proactively.
2. Contracts and grants will increasingly come with requirements for stringent, rigid, and quantitatively oriented approaches to planning, evaluation, and monitoring.
3. Those organizations unable to meet the expanding demands for planning will become increasingly marginalized and may not be able to secure state funding. Such standards for organizational practice will have structural effects, controlling the rise of antiestablishment social movements and pushing marginal groups to produce direct services instead of advocacy outputs.
4. Group activities may become aligned to funding agency needs and expectations for types of services to be delivered. In the process, the type of group output is likely to change toward direct services administered by professionals and away from advocacy and participation.[17]

As anyone who works with nonprofits will know, Wolch's prescience and insights are remarkable. Each of the above predictions leads to the next, creating a cascading effect that ultimately depoliticizes collective action.[18]

The NSWC is a good example. NSWC's funders required annual audits, produced by an outside accounting firm, as well as detailed reports on the number and percent of people helped by NSWC programs. Yet the costs of such reports counted as overhead, or operational costs, that were often not covered by their funding.[19] Over the years, a technocratic emphasis on quantitative measures, reactions to very public scandals exposing nonprofit corruption, and funders' own needs for self-promotion (programs and activities made for sexier advertising than day-to-day operations) shifted funding streams away from organizational expenses and overhead. Even more importantly, program grants more easily mapped onto predetermined funding priorities. As one blogger remarked, "Foundations don't necessarily make grants to support a nonprofit's mission. Foundations make grants to support their own missions."[20] A 2013 Ted Talk by AIDSRide founder Dan Pallotta, entitled "The way we think about charity is dead wrong," rethought the value of directing funds toward overhead spending. Although the talk got over four million hits, potentially marking a nascent trend, a follow-up study found that only 7 percent of nonprofits reported receiving funds for administrative costs.[21]

Such restrictions ensnared environmental justice activists in a complex trap. Those who organized full time often had sick family members or were ill themselves. They needed some kind of income to live on, or to supplement disability payments. Those with full-time jobs took on a grueling and often unpredictable schedule. Either way, grassroots environmental justice organizations needed some kind of funding to realize their goals. Yet, most organization leaders had little to no experience in grant writing or management; they became activists out of a sense of mission to protect their neighborhoods from environmental harms.[22] Not only was it nearly impossible to find funding for grant writers or administrators, but to be eligible for grants, applicants frequently had to show that they had other sources of funding.

Because grant writing is an area in which I have some expertise, I offered to help NSWC with some of its funding proposals. After Hurricane Sandy hit in 2013, Thurman and I applied for a $50,000 grant from the state's Department of Environmental Conservation, Environmental Justice Community Impact Grant Program. Our application focused on developing a community-based resilience report. We offered to identify locations on the North Shore where flood protections were disintegrating, inadequate, or non-existent. We also promised to create an evacuation plan that accounted for recurring street floods. Thurman believed that existing, official versions of these materials did not adequately reflect on-the-ground realities. The irony of having to ask the state to redo its own work was not lost on her. As she wrote in an email, "if they [city and state agencies] were doing their jobs right, we wouldn't need to figure this stuff out in the first place."

That said, the DEC grant *did* allow us to apply for a percentage of NSWC's personnel costs (perhaps in response to some of the critiques outlined above). All we had to do was estimate the percentage of staff time that would be devoted to the funded project. We decided that Thurman would spend 30% of her time on it. In reality, though, Thurman spent most of her time responding to unanticipated issues, such as permit applications for new housing or industrial developments. Indeed, the work of environmental justice tended to be last-minute. As this book recounts, regulatory agencies often notified residents about permit applications and public hearings a week or two in advance, leaving them scrambling to organize a response. Of course, the agencies that generated these last-minute notices were the very same that asked grantees to plan programs years in advance.

The DEC's 40-page application itself required a Herculean effort. For each expenditure, we had to estimate "the reasonableness of the costs of these items in relation to the number of people in the community who will benefit and the nature and location of the Project."[23] Because Thurman intended for the project to protect the entire North Shore, we decided to divide the total population of people living near the North Shore's waterfront (76,000) by the cost of the budget item. For instance, part of our project involved making a video. Our description read:

> Film Editor (to be hired) $2,500.00. *The film editor will create a short video that can be widely distributed and posted online. The video will illuminate the project findings, and the project process. As well, it will contain information about how residents can protect themselves from hazardous flooding. We estimated this rate based on the film we made in 2010, under a DEC grant. The ratio of people benefitting from our project to this cost is 152 to 5.*

Given that we intended to post the film on YouTube, this calculation seemed more like a creative exercise than a meaningful representation of our plan.

Around 2016, two of NSWC's funders, the NYC City Council and the New York Community Trust (NYCT), decided to address some of the above issues by requiring smaller grantees to participate in capacity-building exercises. In May of that year, Beryl Thurman, Warren MacKenzie, and I joined representatives of other small nonprofits in the City Council's capacity-building webinar. For the next hour, a nonprofit management consultant walked us through a lengthy survey designed to assess organizational capacity. From the beginning, NSWC ran into some roadblocks. The survey was targeted to board members, staff, and volunteers, but NSWC only had one staff member and one regular volunteer (me). Thurman distributed the survey anyway, and she, her five board members, and I returned them to the consultant. A few months later, Thurman received a report summarizing NSWC's strengths and weaknesses as well as a set of suggestions for expanding the board, reaching out to new funding sources, and bringing on more volunteers. The report also suggested conducting regular surveys of board members and volunteers. Thurman later told me that she found the suggestions far from helpful. How would she find the time to design, implement, and analyze more surveys, let alone implement any of the other suggestions?

That same summer, Thurman and I also scrambled to comply with the NYCT's approach to capacity building. In this case, the NYCT provided $5,000 to hire a consultant to help NSWC develop a capacity-building plan. Corporate ideologies and models had created a demand for non-profit management consultants, so they were easy to find. Yet Thurman insisted that she would only take on a consultant who would develop *and execute* a plan. The latter criteria made my task impossible—none of the consultants I spoke with were able to put a plan in motion. Unable to find a consultant that would meet her requirements, Thurman had to let the $5,000 go back to her funder. "They want us to do all this capacity building," she told me. "But what they don't seem to recognize is that capacity building takes time, and that's something I don't have." Without grants, it was difficult to secure grants. Without capacity, it was impossible to build capacity.

A final example of this type of double bind arose in early 2017. Almost every spring, Thurman organized a series of boat tours around Staten Island. She would rent a 50-person passenger ferry from one of the city's water taxi companies and invite Staten Islanders to tour the Island from the water, while Thurman and other local activists pointed out toxic sites, visible erosion, areas of flood risk, and other hazards. The boat tours had become quite popular among residents, local nonprofits, and schools—and they were a major undertaking. A few months after the spring 2017 boat tours, the program's major funder sent Thurman an email with requirements for its final funding report. Part of those requirements included an essay, described as follows:

> In approximately 500 words, write about a participant and/or group that stand(s) out as an example of impact due to activities of the funded proj-

ect. Requirements: (1) The story must be true and personal; (2) It should convey the impact of the project and the needs of the community; (3) It may be published on the website or in *Response* magazine, so please consider confidentiality.

Thurman emailed me in a panic. "My response in my head was 'what?' In truth, I was so busy working the tour that at no point in time do I remember having conversations with people on the tour." To complete this request, Thurman would have to track down attendees, conduct interviews, and "document the true, personal stories" of NSWC's constituents, from hindsight.

In larger terms, by asking for a 500-word story that "may be published on the website or in *Response* magazine," the funder was essentially outsourcing to grantees the promotional copy it needed. Such requests put grantees in a difficult position: they could neither decline, nor charge for their services. While funders' recognition of capacity problems seemed like a step in the right direction, it ultimately reinforced the same system of overload. And yet, like most nonprofit organizations, NSWC could no more turn its back on funding opportunities than it could decline to participate in local governance.

## "It's Called a Steering Committee Because They Are Steering Us"

Much of my fieldwork involved trailing after North Shore activists as they rushed around participating in public hearings, visioning sessions, community panels, and meeting after meeting . . . after meeting. But for all the hours they spent offering testimonies, comments, perspectives, questions, and information about their neighborhoods, their input seemed to have little influence on land use decisions and permits. It was obvious that the emperor of public participation had no clothes, so why was he constantly on parade?

In the late 1950s and 1960s, social unrest was erupting in countries across the globe. Decolonization movements in Africa, and the US civil rights movement, in particular, inspired social justice activists to demand transparent, democratic, and racially just forms of governance.[24] In the wake of civil rights reforms, President Lyndon Johnson's Great Society programs sought to address racism and poverty and to institutionalize mechanisms for public input into federal decision making. This emphasis on social responsibility and collectivism shifted after the fiscal crisis of the 1970s, however. As neoliberal rationalities gained prominence, institutional policies and politics stressed selfhood, personal responsibility, entrepreneurialism, self-esteem, and self-empowerment. Taking up these ideas, social scientists produced a series of studies showing that unemployment, alcoholism, criminality, child abuse, teenage pregnancy, and other urban ills were rooted in a lack of self-confidence. Such studies then gave rise to a spate of social programs designed to build self-esteem and foster individual empowerment among impoverished citizens.[25] The self-esteem movement neatly reflected neoliberal values, as it made individuals responsible for their own health, well-being, and personal fulfillment. In so doing, it bypassed questions of systemic inequality or structural barriers to wealth.[26]

Similarly, neoliberalism reconfigured communitarian ideals from the 1960s, which emphasized collective power, and re-cast them as depoliticized forms of volunteerism. In 1988, George H. Bush famously compared America's clubs and volunteer organizations to "a thousand points of light." In so doing, he entreated Americans to "give back" by helping out in soup kitchens, homeless shelters, and so on, and engaging in civic and political organizations (such as neighborhood watches and planning boards).[27] Civic engagement thus became another form of abandonment, compensating for draconian social welfare policies that dramatically cut public funding for homelessness, affordable housing, food stamps, and so on.[28]

Popular psychology helped integrate these discourses of self and community by producing multiple studies showing that volunteerism improved one's sense of self-worth.[29] In addition, in the 1980s, 1990s, and 2000s, films like *Silkwood*, *Norma Rae*, *Erin Brockovich*, and *A Civil Action* (to name a few) celebrated agentive citizens who stood up on behalf of themselves and their communities. These films highlight how crises bring out individual, psychological strengths like moxie, courage, stamina, and self-worth, all of which enabled protagonists to prevail against multiple odds. Like any good hero, these characters stumble upon activism through a journey that takes them from apathy and denial to self-actualization and empowerment. Such tropes feed neoliberal ideas about the power of individual rational actors to instigate political and economic change, and the importance of political engagement as a means to good citizenship and psychological well-being.

Conversely, images of the feckless couch potato warn us that passive citizenship leads to physical and psychological dysfunction and the general erosion of community values.[30] In his best-selling 2000 book *Bowling Alone,* sociologist Robert Putnam argued that membership in traditional civic organizations had declined significantly since the 1980s. Putnam blames the decline on technology, which was "individualizing" people's leisure time via television, the Internet, and video games. He argues that not participating in civic meetings or local organizations— "bowling alone"—would eventually lead to the erosion of democracy itself. Another popular version of the civic engagement narrative holds that non-participants have only themselves to blame when policy decisions do not favor their interests.

Crucially, such moral rationalities relied on market terms or economized versions of self, community, and government. As political theorist Wendy Brown argues, these rationalities evaluate neoliberal citizens as "better or worse consumers of national or local institutions and services."[31] From this view, participation in governance is a service provided by the state to citizens who consume this particular form of "empowerment."[32] In so doing, citizen/consumers become both subjects to be managed by the state *and* agents of that management.[33] The North Shore 2030 "budget game" illustrates this point. Planners constrained participants' opportunity to prioritize new planning initiatives by providing them with a predetermined list of choices. At the same time, their participation stood for "public buy in," which in turn ratified planners' priorities and formed the basis for at least a decade's worth of planning initiatives.[34]

If bureaucrats are service providers, then one of their main charges is to expand their consumer base by finding new constituencies and "activating" their participatory relationship to the central state.[35] The "usual suspects" problem illustrates this imperative. The "usual suspects" describes those community members who regularly attend—and frequently dominate—public meetings. These folks are not shy about opposing projects they see as reinforcing their and their community's marginalization.[36] A quick Google search revealed dozens of websites advising community engagement professionals on how to manage the "usual suspects," in some cases, by not inviting them in the first place. Even more sites characterized these people as self-interested, eccentric, and not representative of the larger, though absent, community.[37] I found the opposite. Most community residents did not have time to attend endless public meetings. While they might have disliked or disagreed with the usual suspects, they trusted them more than they trusted agency officials. Moreover, they relied on, and trusted, the usual suspects' experience, outspokenness, and ability to represent community-based interests.

The performance of participatory activities became a kind of ritual that conferred some vague standing on public projects or planning initiatives. After a while, activists saw through this mystification and tried to resist it, albeit in limited ways. Over the years, I noticed that they increasingly declined invitations to engagement opportunities. Thurman especially refused to sit on committees that she considered to consist of "busy work designed to make the government look like it's doing its job," or to attend visioning sessions that she suspected would be nothing but "kumbaya" opportunities. Yet, more often than not, she was nonetheless compelled to accept them, lest the organization risk losing even a narrow window of opportunity to insert its concerns into public discourse. A good example is a January 2016 email from the Deputy Director of the New York State DEC's Office of Environmental Justice, which Beryl Thurman shared with me.

> Dear Beryl,
> The New York State Department of Environmental Conservation (DEC) cordially invites you to attend an *Environmental Justice Forum: Communities Shaping Policies and Regulations,* on Thursday, January 26, 2017 from 8:45 a.m.—5 p.m., at 47–40 21ˢᵗ Street, Long Island City, NY, Room 834A.
>
> Because you are a leader in your community, we are soliciting your input on various environmental topics important to low-income and minority communities. Having meaningful involvement from you is the cornerstone of environmental justice, so we are excited about this opportunity to get your feedback on various DEC policies and regulations.

In the next email, she wrote me the following note:

M,
I probably will attend this meeting, I don't trust that the phone communications will be good enough so that I will hear everything being
said or that my concerns will be related to the group that will accurately
project our sense of urgency on the issues that we face. But the hour
that they starting this meeting for a commuter from Staten Island is
ridiculous, I will have to get up at 4:45 AM or 5:00 AM at the latest to
get ready, drive to the ferry terminal, park and catch a ferry and take a
train uptown, walk a block to attend this all-day meeting. Three modes
of transportation just make sure Staten Island's EJ communities are represented and not ignored, can you imagine how pissed I will be if this is
just another bullshit lip-service meeting?

Thurman was fully aware that the meeting might only pay "bullshit
lip service" to addressing environmental justice issues. She was also
aware that the day-and-a-half that she would spend preparing for and
attending this meeting could be spent doing things more central to
NSWC's mission. But Thurman felt compelled to attend the meeting
in order to be able to "accurately project" a sense of urgency on the
issues facing the North Shore, and to make sure that those issues were
not ignored.

Usually, Thurman would express her frustrations about these meetings in follow-up emails to city, state, and federal officials. In a 2016
email, she wrote,

It was misleading to give people in EJ communities hope that their quality of life would be improved when there was no mechanism, then or
now, to make that happen by law. Further, to dupe them into participating in these visioning exercises to which those that were the orchestrators
got paid for their time and energy, while the people who have the very
least, the community, got nothing.[38]

At one point, Thurman tallied all the time she spent on participation.
She then wrote a detailed report on all of her activities and sent it to
elected and agency officials asking for compensation. "You all get paid
for this," she wrote, "Why shouldn't I"?

## "This Is Our Lives They're Wasting"

"I held it up to the light like so," said Victoria Gillen, stretching her arm toward the ceiling and aiming it at a fluorescent light. It was the summer of 2013 and I was attending a meeting of the North Shore Community Coalition for Environmental Justice (NSCCEJ). About seven North Shore residents and I sat at a folding table in the basement meeting room of the Stapleton United American Methodist Episcopal Church. The church's food pantry had just finished for the day, and volunteers hurried to clear away the leftovers. A mellow evening light slanted through the basement windows, dulling Gillen's demonstration. In her outstretched hand, she held a printed piece of paper, about half of which was covered by thick black lines. "They redacted it!" she exclaimed, "Only they didn't do a very good job. You can see right through the lines!" In this case, "they" was the EPA, Region 2's Office of Environmental Justice (EJO), and the document in Gillen's hand was an expense report, obtained through a Freedom of Information Act (FOIA) request. The receipt of the expense report was the culmination of a nearly four-year saga that had begun when the EPA designated the North Shore of Staten Island as one of its ten Environmental Showcase Communities. Each designee was allocated $100,000 for a community-driven project that addressed its environmental justice concerns. Or so recipients thought. As this section shows, community members had so little control over the funds that they never saw an expense report or a budget. Even Gillen's FOIA request yielded only the highly redacted document in her hand.

Briefly, the Environmental Justice Showcase Communities program was the brainchild of Lisa Jackson, EPA Administrator from 2008 to 2013. Jackson's cabinet appointment, perhaps more than any other, emblematized the Obama era. An African American woman born in Philadelphia and raised in a middle-class, black neighborhood in New Orleans, Jackson had earned a Master of Science in Chemical Engineering at Princeton. She had spent sixteen years at the EPA, mostly at its Region 2 office in New York City, until New Jersey Governor Jon Corzine named her Commissioner of Environmental Protection. Appointing Jackson in 2008 signaled Obama's commitment to an urban-focused agenda that included environmental justice issues.

Jackson's vast experience with toxic issues in urban areas gave environmental justice activists more hope than they had had in a long time.[39] In early 2009, I attended her keynote at a regional environmental justice conference. The exuberance in the room—so rare at an environmental justice event—was unforgettable, as Jackson was celebrated as "one of our own." One of Jackson's first major initiatives was to dedicate $1 million to the two-year Environmental Justice Showcase Communities program. Each of the EPA's ten administrative regions would choose one community that had the following characteristics: multiple, disproportionate environmental health-burdens; population vulnerability; limits to effective participation in decisions with environmental and health consequences based on previous experience and existing projects; and opportunities for multiple federal, state, and local agency collaboration, with a focus on green development. According to the EPA website, Showcase communities would receive $100,000 each to "help alleviate environmental and human health challenges."[40]

About eight months after the launch of the Showcase program, I took a crowded bus to St. Mary's Episcopal Church in Rosebank on the eastern edge of the North Shore area. The dimming sky was dramatic that night—a sudden summer storm with near tornado-level winds had just ripped through the area, scattering tree branches across yards and driveways. Luckily, although the storm had shut power off to thousands of homes, St. Mary's remained brightly lit. Inside the stone walls of the 150-year old church, I found about fifty Staten Islanders balanced on round, plastic seats in its parochial-school cafeteria. They watched as a consultant, hired by the EPA to facilitate the meeting, explained the Showcase Community program. He then broke us into groups and charged us with ranking the North Shore's most urgent environmental health problems and coming up with ideas for how the grant could address them. At the follow-up meeting, the consultant said that we would narrow down the list and decide on two or three projects to be funded by the grant. "It's about empowerment," commented one woman as the broke up. "People don't think they can make a difference." This was the largest group I had seen since the meeting to discuss lead in Veteran's Park. In a perverse way, people seemed proud that the EPA had singled out the North Shore as a showcase for environmental injustices. The room buzzed loudly as we conversed with our groups.

"No Fishing" signs at the Kill Van Kull, 2011. Credit: Melissa Checker

The facilitator asked Beryl Thurman (who had helped organized the Showcase meeting) to write each group's top concerns on a piece of chart paper: lead, diesel, sanitation, waterfront cleanup and access, toxic contaminants, and zoning. Then she wrote down project ideas: enforcing laws against idling, installing more multi-source air monitors, improving the regulation of particulate matter[41] and toxics, and remediating toxic contamination. The facilitator explained, however, that the $100,000 was earmarked only for education and outreach, not enforcement, regulation, or remediation. He then suggested consolidating several priorities into one, broader category called "air quality." After taking the names of people willing to be part of an area-wide coalition, the facilitator explained that his role was now finished. Going forward, EPA staff would only attend meetings when invited—the Showcase grant was to be an almost entirely community-based effort.

The following month, a much smaller group of about 10 to 12 people met at the offices of the Northfield LDC. All lived on the North Shore and were active in their neighborhood civic associations, with two exceptions—myself and a staff member from New York Lawyers for the Public Interest (NYLPI). NYLPI had taken up the cause of environmental justice on the North Shore about a year earlier, mainly by monitoring the Jewett White Superfund cleanup and pressuring the EPA to act on the radioactive ADM site. Thanks to the Showcase Community designation, one of their attorneys also facilitated a highly unusual meeting between NSWC and various city, state, and federal agencies, including the Army Corps of Engineers, the DEP, the DEC, the EPA, Fish and Wildlife, the New York State Department of Health, and the NYC Health Department. Thanks to that meeting, Thurman achieved one of her longstanding goals: coordinating the city and state Departments of Health to install No Fishing signs in both Spanish and English.

Finally, NYLPI assigned one of its incoming Post-Graduate Fellows to help coordinate the new coalition. Taye Sayd,[42] a soft-spoken and thoughtful man of Ethiopian descent, kept meeting minutes, coordinated meetings, found venues, and acted as a liaison between the coalition, assorted vendors, and the EJO. Sayd's involvement was instrumental to the coalition, to say the least. Staten Island's collection of small, predominantly homeowner-occupied neighborhoods fostered hundreds of robust civic organizations, and coalition members already participated in more than one of them. To take one example, Susan, a slight woman in her early sixties, had spent the past several decades advocating for environmental improvements on the North Shore and serving on Staten Island's Community Board 1 (CB1). She attended CB1 meetings on the third Thursday of the month and CB1 subcommittee meetings on the fourth Thursday. On the first and second Tuesdays of every month, she went to meetings of the West Brighton Civic Association. She also headed a nonprofit, community-based organization, which required attending various public hearings and City Council meetings, and so on. In between, there was plenty of work to be done. Susan's hectic schedule was typical of other members.[43] In fact, these people were "the usual suspects." They regularly attended public meetings and took on various committee roles. In public participation lingo, they displayed "high levels of engagement" in pursuing the welfare of their communities.

At the coalition meeting, we had two main orders of business. First, we needed to decide on a name, which, according to the EPA, should include the words "environmental justice." After a brief discussion, we decided on the "North Shore Community Coalition for Environmental Justice" (NSCCEJ). Second, we had to narrow down our list of priorities from the last meeting—we chose to focus on diesel and lead. Coincidentally, the EJO had already sent someone to make a presentation on EPA grant programs that addressed diesel exhaust. This became a consistent theme, as EJO staff regularly urged us to apply for tax-exempt status, as well as for additional grants. More than once, the EJO Director informed us, "The Showcase program is meant to leverage other monies." With no time for grant writing, coalition members decided to request that some Showcase funds be used to hire a grant writer.

The following month, we met with the EJO Director to finalize our projects. In addition to asking for a grant writer, our list of priorities included: opening an asthma clinic, creating a truck stop so that trucks would not have to idle on local streets, installing new air monitors around the North Shore, and finding ways to reduce operations at the sanitation garage. The Director reminded us that the grant money could only be used for education and outreach programs, and that almost none of our requests could be funded. Instead, he suggested that we launch a campaign to "educate people in how to be smart in educating themselves about not bringing lead into their homes from the outside."

"[The EPA] is supposed to do that kind of thing," grumbled a coalition member named Lisa. Indeed, the EPA as well as the Department of Housing and Urban Development, Health and Human Services, and state and local Departments of Health all produced lead poisoning protection fact sheets and brochures. Residents saw no need for redundancies, especially given the urgent and widespread pollution problems they faced. Eventually, the EJO director and coalition members reached a compromise and agreed to use the funds for three main projects. First, they decided to implement three Asthma-Free School Zones (AFSZ). This program involved installing signage around designated schools that limited idling. It also included taking ambient air samples around the school and providing asthma and environmental health training to school and community members. Second, they decided to organize the anti-idling campaign described in chapter 3. Finally, coalition members would create a website featuring an environmental justice profile that included demographics, environmental conditions, the location and nature of toxic sites, environmental health concerns and statistics, and other pertinent information that educated people about environmental justice on the North Shore.

Then the EJO director dropped a bombshell. He announced that Showcase funds had to be committed immediately or be returned to the EPA. In order to safeguard the funds, he was planning to sign a contract with an environmental justice consulting firm, one of the agency's regular vendors. That firm had already subcontracted a web designer to work on the website. NSCCEJ members were shocked—and then irate. Seven months had elapsed between the time of the initial Showcase designation and the first public meeting. Now they were being forced to accept the "emergency" hiring of a costly consulting firm with no bidding process and no consultation with community members. Moreover, the EJO director said he was not able to provide details on the terms of their contract with the consultant. NSCCEJ members were especially galled to learn that the firm was based in Washington, DC—Staten Islanders are especially sensitive to "carpet-bagging," or being governed by outsiders.

Nonetheless, NSCCEJ members moved forward in good faith and began working with the consultant and meeting once a month to execute the AFSZs and other agreed-on projects. Without access to a project budget or to cost estimates, however, they were constantly stymied. Was the web developer charging them one lump sum, or was it charging per web page? Would it cost extra to add unforeseen features to the site? Was there enough money in the budget to print brochures in color? Finally, when the senior associate at the consulting firm suggested that she travel to the North Shore for an in-person meeting with the NSCCEJ, members refused. They had no idea how much she was being paid per hour, let alone how much such a visit would cost them.

In late June, the EJO Director delivered more bad news. The AFSZs were not likely to get funded because all the grant monies had been allocated to the consultant. By this point, members had devoted many hours to identifying and confirming potential sites for the AFSZs. Both Sayd and Gillen wrote letters to the EPA expressing their disappointment with the Showcase program. Gillen wrote:

> This is not acceptable. Is the Coalition—is my own group, the Elm Park Civic Association—simply window dressing to meet a paper requirement for "community engagement," while the Agency deems us, denizens of

the "distressed socio-economic strata," constitutionally incapable of an effective role?

Here, Gillen questions whether the coalition's role was merely to provide cover for the EPA's commitment to community engagement. While the EJO repeatedly urged the coalition to become a self-sustaining organization and to apply for additional grants, it also prevented them from managing the Showcase grant.

In the end, the NSCCEJ did accomplish most of its compromise goals. Members worked with the consultant to create a website and an environmental justice profile, although the coalition had to come up with their own funds to print the profile and to host the website. With the help of some college interns, they partnered with the DEC to conduct the anti-idling campaign, and the EPA found a few thousand dollars to hire someone to coordinate the installation of three Asthma-Free School Zones. And, after many, many hours, coalition members produced a set of formal documents including a mission statement, articles of incorporation, bylaws, and an organizational structure. The group did not, however, apply for tax-exempt status after learning that it would cost $2,000 (not reimbursable through the Showcase funds), and none of them had time to apply for additional grants.

Meanwhile, Gillen's repeated requests for copies of the consultant's contract and the Showcase budget were denied. Eventually, she filed a FOIA request and after nearly a year, received the packet of redacted documents. According to Gillen, by reading through the black lines, she discovered that the EJO spent only $50,000 (half of the Showcase grant) on NSCCEJ projects, and had reallocated $50,000 to another Region 2 project in Puerto Rico. I must acknowledge that I myself did not read the redacted document and cannot confirm this assessment. On checking the EPA website, I did find that Region 2 spent $50,000 on a playground project in Puerto Rico, but where those funds came from was not clear. Much clearer was the fact that NSCCEJ members' trust in the EPA had eroded to almost nothing at this point. As an NSCCEJ activist named Kathy said after Gillen revealed the redacted EJO budget, "This is our lives they're wasting."

Instead of highlighting environmental justice, the showcase program revealed contemporary techniques of community governance. By restricting grant monies to education and outreach, the EPA sidelined activists' more urgent concerns while also requiring that they promote the Showcase program. Moreover, by deputizing the Coalition to execute these programs, the agency saddled its members with unpaid administrative responsibilities while hiding critical financial information. This overbearing approach simultaneously patronized coalition members and shifted responsibility onto them. In so doing, it also exploited their most valuable resources—time and energy.

As a final example of activist overload, I discuss neoliberal shifts in the academy. Similar to discourses that valorized civic engagement, an emphasis on engaged scholarship patronized grassroots activists and made even the most well-intentioned academics complicit in the exploitation of their time and energy.

## "Down with the Struggle"

In 2016, Beryl Thurman sent me a frustrated email. She had just received yet another request from an academic institution wanting her to help provide students with an experiential opportunity to learn about environmental justice. In theory, Thurman strongly supported such requests and, in an ideal world, she would find a way to fulfill all of them. However, in the world she actually lived in, such requests had become a significant drain on her time. In her email, she wrote:

> I just got call from Hunter College and they are asking us to participate in a student visioning session about the Bay Street Corridor. There's no compensation in that for us. But will they be using our knowledge? Absolutely. Will it be time consuming? Absolutely! Will there be tangible benefits for the host EJ community? Based on similar experiences over the years, Highly Unlikely.[44]

For Thurman, academic engagements did little to advance environmental justice goals.

This section takes a closer look at the reasons for Thurman's cynicism. I find that the same neoliberal trends that turned nonprofits and community-based organizations into proxies for public agencies, restructured the mission of academic institutions to emphasize public scholarship and community engagement. To carry out such missions, academic researchers increasingly sought partnerships with grassroots activists. However, for reasons I explain below, rather than furthering activists' causes, these efforts tended to add to their overload.

In the early twenty-first century, calls to tear down ivory towers and build bridges between "town and gown" through "engaged" or "public" scholarship resounded throughout academic institutions and disciplines. Public, or engaged, scholars drew on progressive education theorists like John Dewey and David Kolb, as well as the critical pedagogy of Paolo Freire, to stress experiential education and community engagement.[45] By the mid-to-late 2000s, the mission statements of academic institutions across the US emphasized public service.[46] In 2006, the Carnegie Foundation, which classifies and ranks US colleges and universities, instituted a "Community Engagement" category for institutions that demonstrated a mutually beneficial relationship with the community. And in 2009, President Obama signed the Edward M. Kennedy Serve America Act, which allocated over a billion dollars to service-learning programs.[47]

The veneration of volunteerism, participatory politics, and engaged scholarship have all followed a similar path that began with neoliberal restructuring in the 1980s and 1990s. In the case of scholarship, as federal spending on social services shrunk, so too did funding for higher education. Initially, state legislators picked up the slack, and fluctuations in higher education spending generally followed trends in the gross domestic product (GDP) and tax revenues. After the post-9/11 recession, though, public aid to colleges and universities continued to decrease at a fairly steady rate, regardless of tax revenues.[48] The reasons for this decline vary from state to state, but in general they were supported by neoconservative attacks that charged academic institutions with promoting radicalism, elitism, political correctness, liberal bias, and wasting taxpayers' money.[49] At the same time, those on the far left condemned urban universities for their simultaneous indifference to the needs of the poor neighborhoods that surrounded them and rapacious expansion into those neighborhoods.[50] Indeed, cuts to public funding ramped up inter-university competition for revenue and forced academic institutions to adopt market-based and entrepreneurial strategies. In addition to grants, private donors, and tuition from international students, universities produced research and instructional products, as well as professional and vocational degree programs.[51] Capital campaigns built flashy athletic and housing facilities to attract affluent students, while universities replaced tenure-track lines with contingent faculty, expanded class sizes, tightened tenure requirements, and increased pressure on faculty to procure outside funding.[52]

Engaged scholarship emerged as a response to this environment. It countered criticisms from the Left and the Right about "ivory tower" elitism, while also aligning with popular discourses about the value of communitarianism and volunteerism. For those on the Left (who still occupied the majority of faculty and administrative positions), engaged scholarship served as a rejoinder to the voracious entrepreneurism of the contemporary university. As Raddon and Harrison write about service learning, "As a kind of corporate social responsibility strategy, service learning gives visibility to good undergraduate teaching and good works while deflecting attention away from the subsidy to narrowly focused, commercialized research."[53] And yet public service also served the university's entrepreneurial mission, as it attracted donors and helped institutions compete for funding, rankings, and students.[54]

I, too, have devoted much of my career to participating in and promoting public/engaged/activist scholarship.[55] On more occasions than I can count, I have invited grassroots activists to speak to my classes, lead them on toxic tours, provide community support letters, take part in academic grants, and to represent the "community" or the "grassroots" at conferences and seminars. I have also helped connect my academic colleagues with the local activists I know so they can extend similar invitations. But while academics usually receive compensation for speaking engagements, activists are rarely offered travel reimbursements, let alone honoraria. Moreover, academics, and nonprofit professionals earn full-time salaries and are expected to attend such events as part of their job. But for someone like Beryl Thurman, any small, part-time salary she managed to eke out of various grants only covered the time she spent on funded programs and projects. Time spent participating on panels, or visiting college classrooms was always considered "off the clock."

As Thurman's time became more and more overwhelmed with uncompensated invitations, she decided to accept them only when the inviter agreed to make a contribution to NSWC. While some found funding to meet these expectations, Thurman met with surprising resistance from other academics (including those who considered themselves to be radical leftists). In one instance, a colleague and I co-organized a weekly seminar on climate justice, and we invited a mix of academic and activist speakers. As we struggled to allocate our tiny budget for honoraria, my colleague suggested that we pay activists half of the amount we planned to offer our academic speakers. On a second occasion, another colleague wanted to invite Thurman to speak to his class about environmental justice. I put them in touch, and Thurman agreed to speak in exchange for a small donation to NSWC. My colleague responded angrily, accusing her of not being "down with the struggle." He then lectured her about the exploitative nature of the NPIC and urged her to relinquish NSWC's nonprofit status. Similarly, academic grant proposals frequently require community partnerships; yet academic colleagues often balk when I suggest including direct payments to community organizations in our grant budgets.

Embedded in these examples is the common assumption that any kind of institutional recognition has a kind of *a priori* value. Sociologist Nancy Foner argues that just as democratic debate has dissolved into consensus politics and participatory rituals, the right to self-identify has become a political end in itself. But, she warns, this politics of recognition sidesteps and displaces a politics of redistribution and economic inequality.[56] Even though leftist academics generally agree with Foner's critique of recognition politics, they also demonstrate her point through their reluctance to redistribute funding resources directly to community organizations like NSWC, and through their assumption that recognizing an organization's work is payment enough.

In sum, contemporary channels for political action—whether through grassroots organizing, civic engagement, or public scholarship—offer narrow, marketized versions of democracy. Funders, government agencies and academic institutions all became service providers, offering citizen/consumers narrowly defined opportunities for democratic engagement. Under this framework, grassroots leaders are expected to act as subcontractors who further disseminate democratic services to their constituents. Environmental justice activists, however, are not so easily co-opted.

## Conclusion

After Sayd's fellowship ended, a staff attorney ("Linda") replaced him in working with NSCCEJ. Following coalition meetings, Linda and I would ride the ferry together back to Manhattan. One night, Linda told me that she wished Gillen had not filed a FOIA request for the EPA budget reports. She feared this action had "alienated the EPA folks, and ruined [NSCCEJ's] chances of getting more grants from them."

"Well, what did the EPA expect?" I asked Linda, "After all, they're activists." As far as I could tell, Gillen had carefully weighed the value of an EPA grant against its costs to her time and the likelihood that such a grant would advance NSCCEJ's goals. After doing this math, Gillen decided that the FOIA request was worth risking her relationship with the EJO. Linda's patronizing comment missed a crucial point—Gillen was making a conscious decision to opt out of a system that was unlikely to serve her community's interests. Each grant report and application, each public meeting siphoned time and energy away from activists' struggles for environmental justice.

Years of being sucked into activities that were mainly designed to validate institutional agendas left grassroots activists seasoned and jaded. Yet, it also left them obstinate and empowered. They were no longer willing to be wrangled into the quiescence and compliance expected of citizen/consumers. The Harlem residents described in chapter 2 similarly refused to accept a new park that would facilitate green gentrification, and in chapters 3 and 4, Gillen and Thurman wrestled with the choice between environmental improvements and development that might displace themselves and their neighbors. In a sustainaphrenic era, where sustainable initiatives and participatory politics accomplished the opposite of what they promise, the stakes of compliance are high. For environmental justice communities facing contamination, flooding, and displacement, they are a matter of sacrifice or refusal.

# 6

## "This Crosses Party Lines All over the Place"

*Sustainable Solidarities and the Politics of Disaffection*

For years, Sam Manus[1] dreamed of moving into in his childhood home in Oakwood Beach, a tiny neighborhood on Staten Island's eastern shore. Here, one-story and two-story mid-century bunga-lows lined narrow streets that wound their way to the ocean's edge. Oakwood Beach was the kind of place where people worked on their homes and passed them from one generation to the next. In 2008, Sam bought out his siblings' share of the house and set to work renovating it, piece by piece, as money became available. He and his wife Deb-bie finished their back deck—their very last exterior renovation—just as the summer of 2012 approached. All summer, they invited friends and family over to grill on the deck, and "just sat outside, enjoying it," Debbie told me.

But in late October of that year, a fierce hurricane roiling up the At-lantic coast collided with an oncoming snowstorm and a full moon. "Su-perstorm Sandy" slammed into the New York and New Jersey coastline exactly at high tide on October 29, 2012. The storm's tremendous winds sent surges into the New York bight, a narrow indentation in the Atlantic coastline. With nowhere to go, water surged onto Staten Island's south-ern and eastern shores. Sandy devastated the sleepy beachside villages of Oakwood Beach, Midland Beach, South Beach, New Dorp Beach, Oak-wood Beach, Great Kills, and Tottenville, laying hundreds of homes like the Manuses' to waste. As Debbie told me, "We were trapped by flood waters that rose so high so quickly that we barely managed to escape up into a small crawl space in the attic of our home. . . . We struggled to stay calm for the almost twelve hours that we were there, watching the water levels rise to over eight feet in our home, ending just below the ceilings and the space we were hiding in." From the crawl space, Debbie and Sam "could hear each wave come in. You would hear a crash and dishes breaking and everything moving." When they emerged from their attic on the morning of October 30, they found that "everything was in a big pile. It was like a snow globe, like someone shook the house."

Three months later, the Manuses joined one thousand residents of Staten Island's East and South Shores in petitioning Governor Andrew Cuomo to buy out their homes, tear them down, and return the land underneath them to wetlands. Still reeling from 2011's Hurricane Irene, which caused widespread flooding across this part of Staten Island,[2] these residents believed that the worst was yet to come. Like the Manuses, many of them had been living in the area their whole lives, and the thought of relocating broke their hearts. On a Facebook page devoted to Oakwood Beach, one man posted, "This was not just a Neighborhood but it was a small Little town where we created SO MANY wonderful magical memories that will last for generation after generation." And yet residents had been watching their shoreline diminish for years. Now, faced with the gritty reality of sea level rise and intensifying storms they were no longer willing to wait for berms, jetties, and other mitigation measures. They wanted out, and they expected public agencies to foot the bill.

In many ways, Staten Island's South and East Shore neighborhoods served as New York City's alter-ego. With more single-family homes, indoor malls, and green space than any other borough, this part of Staten Island had all the trappings of a suburb, including more conservative political views. In 2017, 30 percent of voters on the Island were registered as Republicans, the largest percentage of any borough in New York City.[3] But 44 percent of voters were registered Democrats, which meant they outnumbered Republicans approximately five to three.[4] Even so, Republican presidential candidates had won Staten Island in all but four elections since 1944. Donald Trump won 57 percent of the vote on Staten Island overall in 2016, and 75 percent of the South Shore vote.[5] Islanders also consistently elected Republicans to their US Congressional District, and they voted for Republican mayoral candidates.

To unpack these political complexities, this chapter leaves the North Shore and travels to Staten Island's South and East Shore neighborhoods. By focusing on environmental activists I find that Staten Islanders, like most people, hold nuanced political beliefs that have grown out of their individual and collective histories and lived experiences. Specifically, attitudes toward buyouts reflected the recent history of development on Staten Island, as well as residents' work and economic histories, and their geographic position—or the fact that they lived on or near the coast of an island. Ultimately, I argue that the increasing precarity of homeownership motivated coastal residents to work across stark political differences and advocate together for more forward-thinking environmental protections and policies.

This is not to say that cross-island environmental activism consisted entirely of "kumbaya" moments. Activists sometimes engaged in heated disagreements, which did not always find resolution. During the 2016 Trump campaign especially, activists engaged in some heated exchanges over email and social media. But cross-Island environmental campaigns moved forward nonetheless, and feuding activists remained involved, even without resolution or apology. These findings urge us to rethink the significance of consensus as a basis for collective action and of dissensus as a stumbling block. More generally, I contend that shared experiences of precarity, disillusionment, and betrayal muck up political binaries. In this case, they brought hundreds of thousands of vulnerable homeowners together to fight for a common cause.

## The Defiant Borough

Along Staten Island's western edge, the Arthur Kill's watery fingers reach inland, forming acres and acres of natural salt marshes. These mineral-rich swamplands brushed the landscape in soft greens, yellows, and blues, and fed verdant forests along with a diverse array of wildlife. Known as the "Everglades of New York City," the marshes once sheltered nearly half of all of New York and New Jersey's wading birds, including herons and egrets. They also nourished the small farms that were scattered across this part of the island. Throughout the early part of the twentieth century, Island residents fought to preserve its forest and marshlands but by the turn of the twenty-first century, only one third of the Island's original marshes remained.[6] Even so, this number comprised approximately 61 percent of New York City's remaining wetlands.[7] Staten Island's fragile natural resources stood in sharp contrast to, and were constantly under threat from, its industrial, urban, and suburban landscapes.

The tension between preservation of natural resources and develop-ment was a theme that helped to shape Islanders' identities as well. In a 1928 *New York Times* article, W. Burke Harmon, President of the Har-mon National Real Estate Corporation, predicted that the mostly rural borough of Staten Island was on the edge of transformation: "This for-gotten borough has suddenly stepped into the limelight."[8] As it turned out, Harmon's statement was hyperbolic. And yet it stuck. Not only did media outlets routinely revive the trope of Staten Island as the next big thing, development-wise, but Islanders themselves adopted "the for-gotten borough" as a rallying cry. Ever-aggrieved Islanders embraced their rural/urban hybridity and wore their outsider status like a badge of honor. It became the source of their sense of victimhood—and their defiance.

Until the turn of the twenty-first century, the Fresh Kills landfill, which stored 90 percent of the city's refuse, served as the Island's most infamous battleground.[9] In 1948, Robert Moses had decided to take ad-vantage of available land on Staten Island and locate a large landfill along the banks of the Fresh Kills estuary in the central-western part of the Island.[10] Over the next four decades, Fresh Kills landfill continued to rise until it became the highest point on the East Coast. According to local legend, its mountainous peaks of garbage could be seen from outer space.[11] A breeding ground for mosquitos, the landfill stank. It leached toxins into the groundwater of surrounding areas, and the trucks that served it increased air pollution. Over time, Fresh Kills would become a metonym for Staten Islanders' defiant victimhood.

Meanwhile, ever since the opening of the Verrazano Bridge, Staten Island's population had been growing by leaps and bounds. By 1968, just four years after the Bridge's opening, population growth went from ap-proximately two thousand people per year to approximately seventeen thousand per month.[12] Many of these settled in the borough's suburban mid-Island and South Shore districts. As the Fresh Kills' trash moun-tains rose higher and higher, they affected a larger and larger population. However, relative to the density of other boroughs, Staten Island still seemed bucolic.

In 1990, Islanders' frustrations over Fresh Kills—and their perceived political marginalization—culminated in a boroughwide secession movement. A year earlier, the US Supreme Court had declared the city's

Board of Estimate (its legislative body) unconstitutional. The Board included all five Borough Presidents, each of whom had one vote, regardless of the borough's population. This configuration led to corruption and the uneven distribution of municipal resources, according to the Brooklyn-based civil rights attorneys who filed the suit. The Supreme Court agreed that the system violated the Constitution's one-person-one-vote requirement and ordered New York City to restructure.[13] The Board of Estimate now became the City Council. Each borough was apportioned seats on the Council according its populations. Out of fifty-one total representatives, Brooklyn had fifteen and one-fifth (it shared one of them with Queens), and Staten Island had three.

With so few City Council votes, the prospects for closing Fresh Kills seemed extremely unlikely to Staten Islanders.[14] Faced with this intolerable future, State Senator John Marichi successfully sponsored a bill to hold a borough-wide referendum on seceding from New York City. In November 1990, 83 percent of Staten Islanders voted to secede and operate as an independent city. Governor Mario Cuomo, however, vetoed their decision, forcing the borough to remain a borough.[15] Defeated in secession but still defiant about Fresh Kills, Islanders continued their fight.

In 1996, Staten Island Borough President Guy Molinari sued the City and State of New York for violating the Clean Air Act by allowing Fresh Kills to expand without proper permits. At the time, Rudolph Giuliani was campaigning for his second term as mayor and he promised to close the landfill by 2002. As it turned out, the state legislature beat him to the punch by voting to close the landfill in 2001. Several months later, the landfill temporarily reopened to absorb refuse from the September 11, 2001 attacks on the World Trade Center. About six months later, Fresh Kills closed again—this time for good.

Within two years of closing, one of the world's largest landfills became one of its largest reclamation projects. The 2,200-acre Freshkills Park showcased state-of-the-art ecological restoration methods (including methane capture) that aimed to make the site a home for local flora and fauna, as well as for hiking, boating, playgrounds, and other kinds of human recreation. Accounts of the reclamation were almost uniformly positive. Project architect James Corner commented, "the whole process of this kind of technologically engineered ecology provides an opportunity for Freshkills to offer a great educational demonstration in environmental sustainability."[16] If the inception of Fresh Kills Landfill reflected human dominance over nature, so too did Freshkills Park. In the latter case, new technologies allowed park developers to assert control over both restored nature and the enduring effects of a massive urban landfill. In addition, the park helped city residents forget that all of their trash was now being exported to other states, by barge, train, and/or truck.

## "We Can't Take a Beating Every Year"

One of the first activists I met on Staten Island was Dee Vandenburg, President of the Staten Island Taxpayers Association. In her mid-fifties, Vandenburg's blond, crimped hair framed bright blue eyes and an easy smile. She wore faded Levi's, a black t-shirt with a fiery logo, and a black leather jacket cinched at the waist, looking every bit the motorcycle enthusiast that she was. Vandenburg, who spoke with a husky, Long Island accent, had moved to Staten Island as a teenager. After working in a variety of jobs, she landed at the Metropolitan Transit Authority in 1989 and spent the next twenty-five years as a general mechanic for the Staten Island Railway. In 1996, Vandenburg joined the Staten Island Taxpayers' Association (SITA), and five years later its members elected her president. As SITA president, Vandenburg assisted local civic associations in achieving their goals. She also served as a liaison to local, state, and federal government officials. She was keenly aware of the borough's infrastructure needs, and she spent years convincing local officials about the urgent need to install storm sewers in all parts of the southern and eastern shores. Vandenburg also spent many years lobbying for other flood protections and against overdevelopment.

Although the southern and eastern shores had been densifying since the mid-1960s, they contained plenty of vacant lots to soak up stormwater and overflow from the area's septic systems. In fact, these small wetland areas were ample enough to obviate the need for storm and sewer lines. But as vacant lots disappeared under duplexes, townhouses, and apartment complexes, it became harder to control local flooding. By 1990, residents frequently complained that their neighborhoods smelled of sewage after heavy rains. Rather than install traditional storm infrastructure, the city decided to piece together a string of public properties, and acquire some private properties to create a storm management area, or blue belt. The program managed to preserve approximately 400 acres of freshwater wetlands and almost eleven miles of stream corridor.[17] Even within the blue belt, however, the Department of Buildings kept allowing variances, and floods kept plaguing South and East Shore residents.

After a 1992 nor'easter caused severe flooding, residents demanded that elected officials improve the area's flood protections and storm management systems. Finally, in 2000, the US Army Corps of Engineers installed some berms and other measures to mitigate beach erosion, although some of those protections began to come undone by the end of the decade.[18] In 2004, the New York City Council answered residents' ongoing concerns about overdevelopment and passed new zoning rules that were meant to stem unchecked growth. But the Buildings Department continued to grant variances that allowed for dense residential development, often adjacent to wetland areas. Between 2001 and 2008, nearly seven hundred new structures went up in a high-risk storm-surge zone, essentially laying Staten Island's southern and eastern shorelines bare of storm protections.[19]

In 2010, a friend of Vandenburg's in New Dorp (whom I will call Mike) asked for her help in opposing the development of a vacant lot next to his house. The lot was part of a wetland, and in heavy rains it held water and prevented flooding. Although Vandenburg, Mike and his neighbors fought hard to preserve the empty lot, development won, and later that year the lot sprouted townhouses.

Twenty-four months later, Hurricane Sandy flooded Mike's street so badly that his house was lifted right off of its foundation. Like most flood survivors, Mike contacted the Federal Emergency Management Agency (FEMA) to make a claim on his flood insurance. Nearly a year later, a FEMA subcontractor came out to assess the damage. "[FEMA] finally sent someone out there to give him an estimate on his house," Vandenburg told me. "Only, they kept calling him because they couldn't find the address. [Mike] was telling them, 'That's because the house isn't there. It's gone.'"

Mike was among many storm survivors throughout the country who find that their dealings with FEMA constitute a second type of disaster. Facing a surfeit of claims immediately after Sandy, for instance, FEMA imported extra insurance adjusters from as far away as Ohio. But home-owners complained that these damage appraisals were not based on New York City prices and vastly underestimated the costs of damages to their homes. A few months after Sandy, Nicole Romano-Levine, president of the New Dorp Civic Association, told me, "A lot of people are only getting half of their policy. So they're getting $125,000 but they need more like $250,000." To supplement recovery funds or inadequate as-sessments, FEMA advised homeowners to apply to the Small Business Administration (SBA) for low-cost loans. But, unbeknownst to most of these applicants, receiving SBA monies disqualified them from receiving grants from Build it Back, a city-managed program to disperse federal disaster funds. Meanwhile, Build it Back was beset by problems of its own. It took eighteen months for the program to make any payments, and many applicants waited five years for construction to begin on their homes. By 2016, Build it Back was half-a-billion dollars over budget and had helped fewer than a third of the homes initially in the program. The Inspector General of the Department of Housing and Urban Develop-ment cited the program for gross mismanagement.[20]

During the first two years after Sandy, Vandenburg devoted herself almost entirely to relocation and restoration plans. One of her major roles was serving on the state of New York's "New York Rising" task force, charged with developing a state-funded recovery plan. Nearly a year after Hurricane Sandy, I traveled to Midland Beach, one of Staten Island's hardest-hit areas, to attend one of several New York Rising pub-lic meetings. The headlights of my taxi illuminated the neighborhood's darkened, hushed streets, lined with still-shuttered homes and busi-nesses. In contrast, the gymnasium of the Olympia Activity Center, a recreation space operated by St. Margaret Mary's Church, was brightly lit and brimming with people. I immediately spotted Vandenburg pacing in the back of the auditorium while a representative from the state stood before the crowd and presented a slide show summarizing a slate of gen-eral recovery ideas. Giving me a quick hug, Vandenburg said she was glad I could make it. "How's it going?" I asked, noticing her nervousness.

Vandenburg had reason to be worried. Almost no residents had set-tled their FEMA recovery claims, and the Build it Back program still had yet to make any payouts. It would not be until April, 2014, before any New York City resident received BiB benefits, although the consulting firm hired to execute the program received $17 million upfront.[21] Meanwhile, many displaced homeowners were still paying mortgages on their houses, on top of paying rents on their temporary homes. As meeting goers poured Dunkin' Donuts coffee into paper cups and loaded plates with baked ziti from a local restaurant, state officials explained the plan for the night. Throughout the gym, they had set up easels with flip charts, one for each category of recovery—infrastructure, housing, transportation, natural resources. Each easel had a stack of sticky notes, markers, and a DEC official to answer questions. Meeting attendees were to write their suggestions on a sticky note and post it on the flip board.

Within the hour, the flip boards were covered with yellow squares that read, "Give us what we're entitled to," "We paid insurance for a house that's gone," "Accelerate the blue belt," "Without proper drainage, what good is anything else?" and "They never should have let them build over there." Over at an easel marked "natural resources," a small crowd scribbled on sticky notes. I struck up a conversation with a woman named Joanne, a fourth-generation New Dorp resident. She remembered that sometime around 2010 she awoke to find city workers cutting down a section of trees at the end of New Dorp Lane, across from Miller Field. The trees were being cleared for a soccer field. "I don't know why," Joanne shook her head. "We already have Miller Field." She explained that the parcel of land was an indentation and its trees held rain water. "As soon as we saw the trees come down, we got nervous." Although Joanne did not want a buyout for herself, she emphasized, "I want people to have the option." After we spoke, she wrote down, "Put the trees back and other natural protections" and stuck her note on the board.

Long-term residents were not the only ones who felt betrayed. I met Dimitri and Alex, two Russian emigres[22] who purchased townhomes a few blocks from Lower New York Bay. "We suspected [the development] was in a wetland when we bought," Alex said. Yet he assumed that if the city permitted a development there, "it must be safe." It turned out that the development covered a marsh and its ground floor apartments flooded often. "We can't take a beating every year," said Dimitri. Both he and Alex signed the petition to be added to Governor Andrew Cuomo's buyout program. "Rising sea levels make it all worse," said Alex. Living in townhomes put Dimitri and Alex in an especially tough spot. Dimitri explained that the recurring floods had created mold problems on the

first floor of all of the houses adjacent to his. While Dimitri had remediated his mold, the neighbors who shared a wall with him had not. In
addition, townhomes could not be raised above sea levels. I heard similar stories from other townhome owners. If the city was going to grant
variances to build higher-density attached housing, then it should also
take responsibility for the circumstances that came with such housing.

In the months following the storm, a total of 2,500 Staten Islanders
joined the Manuses in requesting that the state buy them out of their
homes. In February 2013, Governor Cuomo finally responded to these
requests by announcing that the state would designate certain especially hard-hit areas for a buyout program. The program would leverage federal monies to reimburse eligible homeowners 100 percent of the
pre-storm value of their homes. The homes would then be demolished,
leaving the land underneath to return to wetlands.[23] The governor designated parts of Ocean Breeze, Graham Beach, and Oakwood Beach for
buyouts, and approximately 323 homeowners received them.[24] A larger
area was eligible for a second program that was run jointly by the state
and the city. This program covered parts of New Dorp, Tottenville, Midland Beach, and South Beach, offering to purchase homes for their post-
storm values. Rather than returning purchased properties to nature,
this program allowed them to be redeveloped in a "resilient manner." By
2017, approximately 200 homeowners had opted for this second acquisi-
tion program, and their homes had gone to auction.[25]

For those left to repair and rebuild their homes in the years immediately following the storm—and without the assistance of these
programs—things were about to get much worse. In 2012, the federal
government passed the Biggert-Waters Act, a bill that would defund
federal flood insurance subsidies. If residents of high-risk flood zones
did not pay to elevate their homes, the private market would send these
insurance rates skyrocketing as much as fifteen times their current rates.
Suddenly, hundreds of thousands of coastal homeowners across the
country were staring down the barrel of economic disaster.

## The Waters Prevailed

Since the growth of the real estate industry in the early twentieth century,
floods have presented a vexing social problem. Initially, catastrophic

floods were considered "acts of God," triggering federal emergency relief funds. Homeowners wanting further risk protection could purchase flood insurance on the private market. In 1927, however, widespread damage from the Great Mississippi River Flood necessitated huge payouts from private insurance companies. A year later, insurers claimed that flood payouts were detrimental to their businesses and discontinued their flood insurance offerings.[26] Around that time, new advances in the field of civil engineering promised to create dams and levees that could significantly reduce flooding in many parts of the country. Flood control became a darling of the Progressive movement and New Deal funds generated dams and levees throughout the United States. Not all of these projects were effective, however. In some cases, after especially violent storms, flood waters continued to escape and flood immediate and downstream areas.[27] The costs of flood damage then fell mainly to property owners.

In 1951, after an immense flood in Kansas and Missouri, President Harry Truman proposed federalizing flood insurance legislation. Although Truman's proposal failed three times, his successor, Dwight D. Eisenhower, took up the cause and passed the Federal Flood Insurance Act in 1956. The Act provided up to $10,000 in flood insurance to individual households. However, due to a lack of research on the costs involved in such a program, Congress declined to appropriate the necessary funds.[28] Meanwhile, thanks to the postwar economic boom as well as federal programs that subsidized mortgages, car manufacturers, highways, and other kinds of infrastructure, suburban development was expanding exponentially.[29] Expansion, of course, meant that housing developments increasingly encroached on natural wetland areas, making them more vulnerable to flooding. That vulnerability was apparent by the mid-1960s, when Hurricane Betsy devastated New Orleans on the heels of several other disasters, including the Alaska earthquake. In response to widespread alarms, President Lyndon B. Johnson renewed the call for federal flood insurance. Louisiana Congressman Hale Boggs (Dem) happened to be the majority whip, and he passionately advocated for a new bill. Finally, in August 1968, the National Flood Insurance Act took effect.[30]

The Act's long awaited passage marked a particularly complicated moment in US history. Throughout the 1960s, Johnson's Great Society programs provided federal subsidies to a broad range of American families, encouraging public support for the Keynesian welfare state.[31] At the same time, the US economy was increasingly reliant on the financial and real estate sectors. If homeowners were unable to pay for flood-related losses and foreclosed on their mortgages, widespread recession could ensue.[32] The 1960s also ushered in a new era of environmentalism in the US after Rachel Carson's *Silent Spring* woke people up to the dangers of toxic chemicals and environmental hazards. As part of this trend, a new field of expertise specializing in hazards research emerged. These experts warned that federal flood protections had made homeowners and developers too sanguine about the risks of building in flood plains.[33]

All of these factors contributed to a public consensus that the government should do something to protect homeowners from flood risks. Debates over how to implement these protections again reflect competing trends. Hazards researchers proposed that the federal government establish stricter land-use controls to prevent flood-plain development. But an emerging group of economists—who subscribed to neoliberal ideologies that privileged free markets and individual choice—disagreed. They argued that the decision to live on a flood plain was an individual one, and individuals (not the state) should be responsible for the risks associated with that decision.[34]

The National Flood Insurance Act wrapped all of these competing factors into a unique combination of welfare state-era collectivism and market-based individualism. That is, the Act required private homeowners to pay for their own flood insurance, but pooling their policies nationally lowered individual premiums. In addition, the Act mandated the creation of flood maps to rate individual risks, and the reinsurance of the program, thereby securitizing private insurance and guarding against market failure. Originally, the program was voluntary, and many homeowners declined to participate. However, after five years, Congress adjusted the Act and made flood insurance mandatory for homeowners purchasing properties in areas that FEMA designated as flood-hazard zones. To sweeten this mandate, the National Flood Insurance Program (NFIP) subsidized insurance premiums, discounting rates up to 40 to 45 percent of the market rate that a private insurance company would charge.[35]

In policy terms, NFIP seemed like a relic from a distant, Keynesian past. Federal subsidies to individual homeowners and rate controls were anathema to neoliberalism's entrepreneurial mode of citizenship, which, as Stephen J. Collier has put it, "constitute[d] the individual citizen as a risk-taking agent who is responsible for his or her own security."[36] In other words, good citizens were those who took responsibility for managing their own health and safety.[37] These same ideologies underwrote the expansion of the private insurance industry, a market-based health care system, and other institutions that managed personal risk. In addition, after Reagan and Bush rolled back environmental regulations, real estate developers enjoyed even freer rein to sprawl across natural wetlands and other natural flood protections. This made thousands more homes vulnerable to flooding. Major storms like Hurricanes Andrew, Wilma, Katrina, and Rita flooded some homes multiple times. Katrina, especially, created enormous shortfalls in the federal flood insurance budget.[38]

In 2012, US Representative Maxine Waters (D-Calif.) co-sponsored the Biggert-Waters Flood Insurance Reform Act which ended federal subsidies and reset flood insurance rates to accord with the private market.[39] In addition, the Act responded to concerns about climate change by requiring FEMA to expand its flood maps. In so doing, however, the redrawn maps included thousands of homes that had never flooded. The consequences accumulated—higher flood insurance rates were a hardship for these homeowners, and they made homes more difficult to sell. The new rates also added an extra burden to homeowners still struggling to recover from prior flood disasters. In New York City, for instance, the new FEMA maps placed 32,000 additional properties in Flood Zone A, which raised some owners' insurance premiums from an average of $430 to $5,000 or $10,000.[40] Insurance companies, meanwhile, would profit handsomely from tens of thousands of new customers who were mandated to purchase policies. The Act thus yanked NFIP firmly out of its welfare state roots and replanted it in a privatized, neoliberal present.

Initially, the Biggert-Waters Act received widespread support from both parties in Congress, as well as from the general public. In 2013, though, the New York Times published an unusual op-ed arguing against Biggert-Waters. In it, geologist Nicholas Pinter described the Act as "harsh medicine" for an ailing program that "placed too much of a burden on flood-zone residents."[41] Readers did not exactly share Pinter's opinion. Of the 238 comments on the editorial, only a fraction agreed with him, and nearly all of those were flood survivors. Those whose politics leaned to the left celebrated Biggert-Waters as a rare federal policy that directly addressed climate change. Those on the right welcomed the end of federal insurance subsidies. Both sides expressed disdain for beneficiaries of federal flood insurance. As one person wrote, "The whole problem is that we subsidize people who choose to live in flood-prone areas . . . the rest of us are perpetuating the problem by subsidizing irresponsible behavior." Another comment asked, "Why should we pay for someone's riverside or lakeside or seaside view?"[42] Whether portrayed by the right as mooching off government largesse or by the left as denying the realities of climate change, commenters cast coastal homeowners as the villains of flood insurance narratives. Within a year, however, that tide would turn.

## Stop FEMA Now

George Kasimos,[43] a college dropout-turned-real estate broker in his late forties, often claimed that he had barely followed politics, or voted, prior to Hurricane Sandy. Nor did he post on Facebook or Twitter. Rather, he liked to sit on his back deck, drinking beer and gazing at the lagoon behind his home in Toms River, New Jersey—until October 29, 2012, that is, when Hurricane Sandy sent a foot and a half of water into Kasimos's home and changed his life forever. Kasimos settled his insurance claim unusually quickly. His neighbors, on the other hand, struggled mightily with relief programs that were hamstrung by endless red tape, with insurance assessments, and with countless other obstacles similar to those faced by Staten Islanders.

After hearing about changes to the NFIP, Kasimos decided to take some action. He contacted some of his neighbors and organized a meeting to discuss what they, as private citizens, could do to stop the rate hikes. On a Saturday morning in March, 2013, 120 people crammed into the Yo Way frozen yogurt shop in Ortley Beach. The crowd attracted the attention of local police, who worked crowd control until the fire marshal shut the meeting down.[44] Later on the same day, Kasimos started a Facebook page for "Stop FEMA Now" (SFN), a grassroots effort to repeal the Biggert-Waters Act. Within a few weeks, SFN had more than 8,100 likes on Facebook and 1,000 followers on Twitter.[45] Within a couple of months, homeowners living near oceans, lakes and rivers had created local spin-off groups like Stop FEMA Now–Georgia and many others in upstate New York, Ohio, Tampa Bay, and so on. Using strategies like "Twitter calls to action," they began lobbying their congressional representatives to repeal Biggert-Waters and reframing public debates about national flood insurance and public responsibility.

From the start, Kasimos used SFN's Facebook page to announce meetings and events and to share advice and information about the recovery process. Soon, the page contained hundreds of posts from homeowners who shared disastrous encounters with FEMA contractors and asked for advice in navigating endless red tape and obstacles. A New York homeowner, for example, posted the following description of her meeting with an insurance adjuster on March 2, 2013:

> Lol [the insurance company] sent me this little old man who had problems walking and had to walk on my open floor. I was concerned if he fell I would be sued. On top of that he wrote a report stating that my blown-out walls and damage from having 48" of water inside the house, and the muck, was not caused by water damage. Where do I sign up for help???[46]

In nearly a dozen comments, people sympathized, shared their own experiences and offered concrete advice.

In a second example, on December 8, 2013, Kasimos posted a link to a news story entitled "Flood insurance Falls Short for Many Hurricane Sandy Victims."[47] The link generated a series of comments about insurance underpayments, FEMA inefficiencies and Biggert-Waters. One New Jersey woman wrote:

> We got about half of what it cost to rebuild to live like modern people again. Not to replace what we lost, which some people think we all want. Just heat, electricity & walls.

A second New Jersey woman shared her frustration with FEMA's red tape:

> Yup. And I can't finish [rebuilding] because [FEMA] won't release the funds and they won't release the funds until I finish. So dumb. I can't . . .

A third commenter from Oregon sympathetically shared her concerns about Biggert-Waters:

> It has reached us out in Oregon too. We live on a river .9 miles inside the flood plain. We are NOT subsidized but we can't sell our home because people are afraid of what Biggert-Waters might bring. Really sucks!

A final post is from a man in Pennsylvania who similarly believed that Biggert-Waters had just made his home valueless:

> I live in a small town in PA, never been flooded and FEMA has jacked my premium up to the max, my house is now worth about 30k less than market value, we've been trying to sell but can't, every potential buyer wants nothing to do with flood insurance and FEMA.

Posts and comments like these filled SFN's Facebook page, linking coastal homeowners across the country through their shared frustrations, anger, and fears about their future.

Such reports were so abundant and pervasive that SFN leaders began agitating for an investigation into FEMA fraud. In March, 2015, *60 Minutes* aired an investigation featuring two FEMA whistle-blowers—a contractor and the Deputy Associate Administrator for Insurance. Both revealed evidence of fraud in reports used to deny full insurance payouts as well as the use of unlicensed engineers for flood damage reports. Even worse, top officials at FEMA had been aware of the fraud for over a year but failed to act on it.[48] Shortly after the *60 Minutes* episode aired, FEMA's director resigned, and Congress mandated that the agency reopen all 144,000 Hurricane Sandy-related insurance claims. A year later, most of those claims remained unresolved.[49] Within two years, however, approximately 82 percent of reopened claims had received additional payments.[50] At the end of 2018, the state of New Jersey proposed reallocating an additional $60 million in federal Hurricane Sandy relief funds in order to complete rebuilding projects that remained stalled six years after the storm.[51]

SFN's success in driving public attention to the plight of storm survivors also helped to shift political attitudes about flood insurance reform. By 2014, even Maxine Waters recognized the need to soften her bill's impacts on coastal homeowners. That year, Congress rescinded many of the rate increases called for in the Biggert-Waters Act and limited annual rate increases to 18 percent. These restrictions also applied to properties newly categorized as high risk under FEMA's revised maps. Finally, there would be a $250 surcharge on all policyholders. But in 2019, Congress modified the rules again. Now, homes that suffered repetitive losses were subject to higher premiums and rates increases up to 25 percent. In addition, homeowners had the option to purchase certain limited flood insurance policies that were underwritten by the private market, rather than the federal government. More generally, the program's public funding remained decidedly undecided, caught between ever-fiercer storms and ever-increasing program debt. Between 2017 and 2019, Congress voted for ten short-term extensions of the National Flood Insurance program, but reached no agreement about its long-term future. During that same period, Hurricanes Irma, Maria, and Harvey collectively inflicted over $265 billion in damage.

As the years and the storm damage wore on, SFN's Facebook page remained a robust resource for flood survivors and coastal homeowners. Participants offered practical advice and sympathy. Kasimos posted regular updates on flood insurance policy, as well as on his work on various federal and state committees. Every so often, he issued a call to action, or endorsed a politician who advocated on behalf of coastal homeowners. New Jersey Senator Bob Menendez (D) received Kasimos's most consistent and adamant support, even during Menendez's 2015 indictment, trial, and the eventual dismissal of corruption charges against him. Prior to Sandy, Kasimos considered himself a loyal Republican. Now, however, he insisted on nonpartisanship, endorsing politicians based on their FEMA-related record.

SFN's approximately 9,000 Facebook followers showed a similar reserve in their posts. They regularly exchanged plentiful, creative, and virulent insults aimed at FEMA, fraudulent contractors, and unresponsive insurance companies and elected officials. But even during the notoriously divisive 2016 election season, they deliberately veered away from partisan politics. An exception illustrates this rule. Shortly after the inauguration of President Donald Trump, a woman posted, "The only ones who are making out big from the Gov. is the illegals!! The Gov. has money to give them, yet they screw us!!"[52] Importantly, the post received no "likes," comments, or responses of any kind. Belying a rise in online *in*civility, bullying, trolling, and angry debates, SFN members held to a tacit agreement not to engage such messages. In a Facebook group where members regularly expressed vitriol for certain government agencies and officials, this deft sidestepping of divisive political discussions seemed almost shocking. A 2018 blog post by Kasimos summed up the group's single-issue, nonpartisan ethos, "We don't care if you are a Democrat or Republican, we just want to save our homes."

Kasimos's call for nonpartisanship (and SFN's existence, more generally) complicate common narratives about the degree to which the US is a deeply divided nation. In the next section, I show how environmental activism on Staten Island offers a similarly complex picture of local politics.

## Green Teas and Blue Belts

One late afternoon in the Fall of 2012, Sarah,[53] one of the North Shore Waterfront Conservancy's (NSWC) board members drove me to the ferry after a board meeting. As we drove, I asked Sarah to tell me how she came to join NSWC. Sarah shook her shoulder-length brunette hair and laughed, "It was the Army Corps. That damned dredging project." Sarah was referring to a multiyear project, led by the Army Corps of Engineers, to dredge the Kill Van Kull. Ahead of the blasting, the Corps had inspected a number of houses in the blast range, noted existing damage and told homeowners to file claims if blasts caused any new damage. Once dredging commenced, dynamite blasts shook Sarah's house so ferociously that its foundation cracked. She reported the damage to the Army Corps, but she was unable to prove definitively that the Corps' blasting caused the crack, so the Corps refused to compensate her. As a result, Sarah and her husband, Ben, were stuck with a home that they could not afford to fix and could never resell. As I listened to Sarah's story, I realized that I had heard it a year or so before, sitting next to Ben at an NSWC event. I remembered how his voice had shaken in the retelling, his sense of betrayal as fresh and raw as it had ever been.

Sarah continued her account. Some months into her fight with the Army Corps, a neighbor told her that a local organization, NSWC, was advocating on behalf of homeowners whose property was damaged during the dredging. Sarah attended NSWC's next meeting, and "I never left," she laughed. As we approached the ferry terminal, our conversation turned to the upcoming presidential election. Sarah mentioned that she had recently joined the Tea Party. "Government spending is out of control . . ." she explained. "Enough is enough, you know? It just makes sense."

Along with Sarah, approximately 2,000 Staten Islanders joined the Staten Island Tea Party between 2008 and 2010. The movement's popularity was in keeping with the conservatism that prevailed among Staten Island residents, especially on the southern and eastern shores. Forty-six percent of South Shore residents identified themselves as conservatives, as did 38 percent of Islanders as a whole.[54] After the 2008 federal bailout of failing banks, insurers, and auto companies, the Staten Island Tea Party became especially popular among the Island's furious fiscal conservatives.

And yet, Staten Islanders' individual politics defied common typologies. Like Sarah, NSWC members supported causes that promoted fiscal conservatism *and* calls for increased public spending on environmental protection, infrastructure, and managed retreats. Their Facebook affiliations, for example, could include "Staten Islanders Against the DREAM Act," "NYC Board of Standards and Appeals Approves too Many Variances," "Staten Island Conservative Women," "Stop FEMA Now," the "Natural Resources Protective Association" (a local environmental group), and several East and South Shore neighborhood associations that were lobbying for managed retreat. The Staten Island Taxpayer's Association (SITA)'s agenda reflected a similar political pastiche. SITA, whose members were mainly from the South and East Shores, opposed tax hikes (including a five-cent plastic bag fee under consideration by the New York City Council in 2019) and large economic development projects, especially those that encroached on natural wetlands. The organization also advocated for public spending on storm and waste-water sewers, road improvements, and coastal protections. As its name suggests, SITA members saw tax paying as a civic responsibility. As tax payers, they also had a stake in how those taxes were spent. A tax-paying identity thus empowered Staten Islanders to advocate for the public services they needed and to criticize spending that only benefited a small segment of the population, whether it was super-wealthy developers or noncitizens.[55]

But the complexities and curiosities of conservatism on Staten Island go even deeper. Although the majority of Islanders voted for Republican candidates in national, state, and local elections, registered Democrats outnumbered Republicans by five to three. This misalignment between voting behavior and political party affiliation can be explained, at least in part, by another seeming contradiction. Approximately 22 percent of residents on the southern and eastern shores were employed by the City of New York as teachers, police officers, and firefighters.[56] Most of them were part of a public sector union. The 11th Congressional District, which included all of Staten Island and bits of southern Brooklyn, was the most heavily unionized district in the United States, according to some estimates. Not only did these Islanders support unions in general, but also their union membership influenced their party affiliation.

Local activist Bobby Zahn founded the Richmond County Tea Party Patriots in 2013 after splintering off from the Staten Island Tea Party. Zahn, who liked to say that the Patriots "like their TEA a little stronger," explained the disconnect between party affiliation and voting behavior on his blog, RedBorough.com:

> [Staten Island] is a place where some form of conservatism calls itself home, even among many Democrats. This is not surprising to us at the RedBorough.com, as most of Staten Island is comprised of working families who have no place in the modern Democrat party. These conservative Democrats are made up of a wide variety of folks. From cops and firemen, to teachers and veterans, to people who have been Democrats since the days of Kennedy, when the difference between Republicans and Democrats were [sic] their vision for how to improve America. Some are even shrewd political minds who simply know the best way they, as a single voter, can sway politics is to be a voice in the party that is most likely to hold a primary election.[57]

Zahn argues that conservative Islanders registered as Democrats out of long-standing union allegiances, even if they voted as individuals. In addition, he proposes that savvy conservatives recognized that the only way to have a voice in solid-blue New York was to be able to vote in statewide primary elections.

Staten Islanders also reflected larger, national trends in voting behavior. After the 2016 presidential election, a steady stream of media outlets, polling organizations, and think tanks told us that the country was more politically polarized, antagonistic, and uncivil than ever. But a handful of political scientists took a more nuanced and historical view. Noted political scientist Morris Fiorina argues that in the 1970s, the US electorate was just as divided as it was in 2016.[58] The difference is that, between 2012 and 2018, an average of 40 percent of US voters identified as independent.[59] Researchers attribute the rise in independent voters to a decline in the average voter's satisfaction with a particular political party.[60] This dissatisfaction coincided with the increasing influence of major political donors, especially those with strong points of view on politics or policies.[61] Thus, a growing number of voters rejected partisan identities and held mixed or centrist views on policy, but donor-influenced politicians expressed ever more polarized ideas.[62] When it came to actual elections, this situation left voters in the difficult position of choosing between two parties, neither of which fully aligned with their interests. According to Fiorina, most voters make the choice based on a few standout ideological issues like climate change, gay rights, abortion, or social service spending.[63]

The lived experiences of environmental activists on Staten Island are testament to the willingness and ability of individuals to set aside partisanship and cooperate on immediate, urgent issues. This is not to say that political or ideological differences never arose. Thurman told me that during the 2106 election, she "un-friended" people from NSWC's Facebook group when they posted or reposted racially derogatory or otherwise insulting comments. She also regularly complained that environmental activists from Staten Island's white middle-class neighborhoods lacked concern for issues of environmental racism. At the same time, Thurman knew that partnerships and coalitions were vital to achieving NSWC's goals of environmental protection and remediation. She therefore avoided individuals known to make explicitly prejudiced remarks and remained flexible in forming partnerships with other environmental groups.

In terms of political party affiliations, Thurman considered it "Not my business." Many years after my conversation with Sarah about joining the Tea Party, I mentioned it to Thurman. She raised her eyebrows in surprise. "Really? I had no idea. Wait, don't tell me anymore. I don't want to know." For the activists profiled in this chapter, the need for solidarity around the environmental issues they faced took precedence over political affiliations and proclivities. As Vandenburg told me at the New York Rising meeting, "This crosses party lines all over the place."

## Conclusion

From fighting Fresh Kills to voting for secession to supporting the Tea Party or Donald Trump, Staten Islanders from the South and East Shores maintained a defiant, independent identity. Yet their lived political experiences also offer important insights into national politics. After Hurricane Sandy, Staten Islanders joined forces with coastal residents across the US to challenge a political system that prioritized development while neglecting to maintain infrastructure and protect natural flood barriers. Moreover, as coastlines have eroded and storms have grown more fierce, public resources have dwindled and privatized. Middle-class coastal homeowners were left with little to show for years of investing in mortgages, taxes, and various kinds of property insurance. As Debbie Manus said, "We did everything we were supposed to—we paid our taxes, we paid our property and homeowner's insurance, we paid our mortgage. We did everything right, and now you're telling us that we're not entitled."

Already, middle-class Americans struggled against wage stagnation and rising health care costs. Now, they were being asked to bear the risks of climate change and to shoulder the burden of overdevelopment. Political theorist Wendy Brown argues that in times of economic crisis and austerity, neoliberalism reworks citizen virtue as "shared sacrifice." She explains,

[These sacrifices] entail sudden job losses, furloughs, or cuts in pay, benefits, and pensions, or [they] may involve suffering the more sustained effects of stagflation, currency deflation, credit crunches, liquidity crises, foreclosure crises, and more. "Shared sacrifice" may also refer to the effects of curtailed state investment in education, infrastructure, public transportation, public parks, or public services . . . [64]

Equating shared sacrifice with patriotism deflects blame for economic crisis away from capitalist institutions and shifts responsibility onto individual citizens. I would add that we see a parallel process with climate crisis and natural disasters. With each type of crisis, citizen sacrifices accumulate, and a greater portion of the citizenry becomes vulnerable.

And yet this precarious vantage point also offers some glimpses of hope. The case of environmental activists on Staten Island and Stop FEMA Now demonstrate how coastal homeowners refused to accept the sacrifices imposed on them. This refusal became the basis for their solidarity and enabled them to sidestep divisive issues and organize collectively. Such experiences show us that the political landscape of everyday life is far more dynamic and fungible than we realize, shaping a vast array of political possibilities. In the case of the activists depicted in this chapter, the differences that might have driven them apart were far outweighed by their growing awareness that the sustainaphrenia would eventually sacrifice them all.

# Conclusion

## *Unsticking from Stupid*

"Black people have been through this kind of shit before." It was the night after the 2016 US Presidential election. Beryl Thurman and I sat in a corner booth at one of our favorite bistros. Over dinner, we planned to discuss a new funding proposal as well as NSWC's progress on a couple of ongoing grants. As we sipped gin martinis and waited for our food, I asked Thurman for her thoughts on the Trump victory and the general hysteria it was generating. "Black folks are used to things not going our way," she shrugged. "Now the white folks get to see what it's like." For Thurman, white liberal voters' shock and horror at the results of the 2016 presidential election reflected the privileged assumption that their voices would be heard and paid attention to; their inference that the political system worked in their favor. Black activists believed in, and spent much of their lives fighting for, such democratic ideals. But they also learned to expect disappointment, outrage, and to feel under siege, regardless of who was in office.

"Where were these people when we were protesting about Arlington Marsh, or when the Bayonne Bridge was wrecking people's lives, or when we were trying to get the radioactive site cleaned up?" Thurman asked. "Did they ever come to one of our meetings? Do they even know what environmental justice is?"

In 2014, the People's Climate March in New York City drew 310,000 participants. Indigenous and environmental justice groups (including NSWC, WEACT, and UPROSE) marched at the front of the procession, signifying that they were the populations most vulnerable to climate change. Yet, in the months and years that followed, this enormous outpouring of enthusiasm never carried over into greater support for New York City's localized environmental justice battles. For all their pro-environmental intentions to recycle, to ban plastic straws, drive electric

Beryl Thurman, People's Climate March, 2014. Credit: Melissa Checker

cars, and to support offshore wind farms and climate agreements, environmentally concerned New Yorkers tended to march right past neighborhood struggles against environmental racism. This was especially true in an easily forgotten place like the North Shore. Taking another sip of her martini, Thurman shook her head and said, "I'm just going to keep my head down and keep doing what I've been doing."

As Thurman anticipated, the Trump presidency did little to alter NSWC's over-full agenda. In the years since Hurricane Sandy, state and municipal programs had already devoted millions of dollars to boosting resiliency on Staten Island's southern and eastern shores, including expanding the blue belt, building sand dunes, and funding an oyster reef to control storm surges in the New York bight. These measures deserve applause for creating much-needed protections for residents living in this hard-hit part of Staten Island. But, as Thurman has pointed out time and again, state and municipal resiliency plans bypassed the North Shore.

In 2019, the city opened Van Name Van Pelt Plaza, a small waterfront park on the northern edge of Mariner's Harbor, after eighteen years of effort by NSWC and other local groups. But this one-block sized park did little to balance out the new developments and dredging operations that were accelerating shoreline erosion, year by year.[1] In fact, regulatory agencies continued to permit development in its wetlands, marshes, and old growth forests. For instance, in the Fall of 2019 (around the time of the seventh anniversary of Hurricane Sandy), the New York Department of Environmental Conservation (DEC), gave the go-ahead to a new strip mall development that included approximately half an acre of the Graniteville Tree Swamp, a freshwater wetland and New York State Coastal Management area. In a post-Sandy era, paving over a wetland seemed unthinkable to NSWC and other local environmental groups. In this case, Graniteville served as a flood barrier that protected Mariner's Harbor and Arlington, two nearby neighborhoods populated predominantly by African Americans and nonwhite Hispanics.[2]

Indeed, the North Shore continued to be a flash point for the contradictions of the sustainable city. In the summer of 2019, the City Council rezoned twenty blocks of Stapleton and Tompkinsville for medium-density residential development. The rezoning was as contentious as it was curious.[3] Borough President James Oddo called the plan "reckless, detached, and weak-willed" for not including transportation and other infrastructure improvements.[4] Existing infrastructure was already in-

Erosion on the Kill Van Kull, 2017. Credit: Robert Cluesman

adequate; a population boom could be disastrous. According to Oddo, "this behavior shows a complete disregard for the interests of Staten Island." NSWC and other local groups also noted with alarm that the rezoning plan did not include any flood protection measures, even though the entire area was located on a flood plain.

Meanwhile, North Shore neighborhoods continued to contend with contamination. Port Richmond's Industrial Business Zone was in effect while only four of the twenty-one contaminated sites that Thurman identified in her 2007 booklet had been remediated. These included Mariner's Marsh Park (a former ironworks, then a shipyard), Heritage Park (a shipyard), the Sedutto's site (former Jewett White Lead Company), and Van Name Van Pelt Plaza (a former illegal dump site). Residents cheered the fact that three out of four of these remediated sites became parks; but they still worried about the long-term health implications of living amid so many contaminants. A New York State Department of Health report released in the Fall of 2019 showed that rates of thyroid cancer on Staten Island were approximately two-thirds higher than the rest of the city and the state.[5] In other words, the city's development priorities continued to oscillate between providing a home for heavy industrial facilities and extending the residential and commercial gentrification that had overtaken waterfronts in Brooklyn, Queens, and Manhattan.

Missing from these priorities were the needs of the low-income neighborhoods and communities of color living along the North Shore, who remained stuck in the paradox of environmental gentrification. Either they faced the risks of a heavily contaminated waterfront subject to ever-intensifying floods and storms, or they faced the displacement risks associated with upscale redevelopment. In a 2019 email about the Graniteville Tree Swamp, copied to local politicians and top officials at the US Environmental Protection Agency and the Army Corps of Engineers, Beryl Thurman summarized this double bind: "The cleaning up and the remediation of contaminated properties and waterways should not automatically equal the displacement of people of color and low-income people from their communities" (email dated October 30, 2019). Taking Thurman's premise as its starting point, this book has examined the promises, politics, and paradoxes of sustainable redevelopment in the twenty-first-century city.

## From Environmental Justice to Environmental Gentrification

Environmental justice activists advocate, first and foremost, for all people to live in healthier, cleaner environments. They call for wide-spread reductions of fossil fuel use and waste production and for an overall reduction in hazardous and polluting facilities. They also seek equal protection from environmental harms. To the extent that waste processing and producing facilities must exist, activists believe that they should be more equitably distributed throughout the city. Herein lies to the rub. In the preface to his groundbreaking book *Faces at the Bottom of the Well,* critical race scholar Derrick Bell writes, "Black people, then, are caught in a double bind. We are, as I have said, disadvantaged unless whites perceive that nondiscriminatory treatment for us will be a benefit for them."[6] For Bell and other critical race theorists and activists, those with privilege will not relinquish it unless it is in their own self-interest to do so. This proposition underlies Thurman's pointed question about why environmental justice causes received relatively little support from white liberals. Fighting for environmental justice means relinquishing a system that advantages white and affluent communities by enabling them to live in greener and cleaner environments.

This book has traced the ways such patterns of privilege were etched into the environmental geography of New York City. The term *environmental gentrification* serves as a framework for exploring how urban development unevenly distributes environmental benefits and burdens. To describe this process in detail, I have divided it into three subcategories—green, industrial, and brown.

### Green Gentrification

A growing body of scholarly literature focuses on green gentrification, documenting how the installation of new parks and other green spaces coincides with, and serves, high-end redevelopment.[7] To contribute to these studies, I developed an historic context for the role of urban green spaces in driving property values. I began by tracing the veneration of urban nature to the mid-1800s and the rise of industrialism. The more that the former brought noise, pollution, and hordes of people to the city, the more urban dwellers longed to escape to natural habitats. Nature was prized for being all things the industrial city wasn't—serene, pristine, and uplifting. It transcended the money-grubbing hustle and bustle of urban life. But urban green space was never neutral or value free. Paradoxically, the ideals associated with it gave it both material and symbolic value. Materially, parks, gardens, and other green spaces became commodities that elevated property values and rearranged urban space according to wealth and privilege. Symbolically, the creation of urban green space provided cover for land grabs that displaced marginalized communities. From Seneca Village, the community of freed slaves living on part of Central Park, to the low-income populations of the Lower East Side and Central Harlem, green was a guise for high-end redevelopment.

Despite the populist discourses surrounding urban parks and other green spaces, access to them has historically excluded low-income residents and communities of color. Economic downturns, however, provided an exception to this rule. During the Great Depression of the 1930s, and the economic recession of the 1970s, funding for parks declined significantly, and abandoned and vacant lots proliferated throughout the city's poorest areas. While city leaders turned their attention away from these spaces, low-income New Yorkers reclaimed them—as encampments, as sites of protest and of celebration, and as DIY gardens.

As the twentieth century wore on, real estate increasingly churned the city's economic engine. A constant quest to remake urban neighborhoods fueled this engine, and green spaces became an even more instrumental part of the project. After the post-9/11 recession, newly elected Mayor Michael Bloomberg's aggressive pro-growth policies sought to take advantage of new, global mechanisms for financing real estate development. Initially, Bloomberg's rezoning proposals met with community-based resistance, but the broad appeal of "sustainability" provided the perfect discursive cover for his quest to remake New York into a luxury city. Under the mantle of "greening," Bloomberg encouraged private investments in public spaces. This allowed real estate developers to shore up their ventures by privately funding parks, greenways, and plazas that would help attract affluent new residents. Moreover, such amenities raised property values, enabling developers to raise prices and offset their initial investments. Bloomberg also expanded private funding models for the construction and maintenance of public parks, making them less dependent on the waxing and waning of tax revenues. But just as Bloomberg's emphasis on private industry intensified the gap between the city's rich and poor, it also created a "green space gap," the vast difference between parks in non-gentrifying neighborhoods and those in areas that had undergone, or were ripe for, gentrification.[8]

## Industrial Gentrification

Green spaces tell only part of the environmental gentrification story. Historically, the apportionment of green space worked in conversation with the distribution of industrial space. Beginning in 1916, zoning regulations provided the grammar that structured these conversations. Residential zones protected property values by insulating wealthy areas from the encroachment of industries and immigrant workers. Unrestricted zones, meanwhile, reserved plenty of space in lower-priced areas for manufacturing businesses and blue-collar workers. For four decades, these arrangements attracted industrialists and fostered a thriving industrial economy in New York City. But in the late 1950s, advances in technology and transportation came smack up against the city's spatial limitations. New technologies, which enabled mass production, required up-to-date buildings and large spaces. In New York City, such amenities were cost prohibitive. Taking advantage of new truck routes and more efficient trucking technologies, some manufacturers left for the suburbs. Even so, New York continued to house a number of smaller, niche industries that needed to remain in close proximity to their customer bases.

But the city's elites had different ideas. Influential bankers like David Rockefeller envisioned a future that put New York City at the center of global finance. To achieve this vision, city leaders would have to make more room for finance-related industries and their employees. In 1961, zoning reforms provided a structure for this new spatial conversation. The new codes pushed manufacturing zones to the city's margins, reserving its central areas for commercial and office space as well as high-end residences. FIRE-related businesses began flowing into New York City, along with their employees and a new demand for upscale housing. Urban renewal projects met much of this demand initially, thanks to Robert Moses who cleared working-class and low-income neighborhoods to make way for massive apartment complexes for middle and upper-middle-class families. To house displaced residents, Moses built equally massive public housing projects in mixed manufacturing zones at the city's edges. Low-income communities and people of color thus continued to live either side-by-side with noxious facilities or in apartment complexes meant to buffer those facilities from wealthy neighborhoods.

By the late 1960s, however, the loss of tens of thousands of manufacturing businesses—and jobs—started to catch up with the city's economy. These losses, combined with white flight and large-scale public investments made during the 1960s, emptied the city's coffers. Larger economic trends such as stagflation and oil shocks catalyzed a global recession, and sent New York City into a serious fiscal crisis. Federal and state-mandated recovery efforts finally put banking and finance elites directly in charge. Doubling down on economic strategies that emphasized tourism as well as FIRE-related businesses, city leaders discovered new ways to clear low-income neighborhoods. Specifically, by shrinking public services in the name of austerity and devaluing an area's property values, they paved the way for real estate speculators. Redlining and other forms of housing discrimination prevented people of color from moving out of these divested neighborhoods. Furthermore, racial discrimination in employment, education, criminal justice, health care, and other urban institutions obstructed their opportunities to rise out of poverty. As a result, communities of color were stuck living in underserved, industrialized, or formerly industrialized neighborhoods.

Meanwhile, a scattering of municipally funded housing programs and incentives encouraged artists to locate in certain downtown neighborhoods in Manhattan and Brooklyn. Such incentives effectively outsourced the creation of arts and entertainment-related amenities, which in turn brought more consumers, speculators, and eventually new home buyers. Again, the Bloomberg administration accelerated this process. All told, Bloomberg rezoned one-third of the city, largely by replacing manufacturing zones with residential and commercial districts and by lifting height and density restrictions. After the 2008 recession, though, Bloomberg faced pushback for decimating the city's manufacturing sector. In response, he announced a sustainable reboot of the industrial economy, featuring ecologically friendly, small-scale, and high-tech manufacturing. These businesses resonated with consumer trends that favored local, small-batch production, and artisanship. Just as green spaces attracted upwardly mobile, eco-friendly gentrifiers, small-scale manufacturers became another urban amenity that boosted the appeal of gentrifying neighborhoods. But the new manufacturing was not the same as the old. Rather than reviving a lost employment sector, it offered high-priced items produced by a small number of nonunionized, low-wage workers.

## Brown Gentrification

If green spaces and clean industries facilitated gentrification, so too did the selective remediation and repurposing of toxic properties. Brown gentrification describes this third aspect of environmental gentrification. In this case, I focused on brownfield cleanup programs, which incentivize private developers to clean up and repurpose contaminated properties, especially in neighborhoods in need of revitalization. Initially, such programs appeared to respond directly to the needs of environmental justice communities. In particular, brownfield opportunity areas, which targeted areas containing multiple contaminated sites, promised to solve some of the most pernicious environmental problems facing communities of color. However, residents of these neighborhoods soon learned that because cleanups were predicated on private investment, they inevitably favored neighborhoods where property values were set to rise. Conversely, hitching toxic cleanup to real estate development left non-gentrifying neighborhoods with no mechanism for remediating contaminated properties. By outsourcing the cleanup of contaminated properties to private investors, brown gentrification thus subordinated public health to property values.

Environmental gentrification did not just distribute environmental improvements to gentrifying neighborhoods; it also concentrated environmental burdens in non-gentrifying neighborhoods. As neighborhoods upscaled, they excised heavy manufacturing businesses, waste treatment and transfer stations, sanitation garages, and recycling centers. These facilities then accumulated in poor and out-of-the way neighborhoods and communities of color that already hosted more than their share. The same infrastructure that sustained the sustainable city sacrificed the environmental health and well-being of its marginalized residents.

## Contradictory Politics and the Politics of Contradiction

Environmental gentrification, and the sustainable rubrics under which it operated put environmental justice activists in a no-win situation. If they fought for environmental improvements, they risked gentrification and displacement. But if they stopped fighting, they faced ever-increasing risks from contamination, worsened by the effects of climate change. This was not the only double bind that environmental justice activists had to confront.

In the late twentieth and early twenty-first centuries, community activism itself had become a kind of contradiction. Along with sustainability, public participation became a pervasive part of urban planning discourse. Neoliberal logics of individual responsibility and privatization valorized volunteerism and civic engagement while simultaneously justifying the defunding of public agencies. People in low-income communities, who were especially affected by the defunding of public services, lacked the economic resources and leisure time that would enable them to participate in civic organizations. Environmental justice organizations, for instance, competed with one another for scarce streams of funding that were shot through with contradictions. First, many grant applications required that environmental justice organizations have other sources of revenue in place. Second, applications asked for elaborate metrics and outcomes assessments that had little relevance to the actual work these organizations performed. Third, funders' priorities often centered on education and outreach, rather than concrete initiatives that would protect communities' health and safety. If funded, environmental justice groups found themselves saddled with onerous reporting requirements. Finally, after demanding endless hours of administrative work, funders rarely provided grants to cover administrative costs. In all, the funding cycle ensnared environmental justice organizations in a series of byzantine administrative traps that depleted their time and energy.

Public participation rituals were equally depleting and Kafkaesque. "Participation" typically consisted of commenting on predetermined development projects or helping to execute a predetermined agenda. Over the years, activists became skillful at inserting some of their own needs into these agendas; their success at doing so, however, was tenuous at best. Ultimately, public agencies retained control over a public process that was based on conciliation. If activists criticized this process, they risked being exiled "from the table." But taking part in it meant sacrificing their time and energy. Moreover, participation typically meant validating a project or policy that did not advance—or worse, ran counter to—their goals. Just as sustainability came to serve as a euphemism for profit-minded redevelopment, public participation became a ritualized, but ultimately empty performance of democracy and shared decision making.

Chapter 6 shines a light on new political formations and possible alternatives to sustainaphrenia. Looking beyond the animosities and vitriol of national, partisan politics, this chapter calls attention to everyday instances of bridge-building. I show how environmental activists on Staten Island formed ongoing partnerships across geographic, political, racial, ethnic, and economic divides. Similarly, flood survivors came together from throughout the US to create the Stop FEMA Now (SFN) movement. From red states, from blue states, and from every gradation in between, they offered one another sympathy, moral support, and strategies for collective action. Without erasing or glossing over their differences, activists managed to sidestep them and focus on their collective demands for more careful development and better protections from rising sea levels and intensifying storms.

In a larger sense, coastal residents' visceral experiences clarified a nonpartisan, issue-based politics of disaffection. Over the years, they watched their coastlines erode while elected officials, regulatory agencies, and financial institutions enacted policies and practices that favored profits over coastal protection. Developments proliferated and sprawled across the country, beckoning homebuyers with promises of insurance, equity, and nest eggs. Coastal homeowners invested in this promise, dutifully paying their mortgages, property taxes, and insurance premiums. But, when waves began surging over disappeared beaches and rivers started overflowing their banks almost annually, homeowners got stuck paying the price of overdevelopment. In fact, all those years, they had been investing in a system that created their precarity and then abandoned them to it.

Out of this bipartisan crisis of abandonment, flood survivors and other coastal residents formed coalitions and practical solutions. They lobbied for less costly, more effective, natural flood protections such as storm management easements, sand dunes, and other kinds of shoreline restoration, living breakwaters, and oyster reefs. And they called on Congress to reauthorize the National Flood Insurance Program, while raising premiums at a rate of 9 percent per year. For those homes still in harm's way, they advocated for managed retreats like the original Staten Island buy-out program, which compensated homeowners for their properties and returned the worst-flooded areas to wetlands. Importantly, this last solution eschewed short-sighted, technological fixes like sea walls, gates, and berms. It also turned profit-driven development on its head by sacrificing profit and revaluing land for its ecological worth.

## The End

On the 10:30 pm ferry back to Manhattan, I huddled against the chill and watched the Statue of Liberty pass by. It was mid-December 2017, and in the midst of a chaotic evening, I had forgotten my sweater at Beryl Thurman's house. Along with NSWC board members Warren MacKenzie and Diana Ramos, I had spent the evening helping Thurman finish packing up her house. The following morning, a moving company would arrive and take her belongings to Cleveland, Ohio. Thurman had sold "Villa Villekulla"[9] (my nickname for her gabled, gingerbread Victorian) and was moving back to Cleveland, Ohio, her native city, to look after her father, who was close to ninety. When I arrived, she and Ramos were moving boxes from one half-packed room to another. I had never seen Thurman in such disarray—she was one of the more prepared and organized people I knew. "What happened?" I asked, "I thought you'd been packing for the last two weeks!"

"I don't know," she responded in a small, bewildered voice. "I guess I just got lost in all the memories. . . ." Thurman decided she needed us to help her empty the attic. For the next hour, we carted file boxes down the rickety attic stairs to the second-floor landing, and then down the slightly less rickety stairs to the ground floor. The boxes contained two decades' worth of NSWC meeting agendas, notes, budgets, grant proposals, and flyers as well as pages and pages of information about environmental issues on Staten Island. Thurman decided to store most of them at the Staten Island Reformed Church, in hopes that they would be useful to whoever might step up to be the next President of NSWC. So far, however, her successor was not immediately apparent. She had started searching for someone to fill the position back in the summer, when she announced that she was putting her house on the market. But no one ever came forward. Perhaps it was because no one wanted to believe that Thurman would really leave. For a while, her departure seemed iffy. None of the families looking at the house seemed right, and she rejected several offers. Eventually, the real estate agent's gentle urging wore her down, and Thurman agreed to sell Villa Villekulla to a couple—a Latinx contractor and his Caribbean-born girlfriend—who seemed to love it as much as she did. She agreed to stay on as NSWC President in absentia, until we could find a suitable replacement.

Back on the ferry, as we glided across the dark waters of the Bay toward Manhattan terminal, I tried to imagine what came next. I remembered a recent conversation with Thurman about her position on a new state task force. Convened by the DEC, the task force's job was to help the DEC draft language for statewide environmental justice guidelines. The task force had only met a few times, but Thurman was not impressed. She and the other environmental justice activists on the committee spent most of their time rehashing the same issues they had been raising with the DEC for the past decade or so. As usual, Thurman cut to the chase. "It's like we are all permanently stuck on stupid," she said. "They know what the problems are—we've told them—they need to fix some shit."

In this book, I have detailed the costs of New York City's growth imperative. As this zero-sum game accrues benefits to some residents, the city's natural resources, and its low-income communities of color inevitably lose. To truly "fix some shit" we will have to think beyond quick fixes and win-win scenarios. In her classic analysis of systemic racism, political scientist Jennifer Hochschild writes, "The American garden is rooted in and nurtured by blacks' second-class status. To eradicate it, we must be willing and able to change the whole shape and ecology of the American landscape. Only then can the American creed blossom."[10] As Hochschild's metaphor implies, eradicating racism and environmental degradation go hand-in-hand. Just as it is a fallacy to think that these two forms of exploitation can be separated, or easily remedied, is a fallacy to believe that anyone is insulated from their costs. Every year more intense hurricanes and storms put more and more families at risk. Homeownership no longer shores up middle-class prosperity. As the tides rise around us, the stakes have never been higher or more urgent. Rather than being lulled by sustainaphrenia, I hope that readers will be inspired by the activists depicted in this book to build political solidarities based not on partisanship but on opposition to our shared environmental and economic precarity. Then, we can set to work assembling new sets of tools that can build a raft sturdy enough to carry us all.

In the last scene of a video about NSWC's boat tours, Dee Vandenburg stands on a dock in front of the Kill Van Kull. Hands in her pockets, feet planted against the wind coming off the Kill, Vandenburg addresses the camera. She remembers how she, Thurman and other activists spent years warning public officials that if they did not bolster Staten Island's coasts, one fierce storm could destroy thousands of lives. Turning her head to look out at the water, her blue eyes fill with tears. "We didn't want to be right," she says. "But we were right."

## ACKNOWLEDGMENTS

This project was many years in the making, and I cannot possibly name all those who extended themselves to help it come to fruition. With apologies to those I have inevitably left out, I would like to thank the following people.

Beryl Thurman, for her intelligence, wit, determination, and most of all her friendship; Dee Vandenburg, Victoria Gillen, Diana Ramos, Warren MacKenzie, Linda Eskenaz, and other environmental activists on Staten Island, for welcoming me and giving me the generous gift of their time, energy, and insights, not to mention all those rides to the ferry terminal.

Arthur Smith and Charles Utley, for introducing me to Peggy Shepard and Cecil Corbin Mark. And Cecil Corbin Mark himself, for sharing his scarce time and abundant knowledge, and for putting me in touch with Beryl Thurman.

Ann Neumann, editor and writer extraordinaire, for seeing both the trees and the forest, for her sharp and perceptive comments, for her cheerleading, and for her bountiful warmth and empathy. Truly, I could not have done it without her. I am also thankful for enduring friends who double as incisive editors: Laura Helper-Ferris's masterful comments improved a much earlier draft, and Maggie Fishman and James Garfield came through with vital editing acumen and compassion. Stephen Steinberg, my colleague, mentor, and friend, read my over-long proposal, offered endless amounts of encouragement, and, most of all, came up with "sustainaphrenia," one afternoon over coffee.

Many, many thanks to Ilene Kalish at NYU Press, for her willingness to take me on again, for her keen insights and guidance, and for graciously keeping the faith. I am also grateful to Sonia Tsuruoka and Martin Coleman at NYU Press for cheerfully shepherding the manuscript through production and to the anonymous reviewers for their constructive feedback. I owe much to Miriam Greenberg who offered game-changing comments early on, and to Tom Angotti whose attentive and discerning advice strengthened the manuscript considerably.

I am eternally grateful to Marty Kirchner for being willing and able to face the citations, as well as Jah Sayers and Rosalie Ryan. Ruchika Lodha designed a unique and exquisite map, and Troy Simpson provided mapping and graphic expertise as well as patience and precision. And I thank Robert Cluesman for taking many well-composed photos of seemingly random scenes.

I am also thankful for the largesse and support of many colleagues. I especially thank Jeff Maskovsky for supplemental deadline enforcement and for many stimulating conversations that helped me germinate and refine the ideas in this book. Alice Sardell provided sage advice as well as unlimited empathy and reassurance, and Setha Low and Natalie Bump Vena graciously buoyed me at some very low points.

To say that the abiding encouragement of my friends made this project possible is an understatement. In particular, I extend profound appreciation to Valerie Stivers for stern deadline enforcement, and extraordinary friendship. Julie Brandt, Tony Conniff, Stephanie Foxman, Sharon Freedman, Jane Herring, Jeff Howe, Greg Milner, Jennifer Patico, Julie Reed, Maggie Rickard, Alyssa Senzel, and assorted others provided extra commiseration, counseling, spirit-lifting, distractions, and/or chocolate.

The lasting support of my family is invaluable—Alison, Byron, Emily, Lily, and Rosie McWilliams patiently put up with too many truncated visits and tardy birthday cards and gifts to count. Last but never least, I am ever so grateful to my sister, Jill Checker. From riding along on my first visit to the North Shore to helping me select final images, her support and faith in me mean more than I can ever express.

The research for this book was funded in part by the Professional Staff Congress-City University of New York *(PSC-CUNY) Research Award* Program.

# NOTES

## INTRODUCTION

1 Johnston 2012.
2 US Census Bureau 2018.
3 Environmental Justice Showcase Communities by Region n.d.
4 Mikati and Benson 2018.
5 Di et al. 2017.
6 See Checker 2005.
7 As quoted in Rizzi 2012.
8 Rizzi 2015; Jorgensen 2013.
9 Sammon 2019.
10 Bateson et al. 1956.
11 Bateson 1972.
12 Singh 2008.
13 The Real Estate Group 2010.
14 McGeehan 2010.
15 Oh 2014.
16 Mahawaral 2017.
17 Sobel 2014.
18 See Gould and Lewis 2016; Isenhour et al. 2015; Curran and Hamilton 2017.
19 Savitch-Lew 2017.
20 Routhier 2019. In addition, the mayor's standing with housing advocates dropped after reports revealed that New York City Housing Authority (NYCHA) officials falsely certified lead paint inspections and conspired to hide poor conditions from federal inspectors. Making matters worse, de Blasio publicly declared that only four children had tested positive for elevated lead levels, though a subsequent investigation revealed that he had concealed the real number, which was 202 (Spivack 2019a).
21 Exceptions were included for houses of worship, buildings with any rent-regulated units, income-restricted co-ops, public housing, and city-owned buildings.
22 Muoio and Giambusso 2019.
23 Spivack 2019a.
24 Muio and Giambusso 2019.
25 One of these bills capped the amount of waste handled by private waste-transfer stations in the three areas of the Bronx, Brooklyn, and Queens that had the highest concentration of permitted facilities. The other bill designated specific zones for hauling waste and limited the number of companies that could operate in each zone.
26 Small 2017.

27 Acitelli 2018.
28 "Mother" Clara McBride Hale was a widow raising three children in Harlem in the late 1940s. She began using her home for a daycare center and eventually began taking in drug-addicted infants, free of charge (Lambert 1992).
29 In 2010, the roof of the George Cromwell Recreation Center collapsed, pushing half of the structure into New York Bay. Two years later, Hurricane Sandy destroyed the rest of the building. The Cromwell Center had been built in 1934 atop a North Shore pier. Over the years, worms ate away at the pier and the roof deteriorated. In 2014, the City demolished the remaining structure. In 2019, it allocated funds to rebuild it, as part of the rezoning of the Bay Street Corridor (Kashiwagi 2019).

## 1. SUSTAINABILITY AND THE CITY

1 Not her real name.
2 If an MLM's salespeople make more money from recruitment than they do from selling products, the MLM is considered a pyramid scheme and is therefore illegal. See Federal Trade Commission 2019.
3 Federal Trade Commission 2019.
4 Moritz-Rabson 2018.
5 State of New Jersey Commission of Investigation 2017. In 2015, Italian authorities tracked the biggest European illegal dumpsite in history to the Camorra crime family which had been burning and burying all kinds of hazardous debris since the 1990s, causing cancer rates up to eighty times higher than average (Livesay 2015).
6 Montpetit 2008.
7 See "Mafia Milks Italy's Green Energy Boom" 2015.
8 Marx and Engels [1848] 1947.
9 Harvey 2011, 50.
10 Foster 2000.
11 Marx 1992, 637–38.
12 Foster 2000.
13 Marx 1992, 637–38.
14 Szasz 2009.
15 See Nielson Newswire Newsletter 2018.
16 Lacan 1981, see also Lacan 1997.
17 Deleuze and Guattari 1987.
18 Marx and Engels [1848] 1947.
19 Harvey 2014, 118.
20 Steinberg 2015.
21 Campbell-Dollaghan 2013.
22 Steinberg 2015, xxi.
23 Gandy 2002.
24 Page 1999.
25 McDowell 1984. See Chapter 3 for a more detailed discussion of Harlem during the Great Depression.
26 Honey 1999.
27 There are many good books on this topic. See, for instance, Brodkin 1998; Jackson 1985.

28   Kotz, McDonough, and Reich 1994.
29   Tabb 1982, 22.
30   Tabb 1982, 25.
31   See Harvey 2007.
32   Although Ford never actually said those words, his speech led to the famous Daily News headline, "Ford to City: Drop Dead." The president would notably later approve short-term support for New York City (Nussbaum 2015).
33   Reichl 1999.
34   Greenberg and Aronczyk 2008, 141.
35   Flood 2010.
36   See Wallace 1988, Suarez 1999.
37   Glass 1964, xviii.
38   Soffer 2012.
39   Smith 1987, 462.
40   Smith 1982, 151.
41   Gotham and Greenberg 2014.
42   Mayer 2017; see also Harvey 1973, Hackworth 2002, Smith 1996.
43   Redclift 2005.
44   Escobar 2001.
45   Portney 2013.
46   Brundtland Commission 1987, 8.
47   Escobar 2001; Harvey 2005; Redclift 2005.
48   See Mol and Sonnenfeld 2000.
49   Swyngedouw 2007, 26.
50   Portney 2013.
51   Guggenheim 2006.
52   Moser and Kleinhückelkotten 2018.
53   Gore 2015.
54   See Kanter 2007, Monbiot 2007.
55   The magazine *Good Housekeeping* sponsored this renovation as part of its "green house" program, which sponsored one LEED-certified, green renovation per year (Allen 2008).
56   Greenberg 2015, 119.
57   Greenberg 2015.
58   Greenberg 2010, 2015.
59   Angotti 2008.
60   Greenberg 2015.
61   The City of New York 2007.
62   See The City of New York 2007.
63   Greenberg 2015, 122.
64   As quoted in Greenberg 2015, 122.
65   Greenberg 2015, 114.
66   Cventure LLC et al. 2017.
67   Feng et al. 2015.
68   Plumer 2019.
69   Hausfather 2018.
70   Furman Center 2009.

71 Neuman 2019.
72 Tokmakova 2017.
73 Knafo and Shapiro 2012.
74 ICLEI 2010, 19–20.
75 Shepard, Tyree, and Corbin-Mark 2008.
76 Angotti 2008.
77 ICLEI 2010.
78 Pretty 1995, 1252.
79 ICLEI 2010, 45.
80 See Swyngedouw 2006.
81 Maskovsky 2006; Brash 2011.
82 Redclift 2005, 81.
83 Harvey 2017.
84 As quoted in McNulty 2008, 15; see also Buscher and Igoe 2013; Szasz 2009.
85 See Fiennes 2013; Buscher and Igoe 2013.
86 As quoted in Fiennes 2013.
87 As quoted in Fiennes 2013.
88 Environmental justice activists also pushed mainstream environmental movements (such as the Sierra Club, the Nature Conservancy, and the Audubon society) to address social justice and equity as well as urban environmental issues, and to diversify their staffs (see Checker 2005).
89 Shepard, Tyree, and Corbin-Mark 2008.
90 Bullard et al. 2007.
91 Tessum et al. 2019.
92 Newkirk 2018.
93 Sze 2019, 7.
94 Pulido 2018; see also de Lara 2018; Pulido and de Lara 2018.
95 Essoka 2010; Gamper-Rabindram and Timmons 2013.
96 NEJAC 2006, iii.
97 The following citations represent just a sampling of the burgeoning body of scholarly literature on this topic.
98 Gould and Lewis 2016, 36.
99 Gould and Lewis 2016; McClintock 2018.
100 Dooling 2009; Goldfischer 2019.
101 Carman 2015.
102 Checker 2011a; Lindner and Rosa 2017; Pearsall 2012.
103 Farr, Brondo, and Anglin 2015; Lugo 2015.
104 Baker and Lee 2019.
105 Anguelovski 2015.
106 Alkon and Agyeman 2011.
107 Curran and Hamilton 2017; Miller 2017; Pearsall 2013; Gould and Lewis 2016.
108 Curran and Hamilton 2017.
109 Zavetovski and Ageyman 2014.
110 Curran and Hamilton 2012, 2017; Hagerman 2007; Lubitow and Miller 2013; Pearsall and Anguelovski 2016; Pearsall 2012.
111 See also Curran and Hamilton 2017.
112 Swyngedouw 2006.

113 Wolin 2008.
114 See Deleuze and Guattari 1987.
115 Deleuze and Guattari 1987, 246.

2. WIPED OUT BY THE GREEN WAVE
  1 Adams 2016.
  2 Beveridge 2008; see also Calmes 2016; Plitt 2015; Roberts 2010.
  3 Szekely 2018.
  4 Whitman 1920, 2:11.
  5 Rauch 1869, 83.
  6 Crompton 2005.
  7 As quoted in Doherty and Waldheim 2015.
  8 As quoted by Rosenzweig and Blackmar 1998, 31.
  9 Similarly, in 1903 the city opened Seward Park in the Lower East Side, a project for which Jacob Riis fought long and hard. To build the park, however, the city razed three blocks of tenements and displaced almost 3,000 residents, never to rehouse them (Jackson 1995).
 10 Riker 1881 as quoted in Sanderson 2009, 256.
 11 Crompton 2001.
 12 Crompton 2005, 226.
 13 Rosenzweig and Blackmar 1998.
 14 Purdy 2015. These exclusions persisted well into the 1960s and their legacy in shaping the mainstream environmental movement and its fraught relationship with racial and social justice is well documented (Checker 2005; see also Gottlieb 2005, Cronon 1996; Darnovsky 1992).
 15 Martin 1997.
 16 Sze 2006.
 17 Johnson 1925.
 18 Osofsky 1963, 12.
 19 Beveridge 2008.
 20 Osofsky 1963.
 21 See Locke 1925.
 22 Gates 1997.
 23 Weldon Johnson 1925, 1.
 24 Gates 1997, 11.
 25 Hughes 1926.
 26 James Baldwin said "Urban renewal means negro removal" in an interview with Kenneth Clark in 1963 (see "Conversation with James Baldwin, A; James Baldwin Interview" 1963).
 27 Caro 1975.
 28 Campanella 2017.
 29 Angotti and Morse 2016.
 30 Schomburg Center for Research, Dodson, and Diouf 2005.
 31 Ellison 1964.
 32 Schweber 2011.
 33 WEACT n.d.
 34 Sze 2006; see also Angotti 2009.

35 Naison 2004.
36 Piven and Cloward 1972.
37 Grandmaster Flash and the Furious Five 1982.
38 Ferretti 1977.
39 Cronin 2018.
40 Bradley 2009.
41 As quoted in Gold 2014, 179.
42 Gold 2014.
43 Williams 2008.
44 Cotter 2015.
45 Cotter 2015.
46 Lee 2009.
47 Cotter 2015.
48 Horvath 2010.
49 Horvath 2010.
50 This chapter follows the historic definition of the "Lower East Side" as the area bounded east to west by the East River and Broadway (respectively), and north to south by the Manhattan Bridge and 14th Street (respectively). It included neighborhoods that are now known separately, including the East Village, Alphabet City, Chinatown, Bowery, Little Italy, and Nolita.
51 Ottman, et al. 2012; see also Eizenberg 2013.
52 This story is repeated in a number of websites, including greenguerrillas.org; ecotippingpoints.org and nycgovparks.gov.
53 Brooks and Marten 2015.
54 "About" n.d.
55 Angotti 2008.
56 "About" n.d.
57 Brooks and Marten 2015.
58 "About" n.d.
59 Chaban 2012.
60 See Checker 2005.
61 Smith 1987.
62 Ferguson 1999.
63 Smith 1987.
64 Gibson 2015.
65 Ferguson 1999.
66 As quoted in Shepard and Smithsimon 2011, 158.
67 Waldman 1998.
68 "Where We Stand and How We Got Here" n.d.
69 "Where We Stand and How We Got Here" n.d.
70 Angotti 2008.
71 Voicu and Been 2008, 277.
72 Maantay and Maroko 2018.
73 McClintock 2018.
74 Zukin 2010, 197.
75 Newman and Wylie 2006.
76 As quoted in Smith 1996, 161–62.

77 Taylor 2007.
78 Smith 1996.
79 Taylor 2002; see also Freeman 2006, Jackson 2003, Zukin 2010.
80 Zukin 2010; Zukin et al. 2009.
81 Maurrasse and Bliss 2006.
82 Smith 1996, 161.
83 Shepard 2010.
84 WEACT n.d.
85 Bullard et al. 2007, x.
86 The literature on this movement is extensive. For some overviews, see Bullard 2000; Bryant 1995; Checker 2005; Novotny 1995.
87 Checker 2008.
88 Make the Road New York n.d.
89 Shepard 2007.
90 Title VI states: "No person in the United States shall, on the ground of race, color, or national origin, be excluded from participation in, be denied the benefits of, or be subjected to discrimination under any program or activity receiving Federal financial assistance."
91 "Areas of Work" n.d.
92 Make the Road New York n.d.; Shepard 2007.
93 See "West Harlem Piers Park" n.d.
94 Williams 2008.
95 Furman Center 2011.
96 The Central Park Conservancy was predated by the Southern Queens Park Association, founded in the late 1970s to fund the operation of Roy Wilkins Park (Vanderkam 2011).
97 Bowen and Stepan 2014.
98 O'Neill, Chelius, and Albonesi 2015, 10.
99 David and Hock 2002; see also Lindner and Rosa 2017.
100 Burden 2014.
101 Burden 2011.
102 Brake et al. 2012.
103 The "Privately Owned Public Spaces" or POPS program, which allowed real estate developers in midtown and other particularly dense parts of the city to increase floor areas or receive special waivers in exchange for creating public plazas and atriums (Schwartz 2001). Critics argue that the publicness of such spaces is questionable. Often set back from the street and hidden from public view, security guards typically patrolled these spaces, discouraging certain members of the public from using them (Angotti 2009). A 2017 audit by Comptroller Scott Stringer found that over half of the city's POPS were out of compliance with city requirements for public access and maintenance (Landa 2017).
104 Barbanel 2016.
105 See Lindner and Rosa 2017.
106 Rosenberg 2017.
107 Gould and Lewis 2016; see also Low, Taplin, and Scheld 2005; Zukin 1993.
108 Gould and Lewis 2012.
109 Vanderkam 2011.

110  Foderaro 2015.
111  Foderaro 2015.
112  The blog's author took it down in 2008; no link exists.
113  Williams 2008.
114  Williams 2008.
115  NYC Parks n.d.
116  Moorehouse 2006; emphasis mine. Barbecues continued to be a fiercely contested issue. In 2011, a shooting occurred one evening in Morningside Park. Subsequent discussions included heated debates over barbecue rules (see Leland 2011).
117  "Morningside Park" n.d.
118  Leland 2011.
119  NYPL 2019.
120  Lunke as quoted in Harlem CDC 2010, 2–3.
121  Harlem CDC 2010, 2.

3. "DIRTY DEEDS DONE DIRT CHEAP"

1  US Census Bureau 2010.
2  Cannon 2008; see also Vidal 2009.
3  Papas 2007.
4  Lam 2013.
5  Snug Harbor 2019.
6  Rocco 2004.
7  Bayles 2010; NSWC 2007.
8  Kramer and Flanagan 2012.
9  Curbed 2013.
10  Chappell 1996, 91–92.
11  Page 1999, 90.
12  Fischel 2001, 7.
13  Levinson 2006.
14  Dolkart, Brazee, and Caratzas 2007, 15.
15  NYC Planning Commission, Division of Master Plan 1940, 5, as quoted in Maantay 2002, 70.
16  Freeman 2001.
17  Orleck 1995, 23–30.
18  Sze 2006, 45.
19  As quoted in Fischler 1998, 185n29; see also Sze 2006, 43.
20  Freeman 2001.
21  Levinson 2006.
22  Freeman 2001, 20.
23  Downtown Lower Manhattan Association n.d.
24  Levinson 2006.
25  Freeman 2001.
26  Freeman 2001, 163.
27  Fitch 1993, 12–13.
28  NYC Department of City Planning 2019.
29  Maantay 2002; see also Zukin 1993.
30  Curran and Hanson 2005; Marcus 1991.

31  Zukin 1989.
32  Zukin 1989, 104.
33  In 1982, New York State established the New York City Loft Board to regulate the legal conversion of certain lofts in the city from commercial/manufacturing use to residential use. The Board effectively slowed conversions in SoHo and elsewhere (Angotti and Morse 2016). See also Curran and Hanson 2005; Curran 2004; Harvey 1985; Marcuse 1986; Buck et al. 2005.
34  Zukin 1989, 104.
35  Levinson 2006, 99.
36  Sussna 1970, 481.
37  Sussna 1970, 485.
38  NSWC 2007.
39  This quote is taken from the New York City Department of City Planning Hearing archives, March 1960. See City Planning Commission 1960.
40  As quoted in City Planning Commission 1960.
41  See Jackson 1985; Massey and Denton 1993.
42  Kramer and Flanagan 2012.
43  Beauregard 2001.
44  See Wallace 1988, Suarez 1999.
45  Maantay 2000, 2002.
46  Angotti 2008.
47  Rabin 1989, 101.
48  Kramer and Flanagan 2012.
49  See Mehrotra et al. 2018.
50  Zoellner 2010.
51  Kelly 2009.
52  NSWC 2007.
53  Feiden 2003.
54  Wall Street Journal 2013.
55  Checker 2009; see also Metropolitan Waterfront Alliance 2010.
56  Checker 2009.
57  As quoted in David 2012, 138.
58  Rosenberg 2014.
59  Mistry and Byron 2011, 20.
60  NYCEDC 2019.
61  Skyler and Falk 2005.
62  NYC.gov 2006.
63  Mandel 2013, 2. This report was commissioned in advance of the Second Annual Bloomberg Technology Summit, held in New York City in September 2013.
64  See "Business Programs" n.d.
65  NYCEDC 2013a.
66  Langholtz 2011.
67  Giller 2015.
68  Malewitz 2014.
69  Voight 2014.
70  Ellin 2014.
71  See Szasz 2009.

72 Blain 2015.
73 Humphery 2013, 203.
74 Hatch 2014, 5.
75 Florida 2004.
76 Brooklyn Navy Yard Development Corporation 2019.
77 Brooklyn Navy Yard Development Corporation 2019.
78 Abruzzese 2013; Gould and Lewis 2016.
79 Leon 2015.
80 Hughes 2015.
81 As quoted in Hughes 2015.
82 As quoted in the IAP press release (Adafruit 2015).
83 Adafruit 2015.
84 NYCEDC 2013b.
85 New York City Independent Budget Office 2014, 3.
86 Bureau of Labor Statistics 2014, Table 3.
87 Constable 2015.
88 Katz and Krueger 2016.
89 Bureau of Labor Statistics 2018.
90 Coalition for Clean and Safe Ports n.d.
91 Alliance for a Greater New York 2012.
92 Harsanyi 2015.
93 Even Sunset Park's industrial waterfront was being redeveloped to feature light industrial facilities such as a film studio, a green recycling plant, and artisan spaces.
94 See Hum 2015, 2016.
95 Hum 2016.
96 Jacobs 2017.
97 This quote is taken from an unpublished response to an editorial in *The Architect's Newspaper* (Iovine 2012). The response was written and circulated (via email) by Victoria Gillen the day after the editorial's publication.

4. BROWN SPOTS ON THE APPLE
1 US Census Bureau 2010, 2014, 2015.
2 US Census Bureau 2014, 2015.
3 Make the Road New York n.d.
4 Angotti 2013.
5 Walsh 2006.
6 Sachs 1988, 69.
7 US Census Bureau 2010.
8 US Census Bureau 2010.
9 Spencer 2010.
10 Reddy 2010.
11 Randall 2014.
12 See for instance, Hunter College Urban Planning and Policy 2017.
13 This is not her real name. I am also choosing not to name the nonprofit organization (NPO) she is referring to. It should be noted that most of the North Shore activists I worked with criticized the administrators of this NPO for receiving exorbitant salaries. I could not verify this claim.

14  Russel 2018.
15  New York City Department of Investigation 2015.
16  Spivack 2019a.
17  Honan 2019.
18  "Brownfield Cleanup Program" n.d.
19  "Brownfield Cleanup Program" n.d.
20  New Partners for Community Revitalization 2012.
21  Environmental Advocates 2011.
22  Environmental Advocates 2013.
23  That is, no more than half of the property could be currently in use, for industrial or commercial purposes, *plus* the building had to be in tax arrears or condemned.
24  Office of the Mayor 2011.
25  "Brownfield Cleanup Program" n.d.
26  "Brownfield Cleanup Program" n.d.
27  "BIG Grants" n.d.
28  See Checker 2011b.
29  Mitchell 2010.
30  "NYC Brownfield Cleanup Program" n.d.
31  Furman Center 2018.
32  Newtown Creek Alliance 2012.
33  Furman Center 2018.
34  NEJAC 2006.
35  See Banzhaf and McCormick 2012; Essoka 2010; Gamper-Rabindran and Timmins 2013; Pearsall 2013.
36  In 2015, the de Blasio administration called attention to the role of self-storage facilities in real estate speculation and announced a campaign to rezone them for commercial uses. Two years later, the City Council voted to ban the facilities from Industrial Business Zones. "Mayor de Blasio and Speaker Mark-Viverito Unveil Action Plan to Grow 21st Century Industrial and Manufacturing Jobs in NYC" 2015.
37  "Rules of the City of New York (R.C.U.N.Y.)" n.d.
38  Rotkin-Ellman et al. 2010; Zahran et al. 2010.
39  Valhouli 2012.
40  "Rules of the City of New York (R.C.U.N.Y.)" n.d.
41  I was not privy to those conversations.
42  Eventually, at Thurman and Gillen's request, the OER revised this statement to acknowledge that it received two sets of public comments.
43  Sinha 2011; see also Downs et al. 2009.
44  Checker 2012.
45  Gray 1996.
46  I have used pseudonyms unless requested otherwise by the person quoted.
47  NYCEDC 2011, 6.
48  I never verified whether anything illegal was occurring on these properties.
49  "About DCP" n.d.
50  Mooney 2010.
51  NYC Department of City Planning 2013.
52  Terry 2003.

228 | NOTES

53  Miller 2015.
54  Navarro 2009; see also Pearsall 2013.
55  Navarro 2009.
56  Navarro 2009.
57  Kaysen 2014.
58  "Gowanus Home Prices and Values" n.d.
59  Albrecht 2016.
60  Goldenberg 2016.
61  Albrecht 2016.
62  As quoted in Dobkin 2013.
63  Berger 2013.
64  Musumeci 2013.
65  Rizzi 2013.
66  Clarke 2005, 453; see also Wolin 2008.

5. "DEMOCRACY HAS LEFT THE BUILDING"

1  Checker 2009.
2  In 2019, one of Flag's owners was arrested for covering up a murder. See Hicks, McCarthy, and Jaeger 2019.
3  See Checker 2005.
4  Wolin 2008, 47.
5  Wolin 2008, 65.
6  Swyngendouw 2007; Zizek 1999.
7  Gregory and Howard 2009.
8  Jonker and Meehan 2014.
9  Rodriguez 2016.
10  Wolch 1990, 15.
11  Lemann 1997.
12  Wolch 1990.
13  Wolch 1990.
14  Rodriguez 2016.
15  See Rodriquez 2016.
16  Rodriguez 2016; emphasis in original.
17  Wolch 1990, 206–207.
18  Carmel and Harlock 2008.
19  See Perkins 2009; Smith 2017; Schuller and Farmer 2012.
20  Eugene Chan, as quoted in Stannard-Stockton 2007.
21  Knowlton 2019.
22  See Checker 2005.
23  From DEC Environmental Justice Small Grants Request for Proposals, on file with author.
24  Steinberg 2015.
25  Cruikshank 1999.
26  Perkins 2009.
27  Putnam 2001.
28  Rose 1999, 267; see also Barratt 2014, 266.
29  Pateman 1970; Cruikshank 1999.

30 Acland 2007.
31 Brown 2006, 705; see also Brown 2015.
32 Maskovsky 2006.
33 See Foucault 2003.
34 See Clarke 2013, 216; Foucault 1982, 221; Roy 2008.
35 Barratt 2014, 264; Clarke 2013.
36 Brash 2011; May 2007; see also Clarke 2013, 216.
37 May 2007.
38 Email, April 21, 2016.
39 Tilove 2008.
40 "Climate Showcase Communities Program" n.d.
41 This term refers to particles suspended in air that can be inhaled and that contain organic and inorganic matter including dust, pollen, soot, or smoke (www.epa. gov).
42 I have used pseudonyms unless requested otherwise by the person quoted.
43 Thurman declined to join the coalition as she believed it would distract her from her work with NSWC.
44 Email, October 4, 2016.
45 See Brown 2006; Dean 1999; Rocheleau 2004.
46 Raddon and Harrison 2015, 136; Krause et al. 2008.
47 In general, service learning combines community service and academic learning.
48 American Academy of Arts and Sciences 2015.
49 Gross 2013.
50 Krause et al. 2008; Slaughter and Leslie 1999.
51 Giroux and Giroux 2004; Krause et al. 2008; Slaughter and Rhoades 2004.
52 Schrecker 2010.
53 Raddon and Harrison 2015, 142.
54 Slaughter and Rhoades 2000; see also Kliewer 2013.
55 See Checker 2014 for a more detailed account of these activities.
56 Fraser 2000, 111.

6. "THIS CROSSES PARTY LINES ALL OVER THE PLACE"
1 I have used pseudonyms unless requested otherwise by the person quoted.
2 Residents whose homes were damaged during Irene claimed that they never received insurance reimbursements or Federal Emergency Management Agency (FEMA) recovery money.
3 Murphy 2017.
4 Bredderman 2018.
5 Barron 2018.
6 Tiner 2000.
7 NYC Mayor's Office of Long-Term Planning and Sustainability 2012.
8 Popik 2005.
9 Steinberg 2015.
10 Stamp 2012.
11 GreenBiz Editors 2001.
12 Sussna 1970.
13 Schwarz 2013.

14  Marton 2015. A protracted legal battle to change the Charter and adopt a structure that was more proportional in relation to the population wound up in the US Supreme Court. The Court ruled that affording boroughs of disparate size equal representation on the board violated the one person, one vote standard.
15  Kramer and Flanagan 2012.
16  Corner as quoted in Rogers 2016, 174–75.
17  "The Staten Island Bluebelt" n.d.
18  Rudolf et al. 2012.
19  Benimoff 2010.
20  Toure 2016.
21  Office of the NYC Comptroller Scott M. Stringer 2015.
22  They declined to provide me with their last names.
23  "Programs" n.d.
24  McGhee 2017.
25  McGhee 2017.
26  Knowles and Kunreuther 2014.
27  Collier 2014, 277.
28  Knowles and Kunreuther 2014.
29  There is a vast literature on suburbanization in the US. For examples, see Jackson 1985; Ross and Levine 2011.
30  Knowles and Kunreuther 2014, 335.
31  Kingfisher and Maskovsky 2008.
32  Knowles and Kunreuther 2014.
33  Collier 2014.
34  Collier 2014.
35  Hanscom 2014.
36  Collier 2014, 287; see also Clarke 2005.
37  Clarke 2005; Foucault 1979; Kingfisher and Maskovsky 2008; Harvey 2006, 2007.
38  US Government Accountability Office 2004.
39  Much of the information in this section can be found in Checker 2016.
40  Interestingly, Bloomberg's call contradicted both his free market ideologies, and his emphasis on the dangers of climate change. Bloomberg's successor, Bill de Blasio filed for an official appeal of the newly drawn FEMA flood maps that would refund the flood plain by approximately 2.5 feet (Chayes 2015).
41  Pinter 2013.
42  Pinter 2013. It is interesting to note that these beliefs directly contradict the "right to return" campaigns, popular among liberals, that were developed in the wake of Hurricane Katrina.
43  I consider Kasimos to be a public figure; I have therefore not changed his name. All of his direct quotations are taken from publicly available media sources. The details in this paragraph can be found in Dawsey 2014.
44  Di Ionno 2013.
45  Checker 2016.
46  I have chosen to keep the names of commenters on SFN's Facebook page confidential.
47  United Press International 2013.
48  See Alfonsi 2015.

49 See "Business of Disaster" 2016; "Frontline (PBS) and NPR Investigate Superstorm Sandy Recovery Efforts" n.d.
50 Federal Insurance and Mitigation Agency 2017.
51 Zoppo 2018.
52 Facebook post, January 16, 2017.
53 I have used pseudonyms unless requested otherwise by the person quoted.
54 Kramer and Flanagan 2012, 12–13.
55 See Williamson 2017.
56 Kramer and Flanagan 2012, 6.
57 Barron 2018.
58 Fiorina 2018.
59 Jones 2019.
60 Abramowitz and Webster 2018.
61 Fiorina 2018.
62 Klar and Krupnikov 2016.
63 Fiorina 2018.
64 Brown 2015, 210.

CONCLUSION

1 A few miles east of Graniteville, environmental activists contested a 225-unit residential development in a 15-acre old-growth forest. Along with a series of hills formed by glaciers during the last ice age, the forest comprised the grounds of an historic Jesuit retreat center known as Mt. Manresa. In 2013, the Jesuits sold Mt. Manresa to a local developer who began construction by destroying approximately one hundred native trees believed to be between 300 and 400 years old. The tree slaughter infuriated Staten Island residents, including Borough President James Oddo. Charged with naming the development's streets, Oddo chose Cupidity Drive, Fourberie Lane, and Avidity Place, which in Latin mean inordinate desire for wealth, trickery and deception, and greed, respectively.
2 The DEC determined that the developer's plan for mitigating damage to the wetland was sufficient. Besides, the DEC pointed out, its environmental justice policies only applied to polluting facilities, not wetland development.
3 Urby, a nearby luxury development that opened in 2016, was slow to fill, and then faced a number of issues, including a lawsuit charging its management company with racism, and a stabbing on the premises.
4 As quoted in Spivack 2019b.
5 At a public meeting, representatives from the Health Department suggested that these rates had to do with better diagnostic tools. Unsurprisingly, NSWC and other local activists refused to accept that rationale.
6 Bell 1992, 9.
7 See Gould and Lewis 2016; Curran and Hamilton 2017.
8 Casey et al. 2017.
9 Villa Villekula was the home of Pippi Longstocking, a fictional character created in the 1940s by Swedish author Astrid Lindgren for a series of children's books.
10 Hochschild 1984, 10.

# WORKS CITED

"Programs." n.d. Governor's Office of Storm Recovery, New York State, www.stormre-covery.ny.gov.

"About DCP." n.d. NYC Planning. Accessed March 22, 2020. www1.nyc.gov.

"About." n.d. GreenThumb. Accessed March 22, 2020. www.greenthumb.nycgovparks.org.

Abramowitz, Alan I. and Steven W. Webster. 2018. "Negative Partisanship: Why Americans Dislike Parties but Behave Like Rabid Partisans." *Political Psychology* 39: 119–35.

Abruzzese, Rob. 2013. "High-Tech Manufacturing Hub Opens at Navy Yard." *Brooklyn Daily Eagle*, May 10, 2013. www.brooklyneagle.com.

Acitelli, Tom. 2018. "On the Rise in Central Harlem." *Crain's New York Business*. July 25, 2018. www.crainsnewyork.com.

Acland, Charles R. 2007. *Residual Media*. Minneapolis: University of Minnesota Press.

Adafruit. 2015. "Mayor De Blasio and Speaker Mark-Viverito Unveil Action Plan to Grow 21st Century Industrial and Manufacturing Jobs in NYC." Adafruit. November 3, 2015. www.blog.adafruit.com.

Adams, Michael Henry. 2016. "The End of Black Harlem." *New York Times*, May 27, 2016. www.nytimes.com.

Albrecht, Leslie. 2016. "8-Story 'Boutique Manufacturing' Building Planned for Gowanus." DNAinfo New York, October 5, 2016. www.dnainfo.com.

Alfonsi, Sharyn. 2015. "The Storm after the Storm." 60 Minutes, June 7, 2015. www.cbsnews.com.

Alkon, Alison Hope, and Agyeman, Julian, eds. 2011. *Cultivating Food Justice: Race, Class, and Sustainability*. Cambridge, MA: The MIT Press.

Allen, Jennifer. 2008. "Eco-Friendly Makeover." *Good Housekeeping*. November 13, 2008. www.goodhousekeeping.com.

Alliance for a Greater New York. 2012. "New York-New Jersey Coalition for Healthy Ports Survey Reveals High Prevalence of Dirty Trucks at Ports." Partnership for Working Families. September 12, 2012. www.forworkingfamilies.org.

American Academy of Arts and Sciences. 2015. "Public Research Universities: Why They Matter." The Lincoln Project: Excellence and Access in Public Higher Education. Cambridge, MA. www.amacad.org.

Angotti, Tom and Sylvia Morse, eds. 2016. *Zoned Out! Race, Displacement, and City Planning in New York City*. New York: Terreform.

Angotti, Tom. 2008. *New York for Sale: Community Planning Confronts Global Real Estate*. Cambridge, MA: MIT Press.

Angotti, Tom. 2009. "Zoning without Planning." *Gotham Gazette*, May 26, 2009. www.gothamgazette.com.

Angotti, Tom. 2013. "New York City after Sandy: Who Benefits, Who Pays and Where's the Long-Term Planning?" *Progressive Planning* 194 (Winter): 10–13.

Anguelovski, Isabelle. 2015. "Healthy Food Stores, Greenlining and Food Gentrifica-
tion: Contesting New Forms of Privilege, Displacement and Locally Unwanted
Land Uses in Racially Mixed Neighborhoods." *International Journal of Urban and
Regional Research* 39 (6): 1209–30.

"Areas of Work." n.d. We Act for Environmental Justice. Accessed March 22, 2020.
www.weact.org.

Baker, Dwayne Marshall, and Bumsoo Lee. 2019. "How Does Light Rail Transit (LRT)
Impact Gentrification? Evidence from Fourteen US Urbanized Areas." *Journal of
Planning Education and Research* 39 (1): 35–49.

Banzhaf, Spencer, and McCormick, Eleanor. 2012. "Moving Beyond Cleanup: Identify-
ing the Crucibles of Environmental Gentrification." In *The Political Economy of
Environmental Justice*, edited by Spencer Banzhaf, 23–51. Palo Alto, CA: Stanford
University Press.

Barbanel, Josh. 2016. "The High Line's 'Halo Effect' on Property." *Wall Street Journal*,
August 7, 2016. www.wsj.com.

Barratt, Edward. 2014. "Bureaucracy, Citizenship, Governmentality: Towards a
Re-Evaluation of New Labour." *Ephemera* 14 (2): 263–80.

Barron, Seth. 2018. "New York's Red Borough." *City Journal*. January 11, 2018. www.
city-journal.org.

Bateson, Gregory, Don D. Jackson, Jay Haley, and John Weakland. 1956. "Toward a
Theory of Schizophrenia." *Behavioral Science* 1 (4): 251–64.

Bateson, Gregory. 1972. *Steps to an Ecology of Mind: Collected Essays in Anthropology,
Psychiatry, Evolution, and Epistemology*. Chicago: University of Chicago Press.

Bayles, Richard Mather. 2010. *History of Richmond County (Staten Island), New York
from Its Discovery to the Present Time*. Charleston, SC: Nabu Press.

Beauregard, Robert A. 2001. "Federal Policy and Postwar Urban Decline: A Case of
Government Complicity?" *Housing Policy Debate* 12 (1): 129–51.

Bell, Derrick. 1992. *Faces at the Bottom of the Well: The Permanence of Racism*. New
York: Basic Books.

Benimoff, Alan. 2010. "A GIS Study of Urbanization in Hurricane Slosh Zones on
Staten Island." *Geological Society of America Abstracts with Programs* 42 (1): 146.

Berger, Joseph. 2013. "E.P.A. Plan to Clean Up Gowanus Canal Meets Local Resistance."
*New York Times*, May 5, 2013. www.nytimes.com.

Beveridge, Andy A. 2008. "An Affluent, White Harlem?" *Gotham Gazette*. www.
gothamgazette.com.

"BIG Grants." n.d. NYC Office of Environmental Remediation, www1.nyc.gov.

Blain, Glenn. 2015. "EXCLUSIVE: Brooklyn Has Most Booze Makers in New York
State." *NY Daily News*, October 12, 2015. www.nydailynews.com.

Bowen, Ted Smalley, and Adam Stepan. 2014. "Public-Private Partnerships for Greenspace in NYC: Enter the Conservancy." School of International and Public Affairs,
Case Consortium. Columbia University. May 2014. http://ccnmtl.columbia.edu.

Bradley, Stefan M. 2009. *Harlem vs. Columbia University: Black Student Power in the
Late 1960s*. Champaign: University of Illinois Press.

Brake, Alan G., Molly Heintz, Julie V. Iovine, Branden Klayko, Nicholas Miller, and
Tom Stoelker. 2012. "Agencies of Change." *Architect's Newspaper*. August 22, 2012.
www.archpaper.com.

Brash, Julian. 2011. *Bloomberg's New York: Class and Governance in the Luxury City.* Athens: University of Georgia Press.

Bredderman, Will. 2018. "Last Republican Standing." *Crain's New York Business.* October 23, 2018. www.crainsnewyork.com.

Brodkin, Karen. 1998. *How Jews Became White Folks and What That Says about Race in America.* New Brunswick, NJ: Rutgers University Press.

Brooklyn Navy Yard Development Corporation. 2019. "A History of the Yard." Brooklyn Navy Yard. 2019. https://brooklynnavyyard.org.

Brooks, Steve, and Gerry Marten. 2015. "Green Guerillas: Revitalizing Urban Neighborhoods with Community Gardens (New York City, USA)." June 2015. ww.ecotippingpoints.org.

Brown, Wendy. 2006. *Regulating Aversion: Tolerance in the Age of Identity and Empire.* Princeton, NJ: Princeton University Press.

Brown, Wendy. 2015. *Undoing the Demos: Neoliberalism's Stealth Revolution.* New York: Zone Books.

"Brownfield Cleanup Program." n.d. Department of Environmental Conservation, www.dec.ny.gov.

Brundtland Commission. 1987. *Our Common Future.* New York: Oxford University Press.

Bryant, Bunyan, ed. 1995. *Environmental Justice: Issues, Policies, and Solutions.* Washington, DC: Island Press.

Buck, Nick, Ian Gordon, Alan Harding, and Ivan Turok. 2005. *Changing Cities: Rethinking Urban Competitiveness, Cohesion and Governance.* New York: Palgrave Macmillan.

Bullard, Robert 2000. *Dumping in Dixie: Race, Class, and Environmental Quality.* 3rd ed. Boulder, CO: Westview Press.

Bullard, Robert D., Mohai, Paul, Saha, Robin, and Wright, Beverly. 2007. "Toxic Wastes and Race at Twenty, 1987–2007." Cleveland: United Church of Christ & Witness Ministries. www.nrdc.org.

Burden, Amanda. 2011. "Creating Value with Urban Open Space: Amanda Burden." Urban Land Institute. YouTube video, 4:43. https://youtu.be/SB74k5aqD40.

Burden, Amanda. 2014. "How Public Spaces Make Cities Work." TED. 2014. www.ted.com.

Bureau of Labor Statistics 2014. "Occupational Employment Statistics." United States Department of Labor. 2014. www.bls.gov

Bureau of Labor Statistics. 2018. "Occupational Employment Statistics." United States Department of Labor. 2018. www.bls.gov.

Büscher, Bram, and J. Igoe. 2013. "'Prosuming' Conservation? Web 2.0, Nature and the Intensification of Value-Producing Labour in Late Capitalism." *Journal of Consumer Culture* 13 (3): 283–305.

"Business of Disaster." 2016. Frontline, May 24, 2016, www.pbs.org.

"Business Programs." n.d. NYCEDC. Accessed March 22, 2020. https://edc.nyc.

Calmes, Maggie. 2016. "Wary of Gentrification, East Harlem Braces for Rapid Change." *Gotham Gazette,* April 1, 2016. www.gothamgazette.com.

Campanella, Thomas. 2017. "Robert Moses and His Racist Parkway, Explained." City-Lab, July 2017. www.citylab.com .

Campbell-Dollaghan, Kelsey. 2013. "Watch Manhattan's Boundaries Expand over 250 Years." Gizmodo, May 9, 2013. www.gizmodo.com.

Cannon, J.S. 2008. "US Container Ports and Air Pollution: A Perfect Storm; An Energy Futures, Inc. Study." Boulder, CO: Energy Futures, Inc.

Carman, María. 2015. "Spokespeople for a Mute Nature: The Case of the Villa Rodrigo Bueno in Buenos Aires." In Sustainability in the Global City: Myth and Practice, edited by Cindy Isenhour, Gary McDonogh, and Melissa Checker, 238–60. New York: Cambridge University Press.

Carmel, Emma, and Jenny Harlock. 2008. "Instituting the 'Third Sector' as a Governable Terrain: Partnership, Procurement and Performance in the UK." Policy & Politics, no. 36, 155–71.

Caro, Robert A. 1975. The Power Broker: Robert Moses and the Fall of New York. New York: Vintage.

Casey, Joan A., Peter James, Lara Cushing, Bill M. Jesdale, and Rachel Morello-Frosch. 2017. "Race, Ethnicity, Income Concentration and 10-Year Change in Urban Greenness in the United States." International Journal of Environmental Research and Public Health 14 (12): 1546.

Chaban, Matt. 2012. "El Barrio's Secret Gardens: East Harlem Has Some Unexpected Parks, But It Still Needs Better Ones." Observer (blog). October 25, 2012. www.observer.com.

Chappell, Sally A. Kitt. 1990. "A Reconsideration of the Equitable Building in New York." Society of Architectural Historians Journal 49: 91–92.

Chayes, Matthew. 2015. "NYC Challenges New Federal Flood Maps." AmNY. June 27, 2015. www.amny.com.

Checker, Melissa. 2005. Polluted Promises: Environmental Racism and the Search for Justice in a Southern Town. New York: NYU Press.

Checker, Melissa. 2008. "Working for a Greener Harlem," Gotham Gazette, November 27, 2009.

Checker, Melissa. 2009. "Staten Island's Toxic Stew." Gotham Gazette, 2009. www.old.gothamgazette.com.

Checker, Melissa. 2011a. "Wiped Out by the 'Greenwave': Environmental Gentrification and the Paradoxical Politics of Urban Sustainability." City & Society 23: 210–29.

Checker, Melissa. 2011b. "City Brownfield Program Cleans Sites, But Who Benefits?" Gotham Gazette, May 31, 2011. www.gothamgazette.com.

Checker, Melissa. 2012. "Chicken Little, a Ferris Wheel and Disorderly Development on Staten Island's North Shore." Gotham Gazette, November 26, 2012. www.gothamgazette.com.

Checker, Melissa. 2014. "Anthropological Superheroes and the Consequences of Activist Ethnography." American Anthropologist. 116 (2): 416–20.

Checker, Melissa. 2016. "Stop FEMA Now: Nature 2.0 and the Sacrificed Citizen." In "Nature 2.0: Social Media, Online Activism and the Cyberpolitics of Environmental Conservation." Special issue, Geoforum 79: 124–33.

City Planning Commission. 1960. "Comprehensive Amendment of the Zoning Resolution of The City of New York." March 25, 1960. www1.nyc.gov.

Clarke, John. 2005. "New Labour's Citizens: Activated, Empowered, Responsibilized, Abandoned?" Critical Social Policy 25 (4): 447–63.

Clarke, John. 2013. "In Search of Ordinary People: The Problematic Politics of Popular Participation." *Communication, Culture & Critique* 6 (2): 208–26.

"Climate Showcase Communities Program" n.d. US Environmental Protection Agency. Accessed March 23, 2020. www.epa.gov.

Coalition for Clean and Safe Ports." n.d. Partnership for Working Families. Accessed October 13, 2017. www.forworkingfamilies.org.

Collier, Stephen J. 2014. "Neoliberalism and Natural Disaster: Insurance as Political Technology of Catastrophe." *Journal of Cultural Economy* 7 (3): 273–90.

Constable, Pamela. 2015. "Majority of Undocumented Immigrants Work in Low-Skill Jobs, Report Finds." *Washington Post*, March 26, 2015. www.washingtonpost.com.

"Conversation with James Baldwin, A; James Baldwin Interview." June 24, 1963. WGBH Media Library & Archives, accessed April 20, 2020. www.openvault.wgbh.org.

Cotter, Holland. 2015. "When the Young Lords Were Outlaws in New York." *New York Times*, July 23, 2015. www.nytimes.com.

Crompton, John L. 2001. "The Impact of Parks on Property Values: A Review of the Empirical Evidence." *Journal of Leisure Research* 33 (1): 1–31.

Crompton, John L. 2005. "The Impact of Parks on Property Values: Empirical Evidence from the Past Two Decades in the United States." *Managing Leisure* 10 (4): 203–18.

Cronin, Paul. 2018. *A Time to Stir: Columbia '68*. New York: Columbia University Press.

Cronon, William. 1996. "The Trouble with Wilderness: Or, Getting Back to the Wrong Nature." *Environmental History* 1 (1): 7–28.

Cruikshank, Barbara. 1999. *The Will to Empower: Democratic Citizens and Other Subjects*. Ithaca, NY: Cornell University Press.

Curbed. 2013. "The Equitable Building and the Birth of NYC Zoning Law." Curbed NY. March 15, 2013. www.curbed.com.

Curran, W, and S. Hanson. 2005. "Getting Globalized: Urban Policy and Industrial Displacement in Williamsburg, Brooklyn." *Urban Geography* 26 (6): 461–82.

Curran, W. 2004. "Gentrification and the Nature of Work: Exploring the Links in Williamsburg, Brooklyn." *Environment and Planning A* 36: 1243–58.

Curran, Winifred, and Hamilton, Trina, eds. 2017. *Just Green Enough: Urban Development and Environmental Gentrification*. New York: Routledge.

Curran, Winifred, and Trina Hamilton. 2012. "Just Green Enough: Contesting Environmental Gentrification in Greenpoint, Brooklyn." *Local Environment* 17 (9): 1027–42.

Cventure LLC, Cathy Pasion, Christianah Oyenuga, and Kate Gouin. 2017. "Inventory of New York City Greenhouse Gas Emissions in 2015." New York: Mayor's Office of Sustainability. www.dec.ny.gov.

Darnovsky, Marcy. 1992. "Stories Less Told: Histories of US Environmentalism." *Socialist Review* 22 (4): 11–44.

David, Greg. 2012. *Modern New York: The Life and Economics of a City*. New York: St. Martin's Press.

David, Joshua, and Karen Hock. 2002. *Reclaiming the High Line*. Design Trust for Public Space, Friends of the Highline. www.designtrust.org.

Dawsey, Josh. 2014. "The Super Activist that Sandy Made." *Wall Street Journal*, March 23, 2014. www.wsj.com.

De Lara, Juan. 2018. *Inland Shift: Race, Space, and Capital in Southern California*. Berkeley, CA: University of California Press.

Dean, Jodi. 2012. "The Limits of Communication." *Guernica / A Magazine of Art & Politics*, 2012. www.guernicamag.com.

Deleuze, Gilles, and Felix Guattari. 1987. *A Thousand Plateaus: Capitalism and Schizophrenia.* Translated by Brian Massumi. 2nd edition. Minneapolis: University of Minnesota Press.

Di Ionno, Mark. 2013. "Foes of FEMA Flood Maps Want Answers - and a Place to Meet." NJ.com. February 26, 2013. http://blog.nj.com.

Di, Qian, Yan Wang, Antonella Zanobetti, Yun Wang, Petros Koutrakis, Christine Choirat, Francesca Dominici, and Joel D. Schwartz. 2017. "Air Pollution and Mortality in the Medicare Population." *New England Journal of Medicine* 376 (26): 2513–22.

Dobkin, Jake. 2013. "Environmental Racism? Toxic Gowanus Sludge is Heading for Red Hook: Gothamist." Gothamist, April 26, 2013. www.gothamist.com.

Doherty, Gareth, and Charles Waldheim. 2015. *Is Landscape . . . ?: Essays on the Identity of Landscape.* New York: Routledge.

Dolkart, Andrew S., Christopher D. Brazee, and Michael D. Caratzas. 2007. "Dumbo Historic District Designation Report." New York City Landmarks Preservation Commission. www.neighborhoodpreservationcenter.org.

Dooling, Sarah. 2009. "Ecological Gentrification: A Research Agenda Exploring Justice in the City." *International Journal of Urban and Regional Research* 33 (3): 621–39.

Downs, Timothy, Laurie Ross, Suzanne Patton, and Sarah Runick. 2009. "Complexities of Holistic Community-Based Participatory Research for a Low Income, Multi-Ethnic Population Exposed to Multiple Built-Environment Stressors in Worcester, Massachusetts." *Environmental Research* 109: 1028–40.

Downtown Lower Manhattan Association n.d. "Home." Downtown Lower Manhattan Association. www.d-lma.com.

Eizenberg, Efrat. 2013. *From the Ground Up: Community Gardens in New York City and the Politics of Spatial Transformation.* Burlington, VT: Ashgate.

Ellin, Abby. 2014. "The Brooklyn Brand Goes Global." *New York Times*, December 3, 2014. www.nytimes.com.

Ellison, Ralph. 1964. "Harlem Is Nowhere." *Harper's Magazine*, August, 1964. www.harpers.org.

Environmental Advocates of New York. 2011. "Missing the Mark: New York's Off-Target Brownfield Cleanup Incentives." Environmental Advocates of New York. www.eany.org.

Environmental Advocates of New York. 2013. "New York's Billion Dollar Brownfields." Environmental Advocates of New York. www.eany.org.

Environmental Justice Showcase Communities by Region. n.d. Environmental Protection Agency. Accessed April 4, 2020. www.epa.gov.

Escobar, Arturo. 2001. *Encountering Development: The Making and Unmaking of the Third World.* Princeton, NJ: Princeton University Press.

Essoka, Jonathan. 2010. "The Gentrifying Effects of Brownfields Redevelopment." *Western Journal of Black Studies* 34 (3): 299–316.

Farr, Matthew A., Keri V. Brondo, and Scout Anglin. 2015. "Shifting Gears: The Intersections of Race and Sustainability in Memphis." In *Sustainability in the Global City: Myth and Practice*, edited by Cindy Isenhour, Gary McDonogh, and Melissa Checker, 285–305. New York: Cambridge University Press.

Federal Insurance and Mitigation Administration. 2017. "Sandy Claims Review Division Update." Federal Emergency Management Agency, March 10, 2017. www.fema. gov.

Federal Trade Commission. 2019. "Multi-Level Marketing Businesses and Pyramid Schemes." Federal Trade Commission Consumer Information, October 2019. www. consumer.ftc.gov.

Feiden, Douglas. 2003. "Will Plot Sicken on Staten Is.? Land Stored Fuel for Atomic Bomb." *NY Daily News*, November 2, 2003. www.nydailynews.com.

Feng, Kuishuang, Steven J. Davis, Laixiang Sun, and Klaus Hubacek. 2015. "Drivers of the US $CO_2$ Emissions 1997–2013." *Nature Communications* 6 (July): 7714.

Ferguson, Sarah. 1999. "A Brief History of Grassroots Greening in NYC," In *Avant Gardening: Ecological Struggles in the City and the World*, edited by Peter Lamborn Wilson and Bill Weinberg. Brooklyn, NY: Autonomedia.

Ferretti, Fred. 1977. "New York Parks Face a Touch-and-Go Summer . . ." *New York Times*, May 26, 1977. www.nytimes.com.

Fiennes, Sophie. 2013. *The Pervert's Guide to Ideology*. New York: Zeitgeist Films.

Fiorina, Morris. 2018. "Polarization Is Not the Problem." *Stanford Magazine*, May 8, 2018.

Fischel, William A. 2004. "An Economic History of Zoning and a Cure for Its Exclusionary Effects." *Urban Studies* 41 (2): 317–40.

Fischler, Raphael. 1998. "The Metropolitan Dimension of Early Zoning: Revisiting the 1916 New York City Ordinance." *Journal of the American Planning Association* 64 (2): 170–88.

Fitch, Robert. 1993. *The Assassination of New York*. New York: Verso.

Flood, Joe. 2010. "Why the Bronx Burned." *New York Post* (blog). May 16, 2010. www. nypost.com.

Florida, Richard. 2004. *Cities and the Creative Class*. New York: Taylor & Francis.

Foderaro, Lisa. 2015. "New York City's Low-Profile Parks to Get Conservancies' Help, and Some Cash." *New York Times*, November 13, 2015. www.nytimes.com.

Foster, John Bellamy. 2000. *Marx's Ecology: Materialism and Nature*. New York: Monthly Review Press.

Foucault, Michel. 1979. *Discipline and Punish: The Birth of the Prison*. New York: Vintage Books.

Foucault, Michel. 1982. "The Subject and Power." *Critical Inquiry* 8 (4): 777–95.

Foucault, Michel. 2003. *Society Must Be Defended: Lectures at the Collège De France, 1975–76*. New York: Picador.

Fraser, Nancy. 2000. "Rethinking Recognition." *New Left Review*, no. 3 (June). www. newleftreview.org.

Freeman, Joshua B. 2001. *Working-Class New York: Life and Labor since World War II*. New York: New Press.

Freeman, Lance. 2006. *There Goes the 'Hood: Views of Gentrification from the Ground Up*. Philadelphia, PA: Temple University Press.

"Frontline (PBS) and NPR Investigate Superstorm Sandy Recovery Efforts." n.d. NPR. Accessed March 23, 2020. www.npr.org.

Furman Center for Real Estate and Urban Policy. 2009. "State of New York City's Housing and Neighborhoods Report 2009." www.furmancenter.org.

Furman Center for Real Estate and Urban Policy. 2011. "Distribution of the Burden of New York City's Property Tax." State of New York City's Housing & Neighborhoods 2011. The Furman Center for Real Estate & Urban Policy. www.furmancenter.org.

Furman Center for Real Estate and Urban Policy. 2018. "Making Dirty Land Clean: An Analysis of New York City's Voluntary Cleanup Program (VCP)." Furman Center for Real Estate and Urban Policy. www.furmancenter.org.

FURSAP Considered Sites: Staten Island Warehouse, NY." n.d. Energy.gov: Office of Legacy Management. www.lm.doe.gov.

Gamper-Rabindran, Shanti, and Christopher Timmins. 2013. "Does Cleanup of Hazardous Waste Sites Raise Housing Values? Evidence of Spatially Localized Benefits." *Journal of Environmental Economics and Management* 65 (3): 345–60.

Gandy, Matthew. 2003. *Concrete and Clay: Reworking Nature in New York City*. Cambridge, MA: MIT Press.

Gates, Jr., Henry Louis. 1997. "Harlem on Our Minds." *Critical Inquiry* 24 (1): 1–12.

Gibson, DW. 2015. "How a Gentrification Scam Threatens New York's Community Gardens." *Nation*, October 20, 2015.

Giller, Megan. 2015. "Why Chocolate Experts Think the Mast Brothers Are Frauds." *Slate*, December 18, 2015. www.slate.com.

Giroux, Henry A., and Susan Searls Giroux. 2004. *Take Back Higher Education: Race, Youth, and the Crisis of Democracy in the Post-Civil Rights Era*. New York: Macmillan.

Glass, Ruth. 1964. "London: Aspects of Change." 3. Centre for Urban Studies Report. London: MacGibbon & Kee.

Gold, Roberta. 2014. *When Tenants Claimed the City: The Struggle for Citizenship in New York City Housing*. Champaign: University of Illinois Press.

Goldenberg, Sally. 2016. "Rezoning Gowanus Now a Consideration on de Blasio's Housing Agenda." Politico, August 1, 2016. www.politico.com.

Goldfischer, Eric. 2019. "From Encampments to Hotspots: The Changing Policing of Homelessness in New York City." *Housing Studies* 0 (0): 1–18.

Gore, Timothy. 2015. "Extreme Carbon Inequality." Oxfam International. December 2, 2015. www.oxfam.org.

Gotham, Kevin Fox, and Miriam Greenberg. 2014. *Crisis Cities: Disaster and Redevelopment in New York and New Orleans*. Oxford: Oxford University Press.

Gottlieb, Robert. 2005. *Forcing the Spring: The Transformation of the American Environmental Movement*. Revised ed. Washington, DC: Island Press.

Gould, Kenneth and Tammy Lewis. 2012. "The Environmental Injustice of Green Gentrification: The Case of Brooklyn's Prospect Park." In *The World in Brooklyn: Gentrification, Immigration, and Ethnic Politics in a Global City*, edited by Judith DeSena et al. Lanham, MD: Lexington Books.

Gould, Kenneth, and Lewis, Tammy. 2016. *Green Gentrification: Urban Sustainability and the Struggle for Environmental Justice*. New York: Routledge.

"Gowanus Home Prices and Values." n.d. Zillow. www.zillow.com.

Grandmaster Flash and the Furious Five. 1982. "The Message." Track 7 on *The Message*, Sugar Hill Records SH 268, 33⅓ rpm.

Gray, Christopher. 1996. "Streetscapes/The Music Hall at Snug Harbor Cultural Center; A Low-Budget Revival for a Grand 1890 Theater." *New York Times*, April 7, 1996. www.nytimes.com.

Greenberg, Miriam, and Melissa Aronczyk. 2008. "Branding, Crisis, and Utopia: Representing New York in the Age of Bloomberg." In *Blowing Up the Brand: Critical Perspectives on Promotional Culture*, edited by Melissa Aronczyk and Devon Power, 115–43. New York: Peter Lang.

Greenberg, Miriam. 2010. *Branding New York: How a City in Crisis Was Sold to the World*. New York: Routledge.

Greenberg, Miriam. 2015. "'The Sustainability Edge': The Post-Crisis Promise of Eco-City Branding." In *Sustainability in the Global City: Myth and Practice*, edited by Cindy Isenhour, Gary McDonough, and Melissa Checker, 105–30. New York: Cambridge University Press.

GreenBiz Editors. 2001. "Dumping Ends Today at World's Largest Landfill." GreenBiz. March 21, 2001. www.greenbiz.com.

Gregory, Ann Goggins, and Don Howard. 2009. "The Nonprofit Starvation Cycle (SSIR)." *Innovation Review*. 2009. www.ssir.org.

Gross, Neil. 2013. *Why Are Professors Liberal and Why Do Conservatives Care?* Cambridge, MA: Harvard University Press.

Guggenheim, David. (Director). 2006. *An Inconvenient Truth: A Global Warning* [DVD]. Hollywood: Paramount.

Hackworth, Jason. 2002. "Post Recession Gentrification in New York City." *Urban Affairs Review* 37 (6): 815–43.

Hagerman, Chris. 2007. "Shaping Neighborhoods and Nature: Urban Political Ecologies of Urban Waterfront Transformations in Portland, Oregon." *Cities* 24: 285–97.

Hanscom, Greg. 2014. "Flood Pressure: Climate Disasters Drown FEMA's Insurance Plans." Grist. January 13, 2014. www.grist.org.

Harlem CDC (Harlem Community Development Corporation). 2010. "February Newsletter." www.harlemcdc.org.

Harsanyi, David. 2015. "America, Please Stop Glorifying Manufacturing Jobs." *Federalist*, 2015.

Harvey, David. 1973. *Social Justice and the City*. Athens, GA: University of Georgia Press.

Harvey, David. 1985. *The Urbanization of Capital: Studies in the History and Theory of Capitalist Urbanization*. John Hopkins University Press.

Harvey, David. 2005. *A Brief History of Neoliberalism*. New York: Oxford University Press.

Harvey, David. 2006. *Spaces of Global Capitalism: Towards a Theory of Uneven Geographical Development*. New York: Verso.

Harvey, David. 2007. *A Brief History of Neoliberalism*. New York: Oxford University Press.

Harvey, David. 2011. *The Enigma of Capital: And the Crises of Capitalism*. 2nd edition. Oxford; New York: Oxford University Press.

Harvey, David. 2014.. *Seventeen Contradictions and the End of Capitalism*. London: Profile Books.

Harvey, David. 2017. *Marx, Capital and the Madness of Economic Reason*. London: Profile Books.

Hatch, M. 2014. *The Maker Movement Manifesto*. New York: McGraw Hill.

Hausfather, Zeke. 2018. "Analysis: Fossil-Fuel Emissions in 2018 Increasing at Fastest Rate for Seven Years." Carbon Brief. December 5, 2018. www.carbonbrief.org.

Hicks, Nolan, Craig McCarthy and Max Jaeger. 2019. "SI Garbage Kingpin Who Alleg-edly Helped Cover Up Murder Still Has City License." *New York Post*, May 29, 2019. www.nypost.com.

Hochschild, Jennifer L. 1984. *The New American Dilemma: Liberal Democracy and School Desegregation*. New Haven, CT: Yale University Press.

Honan, Katie. 2019. "New York City Is Investigating Top Homeless-Shelter Operator." *Wall Street Journal*, July 18, 2019. www.wsj.com.

Honey, Maureen, ed. 1999. *Bitter Fruit: African American Women in World War II*. Columbia, MO: University of Missouri.

Horvath, Theresa. 2010. "Health Initiatives of the Young Lords Party." Paper presented at New Directions in American Healthcare: Innovations from Home and Abroad. Hofstra University, March 11, 2010.

Hughes, C. J. 2015. "Staten Island's Turning Point?" *New York Times*, April 17, 2015. www.nytimes.com.

Hughes, Langston. 1926. "The Negro Artist and the Racial Mountain." *Nation*, June 23, 1926. www.thenation.com.

Hum, Tarry. 2015. "There Is Nothing Innovative about Displacement." *Gotham Gazette*, October 21, 2015. www.gothamgazette.com.

Hum, Tarry. 2016. "The Hollowing-Out of New York City's Industrial Zones." *Metropolitiques*, February 2, 2016. www.metropolitiques.eu.

Humphery, Kim. 2013. *Excess: Anti-Consumerism in the West*. New York: John Wiley & Sons.

Hunter College Urban Policy and Planning 2017. "Plan Bay Street: A New Plan for Staten Island's Downtown." www.hunterurban.org.

ICLEI – Local Governments for Sustainability. 2010. "The Process Behind PlaNYC: How New York Developed Its Comprehensive Long-Term Sustainability Plan." ICLEI – Local Governments for Sustainability. www.ilei.org.

Iovine, Julie. 2012. "Carpe Diem & Then What." *Architect's Newspaper*, August 7, 2012. www.archpaper.com.

Isenhour, Cindy, Gary McDonogh, and Melissa Checker, eds. 2015. *Sustainability in the Global City*. New York: Cambridge University Press.

Jackson, John. 2003. *Harlemworld: Doing Race and Class in Contemporary Black America*. Chicago: The University of Chicago Press.

Jackson, Kenneth T. 1985. *Crabgrass Frontier: The Suburbanization of the United States*. New York: Oxford University Press.

Jackson, Kenneth T., ed. 1995. *The Encyclopedia of New York City*. New Haven, CT: New York: Yale University Press.

Jacobs, Sarah. 2017. "A Little-Known Brooklyn Neighborhood Was Named One of the World's Coolest Places—Here's What It's Like." Business Insider Singapore. October 16, 2017. www.businessinsider.sg.

Johnson, James Weldon. 1925. "Harlem: The Cultural Capital." National Humanities Center. www.nationalhumanitiescenter.org.

Johnston, Garth. 2012. "The World's Tallest Ferris Wheel Is Coming To Staten Island!" *Gothamist*, September 27, 2012. www.gothamist.com.

Jones, Jeffrey M. 2019. "Americans Continue to Embrace Political Independence." Gallup. January 7, 2019. www.news.gallup.com.

Jonker, Kim, and Meehan, William F. III. 2014. "Mission Matters Most." Stanford Social Innovation Review. February 19, 2014. www://ssir.org.

Jorgensen, Jillian. 2013. "Lawsuit Alleges Developer Cut Out of New York Wheel Deal on Staten Island." SiLive.Com, April 2, 2013. www.silive.com.

Kanter, James. 2007. "Are Dell, Wal-Mart, Philips Going Green or Just Re-Branding?" New York Times, September 27, 2007. www.green.blogs.nytimes.com.

Kashiwagi, Syndey. 2019. "With No Funding or Timeline, Cromwell Center Remains in Limbo," Staten Island Advance, February 1, 2019. www.silive.com.

Katz, Lawrence, and Krueger, Alan. 2016. "The Rise and Nature of Alternative Work Arrangements in the United States, 1995-2015." NBER Working Paper No. 22667. www.nber.org.

Kaysen, Ronda. 2014. "Gowanus Is Counting on a Cleanup." New York Times, October 3, 2014. www.nytimes.com.

Kelly, Cynthia C., ed. 2009. Manhattan Project: The Birth of the Atomic Bomb in the Words of Its Creators, Eyewitnesses, and Historians. New York: Black Dog & Leventhal.

Kingfisher, Catherine, and Jeff Maskovsky. 2008. "Introduction: The Limits of Neoliberalism." Critique of Anthropology 28 (2): 115–26.

Klar, Samara, and Yanna Krupnikov. 2016. Independent Politics: How American Disdain for Parties Leads to Political Inaction. New York: Cambridge University Press.

Kliewer, Brandon W. 2013. "Why the Civic Engagement Movement Cannot Achieve Democratic and Justice Aims." Michigan Journal of Community Service Learning 19 (2): 72–79.

Knafo, Saki, and Lila Shapiro. 2012. "Staten Island's Hurricane Sandy Damage Sheds Light on Complicated Political Battle." December 6, 2012. www.huffingtonpost.com.

Knowles, Scott Gabriel, and Howard C. Kunreuther. 2014. "Troubled Waters: The National Flood Insurance Program in Historical Perspective." Journal of Policy History 26 (3): 327–53.

Knowlton, Claire. 2019. "Why Funding Overhead Is Not the Real Issue: The Case to Cover Full Costs." Nonprofit Quarterly, September 10, 2019. www.nonprofitquarterly.org.

Kotz, David M., Terrence McDonough, and Michael Reich. 1994. Social Structures of Accumulation: The Political Economy of Growth and Crisis. Great Britain: Cambridge University Press.

Kramer, Daniel, and Richard Flanagan. 2012. Staten Island: Conservative Bastion in a Liberal City. Lanham, MD: University Press of America.

Krause, Kerri-Lee, Sophie Arkoudis, Richard James and Ros McCulloch. 2008. "The Academic's and Policy-Maker's Guides to the Teaching Research Nexus: A Suite of Resources for Enhancing Reflective Practice: Final Project Report." Australian Learning and Teaching Council. https://ltr.edu.au.

La Rocco, Barbara. 2004. Going Coastal New York City. Brooklyn, NY: Going Coastal, Inc.

Lacan, Jacques. 1981. The Four Fundamental Concepts of Psycho-Analysis. New York: W. W. Norton.

Lacan, Jacques. 1997. The Seminar of Jacques Lacan: The Psychoses (Book III) Jacques-Alain Miller, ed. Translated by Russell Grigg. New York: W. W. Norton.

Lam, Joyce. 2013. "The Staten Island Farm Colony's Disturbing Secrets." Untapped Cities. October 15, 2013. www.untappedcities.com.

Lambert, Bruce. 1992. "Clara Hale, Founder of Home for Addicts' Babies, Dies at 87." *New York Times*, December 19, 1992. www.nytimes.com.

Landa, Marjorie. 2017. "Final Letter Report on the Follow-Up Review of the City's Oversight over Privately Owned Public Spaces." City of New York Office of the Comptroller Scott M. Stringer. www.comptroller.nyc.gov.

Langholtz, Gabrielle. 2011. "Brooklyn's Celebrated Chocolatiers Set Sail." Edible Brooklyn, September 30, 2011. www.ediblebrooklyn.com.

Lee, Jennifer. 2009. "The Young Lords' Legacy of Puerto Rican Activism." City Room, 2009. http://cityroom.blogs.nytimes.com.

Leland, John. 2011. "Shooting in Morningside Park Tests Harlem's Bond with Past." *New York Times*, August 12, 2011. www.nytimes.com.

Lemann, Nicholas 1997. "Citizen 501(c)(3)." *Atlantic*, February 1997.

Leon, Alexandra. 2015. "DUMBO Was Brooklyn's Most Expensive Neighborhood for Sales in 2015: Report." DNAinfo New York, December 30, 2015. www.dnainfo.com.

Levinson, Marc. 2006. *The Box: How the Shipping Container Made the World Smaller and the World Economy Bigger*. Princeton, NJ: Princeton University Press.

Levinson, Marc. 2012. "How New York Lost the Apparel Business." *Bloomberg* April 18, 2012. www.bloomberg.com.

Lindner, Christoph, and Brian Rosa, eds. 2017. *Deconstructing the High Line: Postindustrial Urbanism and the Rise of the Elevated Park*. New Brunswick, NJ: Rutgers University Press.

Livesay, Christopher. 2015. "Europe's Biggest Illegal Dump—'Italy's Chernobyl'—Uncovered in Mafia Heartland." VICE News, June 19, 2015. www.news.vice.com.

Locke, Alain. 1925. "Harlem, Mecca of the New Negro." *Survey Graphic* 6 (6): 621-721.

Low, Setha, Dana Taplin, and Suzanne Scheld. 2005. *Rethinking Urban Parks Public Space and Cultural Diversity*. Austin: University of Texas Press.

Lubitow, Amy, and Thaddeus Miller. 2013. "Contesting Sustainability: Bikes, Race, and Politics in Portlandia." *Environmental Justice*, 6(4): 121–26.

Lugo, Adonia E. 2015. "Can Human Infrastructure Combat Green Gentrification?: Ethnographic Research on Bicycling in Los Angeles and Seattle." In *Sustainability in the Global City: Myth and Practice*, edited by Cindy Isenhour, Gary McDonogh, and Melissa Checker, 306–28. New York: Cambridge University Press.

Maantay, Juliana A., and Andrew R. Maroko. 2018. "Brownfields to Greenfields: Environmental Justice Versus Environmental Gentrification." *International Journal of Environmental Research and Public Health* 15 (10): 2233.

Maantay, Juliana. 2002. "Zoning Law, Health, and Environmental Justice: What's the Connection?" *Journal of Law, Medicine & Ethics* 30 (4): 572–93.

Maantay, Juliana. 2000. "Industrial Zoning Changes and Environmental Justice in New York City: An Historical, Geographical, and Cultural Analysis." Ph.D. diss.: Rutgers University.

"Mafia Milks Italy's Green Energy Boom." 2015. The Local, July 27, 2015. www.thelocal. it.

Maharawal, Manissa M. 2017. "Black Lives Matter, Gentrification and the Security State in the San Francisco Bay Area." *Anthropological Theory* 17 (3): 338–64.

Make the Road New York. n.d. "Who We Are." Accessed March 22, 2020. www.maketheroad.org.

Malewitz, Raymond. 2014. *The Practice of Misuse: Rugged Consumerism in Contemporary American Culture*. Stanford, CA: Stanford University Press.

Mandel, Michael. 2013. "Building a Digital City: The Growth and Impact of New York City's Tech/Information Sector. Prepared for the Bloomberg Technology Summit." September 30, 2013, New York City. https://southmountaineconomics.com.

Marcus, Norman. 1991. "New York City Zoning – 1961-1991: Turning Back The Clock – But With An Up-To-The-Minute Social Agenda." *Fordham Urban Law Journal* 19 (3): 707–26.

Marcuse, Peter. 1986. "The Beginnings of Public Housing in New York." *Journal of Urban History* 12 (4): 353–90.

Martin, Douglas. 1997. "A Village Dies, A Park Is Born." *New York Times*, January 31, 1997. www.nytimes.com.

Marton, Janos. 2015. "26 Years Since the Board of Estimate's Demise." *Gotham Gazette*, March 22, 2015. www.gothamgazette.com.

Marx, Karl, and Friedrich Engels. (1848) 1947. *Manifesto of the Communist Party*. Chicago: C. H. Kerr.

Marx, Karl. 1992. *Capital: Volume 1: A Critique of Political Economy*. Translated by Ben Fowkes. New York, NY: Penguin Classics.

Maskovsky, Jeff. 2006. "Governing the 'New Hometowns': Race, Power, and Neighborhood Participation in the New Inner City." *Identities* 13 (1): 73–99.

Massey, Douglas S, and Nancy A. Denton. 1993. *American Apartheid: Segregation and the Making of the Underclass*. Cambridge, MA: Harvard University Press.

Maurrasse, David, and Jaclyn Bliss. 2006. "Comprehensive Approaches to Urban Development: Gentrification, Community, and Business in Harlem, New York." *Northwestern Journal of Law & Social Policy* 1 (1): 127–47.

May, John. 2007. "The Triangle of Engagement: An Unusual Way of Looking at the Usual Suspects." SSRN Scholarly Paper ID 959524. Rochester, NY: Social Science Research Network. https://ssrn.com/abstract=959524.

Mayer, Margit. 2017. "Whose City? From Ray Pahl's Critique of the Keynesian City to the Contestations around Neoliberal Urbanism." *Sociological Review* 65 (2): 168–83.

"Mayor de Blasio and Speaker Mark-Viverito Unveil Action Plan to Grow 21st Century Industrial and Manufacturing Jobs in NYC." 2015. Official Website of the City of New York, November 3, 2015. www1.nyc.gov.

McClintock, Nathan. 2018. "Cultivating (a) Sustainability Capital: Urban Agriculture, Eco-Gentrification, and the Uneven Valorization of Social Reproduction." *Annals of the American Association of Geographers* 108 (2): 579–90.

McDowell, Winston. 1984. "Race and Ethnicity during the Harlem Jobs Campaign, 1932–1935." *Journal of African American History* 69 (3–4): 134–46.

McGeehan, Patrick. 2010. "New York's Recovery Is Stronger Than Nation's, but Still Uneven." *New York Times*, August 30, 2010. www.nytimes.com.

McGhee, Devon. 2017. "Were the Post-Sandy Staten Island Buyouts Effective in Reducing Vulnerability?" Master's project, Duke University. www.cakex.org.

McNulty, Jennifer. 2008. "Shopping Our Way to Safety." *UC Santa Cruz Review*, Spring 2008, 14–15.

Mehrotra, Apurva, Bijan Kimiagar, Marija Drobnjak, and Sophia Halkitis. 2018. "The North Shore of Staten Island: Community Driven Solutions to Improve Child and Family Well-Being." Citizens' Committee for Children of New York. www.cccnewyork.org.

Metropolitan Waterfront Alliance. 2010. "Feds Agree to Remediate Radioactive Waterfront." Metropolitan Waterfront Alliance. February 17, 2010. www.waterfrontalliance.org.

Mikati, Ihab, Adam F. Benson, Thomas J. Luben, Jason D. Sacks, and Jennifer Richmond-Bryant. 2018. "Disparities in Distribution of Particulate Matter Emission Sources by Race and Poverty Status." *American Journal of Public Health* 108 (4): 480–85.

Miller, Jessica Ty. 2015. "Super Fun Superfund: Polluted Protection along the Gowanus Canal." PhD Dissertation, The Graduate Center, City University of New York.

Miller, Jessica Ty. 2017. "The Production of Green: Gentrification and Social Change." In *Just Green Enough: Urban Development and Environmental Gentrification*, edited by Wilfred Curran and Trina Hamilton, 107–20. New York: Routledge.

Mistry, Nisha, and Byron, Joan. 2011. "The Federal Role in Supporting Urban Manufacturing." What Works Collaborative. www.prattcenter.net.

Mitchell, Max. 2010. "Residents Concerned about Pelham Parkway Towers." *Bronx Times Reporter*, August 31, 2010. www.bxtimes.com.

Mol, Arthur, and Sonnenfeld, David. 2000. "Ecological Modernisation around the World: An Introduction." *Environmental Politics* 9 (1): 3–16.

Monbiot, George. 2007. "Eco-Junk - Green Consumerism Will Not Save the Biosphere." Celsias, August 3, 2007. www.celsias.com.

Montpetit, Jonathan. 2008. "Organized Crime Now Shifting to 'Green' Targets." *Toronto Star*, August 23, 2008. www.thestar.com.

Mooney, Jake. 2010. "Sewage, Cement and Staten Island's Future." City Limits, June 22, 2010. www.citylimits.org.

Moorehouse, Lateefa, 2006. "Green Gentrification? New Arrivals in Harlem are Forcing Changes in the Community." *Amsterdam News*, July 27, 2006.

Moritz-Rabson, Daniel. 2018. "A Recycling Smuggling Ring Illegally Earned $16.1 Million Using California's Beverage Container Refund: Authorities." *Newsweek*, December 4, 2018.

"Morningside Park." n.d. Yelp. Accessed March 22, 2020. www.yelp.com

Moser, Stephanie, and Silke Kleinhückelkotten. 2018. "Good Intents, but Low Impacts: Diverging Importance of Motivational and Socioeconomic Determinants Explaining Pro-Environmental Behavior, Energy Use, and Carbon Footprint." *Environment and Behavior* 50 (6): 626–56.

Muoio, Danielle, and David Giambusso. 2019. "De Blasio's Climate Rhetoric on the Stump Doesn't Mirror Reality Back Home." Politico. May 30, 2019. www.politico.com.

Murphy, Jarrett. 2017. "Data Drop: Which Is the Bluest Borough?" City Limits. October 13, 2017. www.citylimits.org.

Musemeci, Natalie. 2013. "Gowanus Sludge Could Be Made into Concrete, Added to Red Hook Coast." *Brooklyn Paper*, February 18, 2013. www.brooklynpaper.com.

Naison, Mark. 2004. *Communists in Harlem during the Depression*. New edition. Urbana: University of Illinois Press.

Navarro, Mireya. 2009. "Plan to Make Gowanus Canal a Superfund Site Draws Opposition." *New York Times*, April 24, 2009. www.nytimes.com.

Nielson Newswire Newsletter. 2018. "Was 2018 the Year of the Influential Sustainable Consumer?" *Nielson Newswire Newsletter*. December 17, 2018. www.nielson.com.

NEJAC (National Environmental Justice Advisory Council). 2006. "Unintended Impacts of Redevelopment and Revitalization Efforts in Five Environmental Justice Communities." Washington D.C. www.epa.gov.

Neuman, William. 2019. "Big Buildings Hurt the Climate. New York City Hopes to Change That." *New York Times*, April 17, 2019. www.nytimes.com.

New Partners for Community Revitalization. 2012. "A Report & Recommendations from NPCR's February Roundtable on Brownfield Financial Incentives." www.npcr. net.

New York City Department of Investigation. 2015. "New York City Department of Investigation: Probe of Department of Homeless Services' Shelters for Families with Children Finds Serious Deficiencies." City of New York: Department of Investigation.

New York City Independent Budget Office. 2014. "Budget Options for New York City." New York: New York City Independent Budget Office. www.ibo.nyc.ny.us.

Newkirk, Vann R. II. 2018. "Environmental Racism Is Real, According to Trump's EPA." *Atlantic*, February 28, 2018. www.theatlantic.com.

Newman, Katherine, and Elvin Wyly. 2006. "The Right to Stay Put, Revisited: Gentrification and Resistance to Displacement in New York City." *Urban Studies* 43 (1): 23–57.

Newtown Creek Alliance. 2012. "Newtown Creek Alliance Brownfield Opportunity Area Report." Newtown Creek Alliance. www.newtowncreekalliance.org.

Novotny, Patrick. 1995. "Where We Live, Work and Play: Reframing the Cultural Landscape of Environmentalism in the Environmental Justice Movement." *New Political Science* 23 (2): 61–78.

NSWC (North Shore Waterfront Conservancy of Staten Island). 2007. "Staten Island's Gold Coast 5.2 Miles from St. George to Arlington." On file with author.

Nussbaum, Jeff. 2015. "The Night New York Saved Itself from Bankruptcy," *New Yorker*. October 16, 2015. www.newyorker.com.

"NYC Brownfield Cleanup Program." n.d. NYC Office of Environmental Remediation, www.nyc.gov/html/oer/html/lbcp/lbcp.shtml.

NYC Department of City Planning. 2013. "Port Richmond Brownfield Opportunity Area Draft Recommendations." New York State Department of State. www1.nyc. gov.

NYC Department of City Planning. 2019. "City Planning History." NYC Planning. 2019. www1.nyc.gov.

NYC Department of City Planning. n.d. "Community District Profiles." Accessed March 18, 2020. www.communityprofiles.planning.nyc.gov.

NYC Mayor's Office of Long-Term Planning and Sustainability. 2012. "New York City Wetlands Strategy." PlaNYC 2030. www.nyc.gov.

NYC Parks. n.d. "NYC Parks Green Thumb." www.greenthumb.nycgovparks.org.

NYC.gov. 2006. "Mayor Bloomberg Announces $30 Million Annual Increase in City Financing for Film Production Tax Credit Program." NYC.Gov/Office-of-the-Mayor, May 10, 2006. www.nyc.gov.

NYCEDC (New York City Economic Development Corporation). 2011. "North Shore 2030: Improving and Reconnecting the North Shore's Unique and Historic Assets." www1.nyc.gov.

NYCEDC (New York City Economic Development Corporation). 2013a. "NYCrafted: State of Local Manufacturing, October, 2013: A NYCEDC Special Report." www. nycedc.com.

NYCEDC (New York City Economic Development Corporation). 2013b. "Industrial Business Zone Boundary Commission: Staff Recommendations." www.nycedc.com.

NYCEDC (New York City Economic Development Corporation). n.d. "Industrial and Manufacturing." www.nycedc.com.

NYPL (New York Public Library). n.d. "About the Harry Belafonte 115th Street Library." www.nypl.org.

O'Neill, Hugh, Anna Chelius, and Stephen Albonesi. 2015. "The Central Park Effect: Assessing the Value of Central Park's Contribution to New York City's Economy." Central Park Conservancy. www,centralparknyc.org.

Office of the Mayor. 2011. "Plan NYC: A Greener, Greater New York." The City of New York Mayor Michael R. Bloomberg. www.nyc.gov.

Office of the NYC Comptroller Scott M. Stringer. 2015. "Comptroller Stringer Audit of Build It Back Reveals Millions Paid out for Incomplete Work, Double-Billing and Undocumented Travel Costs." March 31, 2015. www.comptroller.nyc.gov.

Oh, Inae. 2014. "Half of New York City Is Living in Near Poverty." Huffington Post, April 30, 2014. www.huffingtonpost.com.

Orleck, Annelise. 1995. Common Sense and a Little Fire. Chapel Hill: University of North Carolina Press.

Osofsky, Gilbert. 1963. Harlem: The Making of a Ghetto; Negro New York, 1890–1930. New York: Harper & Row.

Ottmann, Michelle, Juliana Maantay, Kristen Grady, and Nilce Fonte. 2012. "Character-ization of Urban Agricultural Practices and Gardeners' Perceptions in Bronx Com-munity Gardens in New York City." Cities and the Environment 5 (1): Article 13.

Page, Max. 1999. The Creative Destruction of Manhattan, 1900-1940. University of Chicago Press.

Papas, Phillip. 2007. That Ever Loyal Island: Staten Island and the American Revolution. New York: NYU Press.

"Parks Special Event Permit Request." n.d. NYC Parks. Accessed March 22, 2020. https://nyceventpermits.nyc.gov.

Pateman, Carole. 1970. Participation and Democratic Theory. New York: Cambridge University Press.

Pearsall, Hamil, and Isabelle Anguelovski. 2016. "Contesting and Resisting Environ-mental Gentrification: Responses to New Paradoxes and Challenges for Urban Environmental Justice." Sociological Research Online 21 (3): 121–27.

Pearsall, Hamil. 2012. "Moving out or Moving in? Resilience to Environmental Gentri-fication in New York City." Local Environment 17 (9): 1013–26.

Pearsall, Hamil. 2013. "Superfund Me: A Study of Resistance to Gentrification in New York City." Urban Studies 50 (11): 2293–2310.

Perkins, Harold A. 2009. "Out from the (Green) Shadow? Neoliberal Hegemony through the Market Logic of Shared Urban Environmental Governance." Political Geography 28 (7): 395–405.

Pinter, Nicholas. 2013. "The New Flood Insurance Disaster." *New York Times*, August 29, 2013. www.nytimes.com.

Piven, Frances Fox, and Richard Cloward. 1978. *Poor People's Movements: Why They Succeed, How They Fail*. New York: Vintage.

Plitt, Amy. 2015. "Harlem Is Becoming as Expensive As the Rest of Manhattan." Curbed NY, August 27, 2015. www.ny.curbed.com.

Plumer, Brad. 2019. "US Carbon Emissions Surged in 2018 Even as Coal Plants Closed." *New York Times*, January 8, 2019. www.nytimes.com.

Popik, Barry. 2005. "Forgotten Borough." The Big Apple. www.barrypopik.com.

Portney, Kent E. 2003. *Taking Sustainable Cities Seriously: Economic Development, the Environment, and Quality of Life in American Cities*. MIT Press.

Pretty, Jules N. 1995. "Participatory Learning for Sustainable Agriculture." *World Development* 23 (8): 1247–63.

Pulido, Laura, and Juan De Lara. 2018. "Reimagining 'Justice' in Environmental Justice: Radical Ecologies, Decolonial Thought, and the Black Radical Tradition." *Environment and Planning E: Nature and Space* 1 (1–2): 76–98.

Pulido, Laura. 2018. "Geographies of Race and Ethnicity III: Settler Colonialism and Nonnative People of Color." *Progress in Human Geography* 42 (2): 309–18.

Purdy, Jedediah. 2015. "Environmentalism's Racist History." *New Yorker*, August 13, 2015. www.newyorker.com.

Putnam, Robert D. 2001. *Bowling Alone: The Collapse and Revival of American Community*. New York: Touchstone Books.

Rabin, Yale. 1989. "Expulsive Zoning: The Inequitable Legacy of Euclid." In *Zoning and the American Dream: Promises Still to Keep*, edited by C. Haar and J. Kayden. Chicago: Planners Press, American Planning Association.

Raddon, Mary-Beth, and Barbara Harrison. 2015. "Is Service-Learning the Kind Face of the Neo-Liberal University?" *Canadian Journal of Higher Education* 45 (2): 134–53.

Randall, Judy. 2014. "PA Offering Residents Affected by Bayonne Bridge Noise Hotel Vouchers, Window Replacement." *Staten Island Advance*, April 1, 2014. www.silive.com.

Rauch, John H. 1869. *Public Parks: Their Effects upon the Moral, Physical and Sanitary Condition of the Inhabitants of Large Cities: With Special Reference to the City of Chicago*. Chicago: S. C. Griggs & Company.

Redclift, Michael. 2005. "Sustainable Development (1987–2005): An Oxymoron Comes of Age." *Sustainable Development* 13 (4): 212–27.

Reddy, Sumathi. 2010. "A Spike in Bias Crimes in Staten Island." *Wall Street Journal*, July 24, 2010.

Reichl, Alexander J. 1999. *Reconstructing Times Square: Politics and Culture in Urban Development*. Kansas City: University Press of Kansas.

Rizzi, Nicholas 2012. "Residents Fear New York Wheel Will Hurt Staten Island Commutes." DNAinfo. December 6, 2012. www.dnainfo.com.

Rizzi, Nicholas. 2013. "Staten Island Residents Oppose Plan to Dump Dredged Material on Barge - Port Richmond." DNAinfo, September 26, 2013. www.dnainfo.com.

Rizzi, Nicholas. 2015. "Anti-Semitism Cost Early New York Wheel Developer the Contract: Lawsuit." DNAinfo. December 16, 2015. www.dnainfo.com.

Roberts, Sam. 2010. "As Population Shifts in Harlem, Blacks Lose Their Majority." *New York Times*, January 5, 2010. www.nytimes.com.

Rocheleau, Jean. 2004. "Theoretical Roots of Service-Learning: Progressive Education and the Development of Citizenship." In *Service-Learning: History, Theory, and Issues*, edited by Bruce W. Speck and Sherry Lee Hoppe. Westport, CT: Praeger Publishers.

Rodríguez, Dylan. 2016. "The Political Logic of the Non-Profit Industrial Complex." *S&F Online*, no. 13.2. http://sfonline.barnard.edu.

Rogers, Elizabeth Barlow. 2016. *Green Metropolis: The Extraordinary Landscapes of New York City as Nature, History, and Design*. New York: Knopf Doubleday.

Rose, Nikolas. 1999. *Powers of Freedom: Reframing Political Thought*. New York: Cambridge University Press.

Rosenberg, Eli. 2014. "How NYC's Decade of Rezoning Changed the City of Industry." Curbed NY. January 16, 2014. www.curbed.com.

Rosenberg, Zoe. 2017. "Brooklyn Bridge Park's Funding Continues to Be Scrutinized." Curbed NY. February 23, 2017. www.curbed.com.

Rosenzweig, Roy, and Elizabeth Blackmar. 1998. *The Park and the People: A History of Central Park*. Ithaca, NY: Cornell University Press.

Ross, Bernard H., and Myron A. Levine. 2011. *Urban Politics: Cities and Suburbs in a Global Age*. Armonk, NY: M.E. Sharpe.

Rothstein, Richard. 2017. *The Color of Law: A Forgotten History of How Our Government Segregated America*. New York: Liveright.

Rotkin-Ellman, Miriam, Gina Solomon, Christopher R. Gonzales, Lovell Agwaramgbo, and Howard W. Mielke. 2010. "Arsenic Contamination in New Orleans Soil: Temporal Changes Associated with Flooding." *Environmental Research* 110 (1): 19–25.

Routhier, Giselle. 2019. "State of the Homeless 2019." New York: Coalition for the Homeless. www.coalitionforthehomeless.org.

Roy, Ananya. 2008. "Post-Liberalism: On the Ethico-Politics of Planning." *Planning Theory* 7 (1): 92–102.

Rudolph, John, Ben Hallman, Chris Kirkham, Saki Knafo, and Matt Sledge. 2012. "Hurricane Sandy Damage Amplified by Breakneck Development of Coast." Huffington Post, November 12, 2012. www.huffingtonpost.com.

"Rules of the City of New York (R.C.U.N.Y.)." n.d. NYC Rules. Accessed March 22, 2020. rules.cityofnewyork.us.

Russell, David. 2018. "Protest Held against Ozone Park Shelter Plan." *Queens Chronicle*, September 13, 2018. www.qchron.com.

Sachs, Charles L. 1988. *Made on Staten Island: Agriculture, Industry, and Suburban Living in the City*. Richmondtown, NY: University Publishing Association.

Sammon, Alexander. 2019. "The Rise and Fall of the New York Wheel." *New Republic*, March 20, 2019. www.newrepublic.com.

Sanderson, Eric W. 2009. *Mannahatta: A Natural History of New York City*. New York: Abrams.

Savitch-Lew, Abigail. 2017. "The High-Income Neighborhoods the City Could Look to Rezone." City Limits. May 10, 2017. www.citylimits.org.

Schrecker, Ellen. 2010. *The Lost Soul of Higher Education: Corporatization, the Assault on Academic Freedom, and the End of the American University*. New York: The New Press.

Schomburg Center for Research, Howard Dodson, and Sylviane Diouf. 2005. *In Motion: The African American Migration Experience*. Washington DC: National Geographic.

Schuller, Mark and Paul Farmer. 2012. *Killing with Kindness: Haiti, International Aid, and NGOs*. New Brunswick, NJ: Rutgers University Press.

Schwartz, Anne. 2001. "Privately Owned Public Space." *Gotham Gazette*, February 5, 2001. www.gothamgazette.com.

Schwarz, Frederick A. O., Jr. 2013. "Twenty-Five Years Later: Reflections on New York City's 1989 Charter Revision Commission and on Charter Commissions in General." *New York Law School Law Review* 58: 22.

Schweber, Nate. 2011. "Reunion for a Vanished Neighborhood." *New York Times*, October 9, 2011. www.nytimes.com.

Shepard, Benjamin, and Gregory Smithsimon. 2011. *The Beach beneath the Streets: Contesting New York City's Public Spaces*. Albany, NY: SUNY Press.

Shepard, Peggy, Stephanie Tyree, and Cecil Corbin-Mark. 2008. "PlaNYC: EJ Group Takes the Inside Track to Advocate Sustainability." *Race, Poverty and the Environment* 15 (1): 70–72.

Shepard, Peggy. 2007. "On Earth Day, Mayor Announces Completion of PLANYC 2030 – A Sustainability Plan for NY." *In a WEACT Minute*, May 18, 2007. www.weact.nyc.

Shepard, Peggy. 2010. "Expert's Main Page." Upstream. 2010. www.upstrm.org.

Singh, Manoj. 2008. "The 2007-08 Financial Crisis in Review." Investopedia. October 28, 2008. www.investopedia.com.

Sinha, Deb Ranjan. 2011. "The Environmental Kuznets Curve Hypothesis and Legacy Pollution: A Geohistorical Analysis of the Environmental Consequences of Industrialization in Worcester, Massachusetts." *Industrial Geographer* 7 (2): 1–18.

Skyler, Edward, and Jennifer Falk. 2005. "Mayor Michael R. Bloomberg Introduces New Initiatives to Support New York City's Industrial Sector." January 19, 2005. www1.nyc.gov.

Slaughter, Sheila, and Gary Rhoades. 2000. "The Neo-Liberal University." *New Labor Forum*, no. 6, 73–79.

Slaughter, Sheila, and Gary Rhoades. 2004. *Academic Capitalism and the New Economy: Markets, State, and Higher Education*. Baltimore, MD: Johns Hopkins University Press.

Slaughter, Sheila, and Larry Leslie. 1999. *Academic Capitalism: Politics, Policies, and the Entrepreneurial University*. Baltimore, MD: Johns Hopkins University Press.

Small, Andrew. 2017. "The Gentrification of Gotham." City Lab. April 28, 2017. www.citylab.com.

Smith, Andrea. 2017. "Introduction." In *The Revolution Will Not Be Funded: Beyond the Non-Profit Industrial Complex*, by INCITE! Women of Color Against Violence, 1–18. Durham, NC: Duke University Press.

Smith, Neil. 1982. "Gentrification and Uneven Development." *Economic Geography* 58 (2): 139–55.

Smith, Neil. 1987. "Gentrification and the Rent Gap." *Annals of the Association of American Geographers* 77 (3): 462–65.

Smith, Neil. 1996. *The New Urban Frontier: Gentrification and the Revanchist City*. London: Psychology Press.

Snug Harbor. n.d. "History." Snug Harbor Cultural Center & Botanical Garden. www.snug-harbor.org.

Sobel, Adam. 2014. *Storm Surge: Hurricane Sandy, Our Changing Climate, and Extreme Weather of the Past and Future*. New York: Harper Wave.

Soffer, Jonathan. 2012. *Ed Koch and the Rebuilding of New York City*. New York: Columbia University Press.

Spencer, Peter N. 2010. "City Effort to Make Landlords Maintain Buildings Isn't Working, Report Says." Silive. December 9, 2010. www.silive.com.

Spivack, Caroline. 2019a. "How Bill de Blasio's Housing Record Stacks up to His 'Working People' Platform." Curbed New York. May 16, 2019. www.ny.curbed.com.

Spivack, Caroline. 2019b. "East Side Coastal Resiliency Project Moves Forward, but Concerns Linger." Curbed NY. October 4, 2019. www.ny.curbed.com.

Stamp, Jimmy. 2012. "The Transformation of Freshkills Park from Landfill to Landscape." *Smithsonian*, October 15, 2012. www.smithsonianmag.com.

Stannard-Stockton, Sean. 2007. "Restricted Grants vs. Operating Support." Tactical Philanthropy. August 31, 2007. www.tacticalphilanthropy.com.

State of New Jersey Commission of Investigation. 2017. "Dirty Dirt: The Corrupt Recycling of Contaminated Soil and Debris." State of New Jersey. www.state.nj.us.

Steinberg, Ted. 2015. *Gotham Unbound: The Ecological History of Greater New York*. New York: Simon and Schuster.

Suarez, Ray. 1999. *The Old Neighborhood: What We Lost in the Great Suburban Migration*. New York: Free Press.

Sussna, Stephen. 1970. "Land-Use and Zoning: The Staten Island Experience." *Urban Lawyer* 2 (4): 480–94.

Swyngedouw, Erik. 2006. "Power, Water and Money: Exploring the Nexus." United Nations Human Development Report. Oxford University Centre for the Environment. www.hdr.undp.org.

Swyngedouw, Erik. 2007. "Impossible 'Sustainability' and the Postpolitical Condition." In *The Sustainable Development Paradox*, edited by Rob Krueger and David Gibbs, 13–40. New York: Guilford Press.

Szasz, Andrew. 2009. *Shopping Our Way to Safety*. Minneapolis, MN: University of Minnesota Press.

Sze, Julie. 2006. *Noxious New York: The Racial Politics of Urban Health and Environmental Justice*. Cambridge, MA: MIT Press.

Sze, Julie. 2019. *Environmental Justice in a Moment of Danger*. Berkeley: University of California Press.

Szekely, Balazs. 2018. "Downtown LA's 90014 Heads the List of Fastest-Gentrifying ZIPs since the Turn of the Millennium." RentCafé Blog. February 26, 2018. www.rentcafe.com.

Tabb, William. 1982. *The Long Default: New York City and the Urban Fiscal Crisis*. New York: Monthly Review Press.

Taylor, Marsha. 2007. "Saving the Soul of Harlem." Blog post. www.nyu.edu/ classes/ keefer/EvergreenEnergy/.

Taylor, Monique M. 2002. *Harlem: Between Heaven and Hell*. Minneapolis, MN: University of Minnesota Press.

Terry, Virginia. 2003. "Imaging the City: Gowanus Canal". Metropolitan Waterfront Alliance. *Metropolitan Waterfront Alliance*, April 16, 2003. http://waterwire.net/ Resources/.

Tessum, Christopher W., Joshua S. Apte, Andrew L. Goodkind, Nicholas Z. Muller, Kimberley A. Mullins, David A. Paolella, Stephen Polasky, et al. 2019. "Inequity in

Consumption of Goods and Services Adds to Racial–Ethnic Disparities in Air Pollution Exposure." *Proceedings of the National Academy of Sciences* 116 (13): 6001–6.

The City of New York 2007. "PlaNYC: A Greener, Greater New York." Mayor Michael R. Bloomberg. www.nyc.gov.

The Real Estate Group 2010. "Manhattan Rental Market Report." New York: The Real Estate Group. www.mns.com.

"The Staten Island Bluebelt: A Study in Sustainable Water Management." n.d. The Cooper Union. Accessed March 23, 2020. www.cooper.edu.

Tilove, Jonathan. 2008. "Obama Taps New Orleans Native Lisa Jackson to Lead Environmental Protection Agency." NOLA.Com. 2008. www.nola.com.

Tiner, Ralph W. 2000. "Wetlands of Staten Island, New York: Valuable Vanishing Urban Wildlands." Cooperative National Wetlands Inventory. www.fws.gov.

Tokmakova, Anastasia. 2017. "How Glass Buildings Are Making Fighting Climate Change Harder." Archinect. July 18, 2017. www.archinect.com.

Toure, Madina. 2016. "Bill de Blasio's Battle with the Feds over Hurricane Sandy Recovery." *Observer*, November 7, 2016. www.observer.com.

United Press International. 2013. "Flood Insurance Falls Short for Many Hurricane Sandy Victims." UPI, December 7, 2013. www.upi.com.

US Census Bureau 2010. *American Factfinder*. US Dept. of Commerce, Economics and Statistics Administration, US Census Bureau. www.census.gov.

US Census Bureau 2014. *American Factfinder*. US Dept. of Commerce, Economics and Statistics Administration, US Census Bureau. www.census.gov.

US Census Bureau 2015. *American Factfinder*. US Dept. of Commerce, Economics and Statistics Administration, US Census Bureau. www.census.gov.

US Census Bureau 2018. *American Community Survey 1-year estimates*. Retrieved from Census Reporter Profile page for NYC-Staten Island Community District 1—Port Richmond, Stapleton & Mariner's Harbor PUMA, NY. www.censusreporter.org.

US Government Accountability Office. 2004. "Status of FEMA's FY03 Pre-Disaster Mitigation Program." Washington D.C.: US Government Accountability Office. www.gao.gov.

Valhouli, Constantine. 2012. "Mold News: Sandy Leaves Toxic Trouble." *New York Observer*, November 7, 2012. www.observer.com.

Vanderkam, Laura. 2011. "Parks and Re-Creation: How Private Citizens Saved New York's Public Spaces." *City Journal*, Summer 2011. www.city-journal.org.

Vidal, John. 2009. "Health Risks of Shipping Pollution Have Been 'Underestimated.'" *Guardian*, April 9, 2009. www.guardian.co.uk.

Voicu, Ioan, and Vickie Been. 2008. "The Effect of Community Gardens on Neighboring Property Values." www.furmancenter.org.

Voight, Joan. 2014. "Which Big Brands Are Courting the Maker Movement, and Why." *Ad Week*, March 17, 2014. www.adweek.com.

Waldman, Amy. 1998. "Cricket Invaders Turn an Auction Into 'Madness.'" *New York Times*, July 21, 1998. www.nytimes.com.

Wall Street Journal. 2013. "Staten Island Warehouse." Waste Lands: America's Forgotten Nuclear Legacy. October 29, 2013. http://projects.wsj.com.

Wallace, Rodrick. 1988. "A Synergism of Plagues: 'Planned Shrinkage,' Contagious Housing Destruction, and AIDS in the Bronx." *Environmental Research* 47 (1): 1–33.

Walsh, Kevin. 2006. "Port Richmond, Staten Island." *Forgotten New York.* 2006. www. forgotten-ny.com.

WEACT n.d. "Our Story." www.weact.org/whoweare/ourstory/.

Weldon Johnson, James. 1925. "Harlem: The Culture Capital." In *The New Negro: An Interpretation,* edited by Alain Locke, 301–11. New York: Albert and Charles Boni.

"West Harlem Piers Park." n.d. We Act For Environmental Justice. Accessed March 22, 2020. www.weact.org.

"Where We Stand and How We Got Here." n.d. New York City Community Garden Coalition. Accessed March 22, 2020. nyccgc.org/about/history

Whitman, Walt. 1920. *The Gathering of the Forces.* 2 vols. New York: G. P. Putnam's Sons.

Williams, Timothy. 2008. "An Old Sound in Harlem Draws New Neighbors' Ire." *New York Times,* July 6, 2008. www.nytimes.com.

Williamson, Vanessa S. 2017. *Read My Lips: Why Americans Are Proud to Pay Taxes.* Princeton, NJ: Princeton University Press.

Wolch, Jennifer R. 1990. *The Shadow State: Government and Voluntary Sector in Transition.* New York: The Foundation Center.

Wolin, Sheldon S. 2008. *Democracy Incorporated: Managed Democracy and the Specter of Inverted Totalitarianism.* Princeton, NJ: Princeton University Press.

Zahran, Sammy, Howard W. Mielke, Christopher R. Gonzales, Eric T. Powell, and Stephan Weiler. 2010. "New Orleans before and after Hurricanes Katrina/Rita: A Quasi-Experiment of the Association between Soil Lead and Children's Blood Lead." *Environmental Science & Technology* 44 (12): 4433–40.

Zavestoski, Stephen, and Julian Agyeman. 2014. *Incomplete Streets: Processes, Practices, and Possibilities.* Routledge.

Zizek, Slavoj. 1999. *The Ticklish Subject: The Absent Centre of Political Ontology.* New York: Verso.

Zoellner, Tom. 2010. *Uranium: War, Energy, and the Rock That Shaped the World.* New York: Penguin Books.

Zoppo, Avalon. 2018. "$60 Million Proposed for Hurricane Sandy Recovery Efforts." *The Press of Atlantic City.* December 30, 2018. www.pressofatlanticcity.com.

Zukin, Sharon, Valerie Trujillo, Peter Frase, Danielle Jackson, Tim Recuber, and Abraham Walker. 2009. "New Retail Capital and Neighborhood Change: Boutiques and Gentrification in New York City." *City & Community* 8 (1): 47–64.

Zukin, Sharon. 1989. *Loft Living: Culture and Capital in Urban Change.* New Brunswick, NJ: Rutgers University Press.

Zukin, Sharon. 1993. *Landscapes of Power: From Detroit to Disney World.* Berkeley: University of California Press.

Zukin, Sharon. 2010. *Naked City: The Death and Life of Authentic Urban Places.* New York: Oxford University Press.

# INDEX

Page numbers in *italics* refer to figures

academic engagement: activist overload and, 173–76; history, 174; neoliberal trends in, 174–75; recognition politics and, 176; service-learning, 174, 175, 229n47; Thurman and, 173, 175–76

activism: community, 210; environmental gentrification and, 45; environmental justice and, 13–14, 44, 129, 220n88; films celebrating, 162–63; nuclear, 102; sustainaphrenia impacting, 15–16; usual suspects and, 163–64, 169; volunteerism, 162

activist overload: academic engagement and, 173–76; civic engagement leading to, 166–73; conclusions, 177; democracy as unpaid work, 155–61; Environmental Justice Showcase Communities program and, 166–73; overview, 154–55; steering committee and, 161–65; sustainaphrenia and, 15–16, 154–55; Thurman and, 164–65, 173, 175–76, 177

Adams, Michael Henry, 49–50

ADM. *See* Archer Daniels Midlands

AFSZ. *See* Asthma-Free School Zones

Amway, 21–22

anti-idling campaign, 84–85

Archer Daniels Midlands (ADM), 100–101

Army Corps of Engineers, 195–96

Asthma-Free School Zones (AFSZ), 170–72

Augusta, Georgia, environmental racism in, 4

Baldwin, James, 221n26

barbecue rules, 78–79, 224n116

El Barrio, 61–62

Battery Park City (BPC), 74

Bell, Derrick, 205

Biggert-Waters Act: opinions about, 190–91; passing of, 187; SFN Facebook group and, 191–95

black Americans: black national movements, 59; community garden movement and, 63–64; Harlem migration and, 55–56; pollution exposure, 43

black power movement, 1960s: Columbia University gymnasium and, 60; Harlem and, 59–63; Mount Morris Park and, 60–61

Black Woodstock, 60–61, *61*

Bloomberg, Michael: brownfield cleanup program, 127; Central Park effect and, 74; de Blasio and, 11; environmental gentrification and, 10; Ferris wheel and, 1, 4–5; Five Borough Redevelopment Plan and, 37–38; Gowanus Canal and, 144; green gentrification and, 73–76, 206–7; Hurricane Sandy and, 10; IBZ program and, 104; IOC and, 37; Made in NYC program and, 104; manufacturing and, 103–4; Occupy Wall Street and, 9; OSLRP and, 40–41; PlaNYC 2030 of, 8–9, 38–39; questionable accomplishments, 40; rezoning by, 208

Bloomberg Era parks, 73–76

blue-collar workers, gig workers impacting, 111

Board of Estimate, 182–83, 230n14

BOAs. *See* Brownfield Opportunity Areas

Boggs, Hale, 188

*Bowling Alone* (Putnam), 163

munity garden movement, 63–64; deindustrialization, 91–94; deindustrialization by design, 93–94; D-LMA and, 92–93; dock workers, 92–93; economic power of, 92; FIRE and, 93; gig workers, 111; Great Depression and, 57; hazardous facilities and, 98–99; history, 26–31; Hurricane Sandy and, 9–10, 185–86; I Love NY campaign, 33; IOC and, 37; land expansion of, 26–28; Made in NYC program, 104; maker movement, 105–7; Manufacturing 2.0, 104–5, 109–10; manufacturing jobs in, 110; Moses Era, 1930s-1960s, 57–59; New Deal and, 28; 9/11 and, 8; 1960s, 29; 1970s, 29–31; Occupy Wall Street and, 9; OneNYC and, 11, 12, 217n25; parks, 51–55; planned shrinkage of, 31; post-World War II, 28–29; recession, 2008, 9; reindustrialization, 103–5; right to shelter law, 125; as of right zoning clause, 99; segregation, 98; Slum Clearance Committee, 58; spatial fix and, 31–33; zoned out, 98–100. See also PlaNYC 2030; specific boroughs and neighborhoods

New York City Climate Mobilization Act, 11

New York City Housing Authority (NYCHA), 217n20

New York City Loft Board, 225n33

New York State: BOAs, 126; brownfield eligibility requirements revamped, 127, 227n23

New York State Department of Environmental Conservation (DEC): Graniteville Tree Swamp and, 203, 231n2; grant, 158–59; January 2017 meeting of, 16; Thurman on task force of, 213

NFIP. See National Flood Insurance Program

Nicholas Avenue flooding, 102, 102

Nicholas Estates, 103

9/11, 8

nonprofit industrial complex (NPIC), 156

Nonprofit Organization (NPO): foundations and, 157–58; funding, 155–61; so-

cial service agencies and, 124, 226n13; Wolch on, 155–56; Wolch predictions, 157

Northfield Local Community Development Corporation (NCLDC), 140–43

North River Sewage Treatment Plant (NRSTP), 70

North Shore. See Staten Island North Shore

North Shore Community Coalition for Environmental Justice (NSCCEJ), 84

North Shore Waterfront Conservancy (NSWC), 1; capacity-building webinar and, 159–60; dredging project and, 195–96; Facebook group, 198; funding, 157–61, 175–76; NYLPI and, 169; Reformed Church of Staten Island and, 117–18; Thurman move and, 212–13; Trump presidency and, 202–4

NPIC. See nonprofit industrial complex

NPO. See Nonprofit Organization

NRSTP. See North River Sewage Treatment Plant

NSCCEJ. See North Shore Community Coalition for Environmental Justice

NSWC. See North Shore Waterfront Conservancy

nuclear activism, 102

(NYC) Department of City Planning (DCP): Gowanus Canal and, 144–45; grant, 158–59; North Shore 2030 of, 135–37; Port Richmond BOA and, 140–43

NYC Economic Development Corporation (NYCEDC), 135–37

NYCHA. See New York City Housing Authority

Oakwood Beach, 178–79

Occupy Wall Street, 9

Oddo, James, 203–4, 231n1

OER. See Office of Environmental Remediation

Office of Environmental Justice (EJO): AFSZs and, 170–72; coalition meeting and, 169–71; Environmental Justice Showcase Communities program and, 166–73; expense report of, 166, 172–73

ABOUT THE AUTHOR

Melissa Checker is the Hagedorn Professor of Urban Studies at Queens College, and Associate Professor of Anthropology at the CUNY Graduate Center. She is the author of *Polluted Promises: Environmental Racism and the Search for Justice in a Southern Town* and co-editor of *Sustainability in the Global City: Myth and Practice*, and *Local Actions: Cultural Activism, Power and Public Life.*